The·Master·Musicians

BEETHOVEN

Series edited by Stanley Sadie

The Master Musicians Series

Titles available in paperback

Bach *Malcolm Boyd*
Beethoven *Denis Matthews*
Bizet *Winton Dean*
Britten *Michael Kennedy*
Dufay *David Fallows*
Grieg *John Horton*
Mahler *Michael Kennedy*
Mozart *Eric Blom*

Purcell *J.A. Westrup*
Sibelius *Robert Layton*
Richard Strauss *Michael Kennedy*
Tchaikovsky *Edward Garden*
Vaughan Williams *James Day*
Verdi *Julian Budden*
Vivaldi *Michael Talbot*
Wagner *Barry Millington*

Titles available in hardback

Bach *Malcolm Boyd*
Bartók *Paul Griffiths*
Beethoven *Denis Matthews*
Berlioz *Hugh Macdonald*
Brahms *Peter Latham*
Bruckner *Derek Watson*
Chopin *Arthur Hedley*
Dufay *David Fallows*
Dvořák *Alec Robertson*
Franck *Laurence Davies*
Handel *Percy M. Young*
Haydn *Rosemary Hughes*
Mendelssohn *Philip Radcliffe*
Monteverdi *Denis Arnold*

Mozart *Eric Blom*
Mussorgsky M.D. *Calvocoressi*
Ravel *Roger Nichols*
Rossini *Richard Osborne*
Schoenberg *Malcolm MacDonald*
Schubert *John Reed*
Schumann *Joan Chissell*
Stravinsky *Francis Routh*
Tchaikovsky *Edward Garden*
Vaughan Williams *James Day*
Verdi *Julian Budden*
Vivaldi *Michael Talbot*
Wagner *Barry Millington*

In preparation

Liszt *Derek Watson*

Shostakovich *Geoffrey Norris*

A list of all Dent books on music is obtainable from the publishers:
J.M. Dent & Sons Ltd
Aldine House, 33 Welbeck Street, London W1M 8LX

The·Master·Musicians

BEETHOVEN

Denis Matthews

**With eight pages of photographs
and 42 music examples**

J.M. Dent & Sons Ltd
London & Melbourne

First published 1985
Text © Denis Matthews 1985
First paperback edition 1987

Made and printed in Great Britain by
Guernsey Press Co. Ltd, Guernsey, C.I. for
J.M. Dent & Sons Ltd
Aldine House   33 Welbeck Street   London W1M 8LX

This book is set in 10/12 pt Linotron Sabon by
Inforum Ltd, Portsmouth

Music examples set by Paul Courtenay

British Library Cataloguing in Publication Data
Matthews, Denis
    Beethoven. — (The Master musicians)
    1. Beethoven, Ludwig van — Criticism
    and interpretation
    I. Title   II. Series
    780'.92'4   ML410.B4

    ISBN 0–460–02494–9

Publisher's acknowledgement: Extracts from Beethoven letters, translated
by Emily Anderson, are reproduced by permission of Macmillan, London
and Basingstoke

Preface

The task of replacing a familiar and much-loved volume is not an enviable one. Marion Scott's *Beethoven* in the 'Master Musicians' series has won countless friends over the years. Many, like myself, must have returned to it again and again for its warmth and enthusiasm, its sound scholarship, and the charm and fluency of its prose. Over half a century has elapsed, however, since it first appeared in 1934, and although Beethoven's place among the greatest composers is as firm as ever, a vast amount of research and reassessment has intervened. Even within the last decade or two the ramifications of the Beethoven literature, much of it extremely specialised, have been enough to daunt future writers on the subject. New light has been thrown on many aspects of the composer's life and works: on the crisis over the adoption of his nephew Karl, on his ambivalent attitudes to Napoleon, on the search for the identity of the 'Immortal Beloved'; while on the music itself dates have been challenged, methods of analysis questioned, and editorial standards revolutionised. Styles of writing about music have changed too, so radically that one sometimes regrets the decline of the Romantic metaphor that enabled the previous author to liken the gentle opening of the E flat Piano Sonata op. 31 no. 3 to the Evening Star tapping on the casement. Although the modern purist may smile indulgently, Beethoven himself might not have objected, for did he not admit elsewhere that the slow movement of the E minor 'Rasumovsky' Quartet was inspired by a contemplation of the night sky?

In general, however, we have moved into an age of academic precision, preferring to leave the listener or performer to enjoy his or her own flights of extra-musical fancy, but this is also in keeping with the composer's longer-term ideals. Posterity has come to regard Beethoven as one of the greatest masters of 'absolute' music, at least where his instrumental works are concerned, and this would seem to be borne out rather than denied by his guarded comments, including those in the sketches, about the 'programme' of the *Pastoral*

Symphony. One thing is certain: that the present-day advances in Beethoven scholarship, whether in research or analysis, or in their influence on the interpretation of his music, are tokens of the enduring respect and reverence felt by so many for the composer and the apparently inexhaustible facets of his art. The present book, in its scale and scope, cannot pretend to emulate the profound erudition shown in such admirable volumes as Alan Tyson's collections of *Beethoven Studies*, or Joseph Kerman's stimulating analyses of the string quartets, or Maynard Solomon's full-length and well-documented biography, though it owes many debts to these and other sources.

As with most of the 'Master Musicians' series, the plan is to deal in turn with the life and works, following the biographical chapters with a survey of the music in its various categories, and ending with the usual appendices for quick reference – the year-by-year calendar, the lists of works and of important personalia, a bibliography and index. In Beethoven's case the bibliography will inevitably be more concise and selective than ever, in view of the vast proliferation of material. Three items are however of such significance for the Beethoven enthusiast that they deserve mentioning here also: the classic Thayer biography in its revised version by Elliot Forbes, the English edition of the Letters by Emily Anderson, and the Kinsky-Halm *Verzeichnis* (catalogue) of the works themselves. These have been among my most constant companions.

York, 1984   Denis Matthews

Contents

List of illustrations

1

Bonn (1770–92)

It has sometimes been claimed that great men had the good fortune to have been born at the right time. Although this seems like wisdom after the event, it is reasonable to suggest that potential greatness may be nurtured or thwarted by circumstance, and that talent and character may owe as much to environment and opportunity as to heredity. In the game of conjecture can we imagine the way Beethoven might have developed if he had arrived on the musical scene a century earlier or later than he did? It is hard to visualise his resolute independence at work in a society still bound by feudal concepts of class and patronage, one in which a supreme genius like J.S. Bach could dedicate six concertos to the Margrave of Brandenburg in words of apologetic humility. Yet if we delay Beethoven's birth, we confound conjecture itself, since we should have to discount his own overwhelming influence on his nineteenth-century successors. In fact it is impossible to separate Beethoven from his time. He thrived and suffered in an age of transition and political upheaval and gave eloquent voice to it. The upheaval had been foretold and encouraged by such writers and thinkers as Diderot, Rousseau and Voltaire. Ideas of equality and liberty had been brewing long before the drastic denouement of the French Revolution: the so-called Age of Reason, or Age of Enlightenment, had threatened many long-standing traditions and dubious privileges, including the powers of church and state. The arts, and the status and welfare of artists, were inevitably affected by the inexorably changing social background; but as in all periods of transition there were bound to be overlaps, contradictions and paradoxes.

In 1770, the year of Beethoven's birth, Haydn was enjoying the secure patronage of the Esterházys and was to do so for a further two decades and more; while Mozart, in his early teens, was already contrasting the oppressively provincial Salzburg hierarchy with the glamorous world-at-large that he had seen on his tours as a prodigy. The glamour was deceptive, as he discovered in his too-early bid for independence, and the ultimate irony was to come. Haydn, free to travel at last, was on his first triumphant visit to London when he heard of Mozart's early death. 'Friends often flatter me that I have some genius', he said, 'but he stood far above me' – and yet Mozart was buried in an unmarked grave. A year later Beethoven, frustrated in his ambition to study with Mozart, arrived in Vienna to become a pupil of Haydn. Although he might be described as the first great composer to succeed as a free-lance, he still owed much to his patrons and benefactors. His life-story is interwoven with a long series of aristocratic names, but his dealings with most of them reveal an intimacy and equality that would have been unthinkable a generation or so before.

Yet Bonn, in the days of Beethoven's youth, was still a symbol of the old order, despite the varying degrees of Enlightenment that had been displayed by its succession of electors. For over five centuries it had prided itself on being the seat of the Electorate of Cologne, its larger neighbour, Cologne itself, having long been declared a 'free city' within the far-flung dependencies of the Habsburg empire. The countless small states, soon to be swept away in the aftermath of the Revolution and with the eventual unification of Germany, looked to Vienna as their fountain-head. The tenuous links between Bonn and Vienna were to be strengthened by the accession of Maximilian Franz as Elector in 1784. His brother was the Habsburg Emperor Joseph II, an 'enlightened' ruler and reformer whose death six years later occasioned one of the youthful Beethoven's most impressive early works. The 'Joseph' Cantata (WoO 87)[1], which contains a remarkable foretaste of part of the final scene in *Fidelio*, was soon followed by a second one in honour of Joseph's successor Leopold II. In view of the occasions, and of Bonn's reputation for fostering the arts, it is surprising to find no evidence of a performance of either work during the composer's lifetime. By the age of twenty Beethoven, while hardly rivalling the young Mozart, had acquired considerable local fame. Music had been running in his family. His paternal grandfather, also Ludwig, was a bass singer who had ascended to the responsible post of Kapellmeister in 1761. Ludwig senior's only surviving child, Johann, Beethoven's father, sang tenor

---

[1] WoO stands for *Werk ohne Opuszahl* – work without opus-number. Beethoven did not begin to use opus-numbers until the mid-1790s, after his arrival in Vienna.

in the electoral service and had gained a fair reputation as a versatile musician and teacher by the time of the great composer's birth in 1770, though his later career was frustrated by an unstable personality and an increasing addiction to drink. This last had also been a weakness of Johann's mother, Maria Josepha Poll, who spent most of her later years in a cloister.

In 1767 Johann married a young widow, Maria Magdalena Leym, *née* Keverich, to the disapproval of his father. The fact that she had been a chambermaid, her father a cook, and her late husband a valet, albeit in the service of the Elector, was apparently too much for the dignity of a Kapellmeister, even one whose wife was a known dipsomaniac. It is fair to add that Ludwig senior's attitude changed when the new family started to arrive, and that reliable sources depict Johann's wife as clever and kindly, handsome and slender, wholly serious, and a good housekeeper. Beethoven, who only knew his grandfather in infancy, had a lasting respect for his memory and his musical reputation and preserved his portrait to the end of his days. Their shared name of Ludwig had a complex sequel, since Johann and his wife had an earlier son of that name, though the child survived for only six days. This 'other Ludwig' added to the complications of the family records. Beethoven was to betray an eternal confusion over his own birthdate, not helped by rumours that Johann had deliberately falsified his age in order to display him more effectively as a prodigy. More serious allegations concerning his actual parentage were circulated and published during his lifetime, with claims of royal blood that he seemed reluctant to deny with any vehemence. As late as 1826 he wrote to his old friend Wegeler in Koblenz: 'You say that I have been mentioned somewhere as being the natural son of the late King of Prussia. Well, the same thing was said to me a long time ago. . . . I gladly leave it to you to make known to the world the integrity of my parents, and especially of my mother.' Wegeler's accusation of 'culpable indifference' had produced little effect: it had taken Beethoven nearly a year to reply and he forgot to post the letter. Could it have been that lack of respect for his father had made him secretly relish the idea of a nobler lineage, despite the aspersions on his mother whom he had loved dearly?

The nobility fantasy was also encouraged in Beethoven's Vienna years by the confusion between the 'van' in his name and the aristocratic German 'von'. Unlike 'von', however, 'van' had no status significance, simply indicating his Flemish ancestry and harking back to a place of origin. Various derivations have been offered for the name Beethoven in its different spellings, from the simple 'Beet-Hof', literally a beetroot garden, to the old Belgian place-name 'Betouwe', meaning 'bettered land', hence improved or cultivated. In fact the composer's known forebears had been mostly tradespeople – bakers, chandlers and lace-makers – and even the class-conscious Kapellmeister ran a wine business as a side-line. The city archives at Malines (Mechelen) confirm that Beethoven's great-grandfather Michael was baptised there in 1685, the birth-year of Bach and Handel; and further research, involving much conjecture, has traced the family tree back into the fifteenth century and beyond, and to the Brabant region of the Netherlands. The long presence of Spain in those northern lowlands has invited speculation about 'southern' traits in Beethoven's character: his volatile temper, his stubborn pride, and indeed his swarthy complexion that soon earned him the nickname of 'the Spaniard'. By a curious chance his last lodgings in Vienna, up to the time of his death in 1827, were in the Schwarzspanierhaus (The House of the Black Spaniard).

Michael's sons Cornelius and Ludwig moved to the Rhineland in the 1730s, their father following them to Bonn in 1741 to evade the Flemish bankruptcy laws when his lace-making business ran him into serious debt. Ludwig, Beethoven's grandfather, who was born in 1712, had made rapid musical progress as a child and acquired important church posts in Louvain and Liège before being invited to Bonn by the Archbishop-Elector Clemens August on account of his accomplished bass singing. He arrived there in 1733 and was well established as a court musician long before his appointment as Kapellmeister; and his son Johann, born in 1739 or 1740, began his more precarious musical career early by joining the electoral choir as a boy soprano.

History repeats itself, for today Bonn, rather than Cologne, is the capital of West Germany, just as in Beethoven's time it was the home of the Elector. Reports of eighteenth-century travellers none the less suggest that the 'free cities' like Cologne enjoyed a more general prosperity and well-being that was denied to the electorates and principalities, in which a facade of courtly opulence too easily distracted from the squalor of the back streets. The Clemens August who brought Ludwig senior to Bonn was the last in a line of Bavarian electors, succeeding his uncle Joseph Clemens in 1723. Although officially an archbishop, he indulged his secular tastes with extravagant splendour, squandering vast sums on furnishings and festivities. He encouraged music, art and architecture on a lavish scale, but ignored the state of the lower classes in their unpaved and vermin-infested quarters, further aggravated by regular flooding from the swiftly-flowing Rhine. When the next elector, Maximilian Friedrich, took over in 1761 his minister Belderbusch introduced a round of economies that curtailed the luxuries without alleviating the poverty. The reduction in salaries caused the new Kapellmeister, Dousmoulin, to resign; and in that same year Beethoven's grandfather, stressing his dual capacity as singer and musical director, petitioned successfully for the vacated post.

After their marriage in 1767 Beethoven's parents, Johann and Maria Magdalena, took up modest lodgings in the Bonngasse, between the market place and the Cologne gate, in what amounted to a musical colony. Their neighbours included Franz Anton Ries, father of Ferdinand, who was to become Beethoven's pupil and biographer; Nikolaus Simrock, a horn-player who later took to music-publishing; and the parents of Johann Peter Salomon, the violinist and impresario who settled in London and organised Haydn's visits there in the 1790s. Meanwhile Theodore Fischer, a baker who owned a house in the Rheingasse, rented rooms to Beethoven's grandfather, whose initial objections to Johann's marriage did not prevent him from sponsoring the first two children. Both were called after him, for as the first-born Ludwig died in infancy the name passed to the next child, Beethoven himself.

He was baptised on 17 December 1770 and judging from local custom was probably born on the previous day. Since the Kapellmeister died three years later he can have had no inkling of his grandson's remarkable destiny. As for Beethoven, the fact that he remembered his grandfather and, according to Wegeler, clung to him 'with the greatest affection', should have countered his own illusion that he was born not in 1770 but in 1772; but in his obstinacy even the baptismal record was inadequate proof, since to his way of thinking it could still have belonged to that 'other Ludwig' who had died before his own birth. We owe many glimpses of Beethoven's childhood to Theodore Fischer's children, Cäcilia the eldest and Gottfried the youngest, who in the much later days of his fame were persuaded to recall those early days in the so-called 'Fischer manuscript'. We read of the Kapellmeister's splendidly kept apartments where everything sparkled like silver, of the young Beethoven's normal childish pranks but abnormal love of solitude, of Johann's drinking bouts, and of Maria Magdalena's eternal seriousness. Beethoven's mother was never known to laugh, not even on the festive occasions that were arranged on her name-day each year with music, food and dancing. Her view of marriage was already an embittered one, as she told Cäcilia Fischer: 'a little joy – and a chain of sorrows'.

Ludwig senior's death in 1773 removed a figure-head and a stabilising influence hardly replaceable by the intemperate and ambitious Johann, who, needless to say, lost no time in applying for the post of Kapellmeister himself. His lack of success and loss of face did not help his drinking habits, which became notorious, and these in turn did not temper the severe musical instruction that he began to inflict on the young Ludwig. Other neighbours confirmed Cäcilia's memories of Johann's 'lessons': of a child of four or five being literally forced to play the clavier and the violin, of being beaten or locked in the cellar for disobedience, or observed standing and weeping on a little footstool in front of the keyboard. Such scenes hardly augured well for any child's future love of music, but Beethoven's innate gifts soon showed themselves in a flair for improvising, for which he was duly reprimanded by his father. If Johann's aim had been to turn his son into another Mozart and thus a 'marketable commodity', his methods seemed pathetically misguided, though Beethoven's talents developed in spite of them. In 1778 he made his first public appearance in Cologne along with another of Johann's pupils, the contralto Johanna Averdonk, but since no reports survive and there was no follow-up it can hardly have been the wished-for Mozartian sensation.

Beethoven's mother apparently made no attempt to interfere in these musical activities, but she had worries enough in holding the family together as Johann's drinking increased to the detriment of his singing and his earnings. They moved several times, from the Fischers' house in the Rheingasse to lodgings in the Neugasse, returning to the Rheingasse after a devastating fire at the nearby palace in January 1777. Five more children were born between 1774 and 1787 but only the two eldest survived infancy. These were the brothers who figured in various ways in Beethoven's later life, not least as the intended recipients of the Heiligenstadt Testament of 1802: Caspar Anton Carl was born in 1774 and Nikolaus Johann in 1776.

After the Cologne concert Beethoven's father, presumably

realising his own limitations, began to search for other teachers. There was the aging Gilles van der Eeden, the court organist, who may have looked on the young Beethoven as his possible successor and was said to have taught him keyboard and thorough-bass. There was Franz Rovantini, whose lessons in violin and viola were cut short by his premature death in 1781. Beethoven also studied the violin with Franz Ries, the organ with Willibald Koch, and the horn with Nikolaus Simrock. There was also the strange case of Tobias Pfeiffer, an eccentric musician-cum-actor who was engaged by the theatre at Bonn in 1779 and invited to stay with the Beethoven family to help with the tuition. This turned out to be a mixed blessing, for Pfeiffer and Johann soon became drinking companions and thought nothing of returning home in the small hours, waking up the nine-year-old Ludwig, and making him play throughout the night. Beethoven probably assimilated far more by hearing, overhearing and participating in the informal domestic music-making of Johann and his colleagues. The most significant event of that time, however, was the arrival in Bonn of Christian Gottlob Neefe, who was to become Beethoven's first real teacher.

Neefe was born at Chemnitz in 1748 and at his father's insistence entered Leipzig University in 1769 to study law, which he soon abandoned for music. He composed piano music and songs but was best known for his numerous Singspiele and other stage works. In 1778 he married the actress Susanne Zink and came to Bonn in the following year to join Grossman's theatrical company, though he eventually took over van der Eeden's post as organist in 1781. Whether Johann or the Elector himself persuaded him to accept the young Beethoven as a pupil matters little: more important is the fact that Neefe at once recognised his talent and went on to help him through his crucial formative years. As a mentor the contrast with Johann could not have been greater. Neefe was a man of strong ethical principles, well-versed in literature and philosophy, and a rare enthusiast for the music of J.S. Bach. He encouraged his pupil to study the preludes and fugues of *The Well-tempered Clavier*, still unpublished and only available in manuscript copies. It is interesting to reflect that as Beethoven was enjoying his initiation into the older 'learned' style, the 26-year-old Mozart was also discovering Bach and Handel fugues for the first time at the home of Baron van Swieten in Vienna. Both were to be enriched by the exposure to Bach's expressive mastery of counterpoint, without which we should hardly have had the miraculous finale of Mozart's 'Jupiter' Symphony or, looking much further ahead, the increasingly contrapuntal textures of Beethoven's last-period works.

At eleven Beethoven had become a full-time musician. His general education ceased when he left the Tirocinium, an elementary school where he was taught Latin to the exclusion of arithmetic, leaving him with a shortage of mathematics that was to plague him in later years. At school his friends had found him self-contained but aloof, and an indifferent learner, showing little of the divine spark that was to illumine his musical genius. Away from school, too, the impression remains of a shy withdrawn child, ill-kept and dishevelled, and seldom happy except when left to his own devices, such as wandering in the countryside or observing the Sieben Gebirge, the hills across the Rhine, through the Fischers' telescope. In music at any rate his thirst for knowledge and criticism was growing and the lessons with Neefe soon produced results. Within a year he was able to deputise for him at the organ, and he gained orchestral experience as assistant harpsichordist in the Elector's Kapelle. In 1784 he was officially appointed second organist at a salary of 150 florins, though embarrassingly at Neefe's expense. The ironic situation arose when the new Elector, Maximilian Franz, ordered a general survey of finances and received a slanderous report that Neefe 'might well be dismissed, inasmuch as he is not particularly versed on the organ, moreover is a foreigner[!], having no *Meritten* whatever and of the Calvinist religion.' This malicious campaign that set the young Beethoven up in opposition to his teacher was fortunately short-lived: Neefe's salary was restored in full in 1785 and the good relations with his pupil continued.

Two years earlier Neefe had published an account of Beethoven's progress in Cramer's *Magazin der Musik*, mentioning his excellent sight-reading, his studies in thorough-bass and composition and his playing of Bach's '48' and ending with the prophetic words: 'This youthful genius is deserving of help to enable him to travel. He would surely become a second Wolfgang Mozart were he to continue as he has begun.' He also referred to Beethoven's first known composition, some clavier variations on a march by Ernst Christoph Dressler which 'for his encouragement' Neefe had had engraved at Mannheim. It is amusing to note that Dressler's little march was in the Beethovenish key of C minor – another prophecy? – and that the age confusion continued, the title-page describing him as ten instead of twelve. Other works soon followed: a fugue for organ, two rondos for piano, some songs, and a clavier concerto in E flat, surviving only in short score. More interesting for posterity are the three keyboard sonatas of 1783 (WoO 47), dedicated to the Elector Max Friedrich, and three piano quartets (WoO 36) dating from 1785, from which Beethoven was to draw some material for the mature op. 2 piano sonatas of the following decade. It is hard to date his next Bonn compositions with certainty, though there are signs of a lull after this promising beginning. He had plenty to occupy him with his court duties and family worries, and may even have been put off, or had his critical powers alerted, by a patronising notice in Forkel's *Almanach* (1784) likening his first published works to those of 'a third or fourth-form student'.

Neefe obviously thought otherwise, and his recommendation that Beethoven should travel was to be fulfilled. In 1787 funds were somehow raised to send him to Vienna, though it was a frustrated venture, cut short after only two weeks by news of his mother's illness and entreaties from his father to return home. In Vienna he recalled catching a glimpse of the Emperor Joseph II; but, far more important, he played to Mozart, who is said to have praised him rather coolly until he heard him improvise and then to have made his much-quoted aside: 'Keep an eye on him: some day he will give the world something to talk about.' According to Ferdinand Ries, Beethoven took some lessons from Mozart but never heard him play; but Czerny insisted that he must have done, since he later commented on his 'choppy' style and lack of legato, surprisingly at variance with Mozart's own dictum that passages 'should flow like oil.' However, the fortepiano was still a newcomer to the family of keyboard instruments, and opinions on the right and wrong ways of playing it were debatable. Mozart had described the piano specialist, Clementi, as a 'mere mechanicus', and Beethoven's own approach, which was to become so personal and eloquent, was obviously affected at that time by his regular duties as organist and harpsichordist at Bonn.

On his return journey Beethoven stayed in Augsburg where, like Mozart before him, he met the piano-maker Andreas Stein and his family and was also befriended by the advocate Dr von Schaden, whose wife was an accomplished pianist and singer. Schaden later received the earliest surviving letter from Beethoven, apologising for the delay in thanking him for a loan he was unable to repay and describing the sad circumstances of his hasty return to Bonn, where he found his mother dying of consumption: 'Who was happier than I, when I could still utter the sweet name of mother and it was heard and answered; and to whom can I say it now?' Maria Magdalena had died on 17 July 1787, and to add to the general despondency his infant sister Margareth passed away four months later. Faced with the family problems of an alcoholic father whose voice had become 'stale' and with two younger brothers to support, Beethoven petitioned for half his father's salary, which the Elector granted in a decree of 20 November 1789. Thus Johann was effectively retired and Beethoven, not yet nineteen, became head of the household, though he left his father a vestige of personal dignity by allowing him to pay over the quarterly instalments himself. Outside the family Beethoven had his staunch colleagues in the newly-formed opera orchestra, in which he played the viola: the violinists Franz Ries and Andreas Romberg, the cellist Bernard Romberg, the flautist Anton Reicha, the horn-player Nikolaus Simrock, and his teacher Neefe who acted as pianist and stage manager. He had also acquired other close friends: the von Breuning family, Franz Wegeler, and Count Waldstein.

Beethoven probably met the von Breunings and the young medical student Wegeler in 1784, and we owe much of our knowledge of their relationship to the biographical *Notizen* that Wegeler and Ferdinand Ries compiled and published after the composer's death. In the absence of secondary schooling Beethoven learnt a good deal about German literature and poetry in this cultured but informal circle. After his mother's death Frau von Breuning, herself a widow, befriended him especially, noting his moods of shyness and introspection – his 'raptus' – and keeping a watchful eye on his friendships and impulses. 'She knew how to keep the insects off the flowers' he said later. Discussions at the von Breunings undoubtedly touched on such topics of the day as Rousseau and Voltaire, and Beethoven's lasting absorption in the Greek and Roman classics as well as his knowledge of recent philosophy, notably Kant and Hegel, must have dated from this time. Count Waldstein entered this circle in 1788, having come to Bonn as a novitiate of the ancient, but declining and foredoomed, order of Teutonic Knights of which the Elector was a Grand Master. His love of music drew him to the young Beethoven, and his friendship with the von Breunings along with his closeness to the Elector probably exercised a strong influence on the composer's future welfare, culminating in the decision to send him back to Vienna.

Waldstein's name is forever associated with the magnificent middle-period sonata, the C major op. 53, that was dedicated to him (1804), and in Bonn Beethoven expressed his gratitude to the Count by writing the music for a *Ritterballet* in 1791, supposedly composed by Waldstein himself. Beethoven had already shown his ability to write for orchestra in the two cantatas, already mentioned, of the previous year; and his experience of the orchestral and operatic repertory had been greatly enriched by his viola-playing in the Electoral chapel and the Court theatre, which the enlightened Max Franz had re-established on a firm financial basis with a regular company in the year of Waldstein's arrival. The first of the new opera seasons had opened on 3 January 1789, in the Elector's absence, with *Der Baum der Diana* by Vincenzo Martin but soon turned to more important contemporary composers such as Benda, Cimarosa, Grétry, Paisiello and Salieri. Still more significant for Beethoven was the production of Mozart's *Die Entführung*, to be followed in the second season by *Figaro* and *Don Giovanni* and by Gluck's *Die Pilgrimme von Mecca*. The influence of the Mozart operas on Beethoven was far-reaching, though it disturbed him that such sublime music could have been inspired by such frivolous plots, and *Die Zauberflöte* was eventually to become his favourite of all. Although he played in a large number of operas during his last four years at Bonn, this did not prevent Beethoven the composer from having a life-long problem with the medium itself, summed up in the protracted rewritings of his only opera, *Fidelio*.

Apart from his various musical activities, which included giving lessons to the von Breuning children, and his new responsibilities as head of the family, Beethoven found a further intellectual stimulus in his visits to the Zehrgarten, a tavern in the market place much frequented by professors and students of the new University, an academy that had been elevated in status in the Elector's educational reforms and in which he enrolled for a time. His desire to set Schiller's 'Ode to Joy', with its topical idealistic call to universal brotherhood, probably dated back to these last years in Bonn since it was already absorbing him on his arrival in Vienna, but this did not come to its fruition in the finale of the Ninth Symphony for over thirty years.

Thayer was the first biographer to mention a visit Beethoven made with his mother to Holland in 1781. It is not clear whether he actually appeared there as a prodigy, but he apparently told the Fischers that the Dutch were skinflints and vowed never to return. Whether that story is true or not, his later excursions with the Electoral orchestra from Bonn to Mergentheim, where Max Franz presided over sessions of the Teutonic Order, were far happier affairs; and at Aschaffenburg he astonished the well-known pianist Abbé Sterkel with his sight-reading and improvisations. Carl Ludwig Junker, chaplain at Kirchberg, also heard the Bonn musicians at Mergentheim and in November 1791 wrote a vivid account of Beethoven's playing:

> The greatness of this amiable, light-hearted man, as a virtuoso, may in my opinion be safely estimated from his almost inexhaustible wealth of ideas, the altogether characteristic style of expression in his playing, and the great execution which he displays. I know, therefore, no one thing which he lacks, that conduces to the greatness of an artist . . . . Even the members of this remarkable orchestra are, without exception, his admirers, and all ears when he plays. Yet he is exceedingly modest and free from all pretension.[2]

In 1790 and 1792 Haydn stopped at Bonn on his way to and from his first visit to London. He was greeted with great enthusiasm by the Elector and the local musicians, and Wegeler recalled that it was on his way back that he was shown one of Beethoven's recent cantatas and at once agreed to take him as a pupil. As a result Beethoven departed for Vienna again in early November 1792, having been granted leave of absence with salary and expenses by the Elector. Waldstein may have had a hand in the decision, and in his farewell message he exhorted Beethoven to work hard and 'to receive Mozart's spirit from the hands of Haydn'. Haydn, whose admiration for Mozart knew no bounds, could not have minded the allusion and the implication. The Elector's concern for his promising young Court musician was however clouded over by more drastic events. In April that year open war had broken out between France and the Habsburgs, and by the time of Beethoven's departure the Revolutionary armies had already reached the Rhine and captured the city of Mainz. The early stages of the long journey from Bonn gave him

[2] Letter of 23 Nov. 1791 to Bossler's *Correspondenz*, quoted by Thayer.

his first taste of the turmoil of military manoeuvres. Together with a travelling companion he kept an account of expenses, including fares, tolls and 'road money', to be enlivened by a more detailed entry after leaving Koblenz: 'Tip – because the fellow drove us at the risk of a cudgelling right through the Hessian army going like the devil – one small thaler.' They narrowly missed being cut off by a French corps at Limburg; but after arriving safely in Frankfurt the rest of the journey, by public stage-coach, presumably passed without incident.

Although Bonn was already under threat from the French, the pros and cons of Beethoven's fortunes during the next two or three years could hardly have been foreseen: the easing-off of his obligations, the indefinite extension of his leave, and the rapid drying-up of his salary and subsistence. Once in Vienna, however, he did not take long to establish himself. Armed with introductions from Waldstein and others, and helped by Haydn as well, he soon won his way into the highest circles. Yet despite domestic problems and sorrows Bonn must have held some happy memories for him. Its orchestra and opera had thrived with Max Franz's support; it had its University and other cultural bodies, such as the Lese-Gesellschaft that had commissioned, even if it could not perform, the two cantatas. He had many loyal friends, some of whom – like his two brothers – were to follow him to Vienna sooner or later.

Following on the cantatas of 1790 Beethoven's last Bonn compositions make an impressive list: songs, piano music, chamber music. They include the attractive Octet and Rondino for wind ensemble, written as *Tafelmusik* for the Elector. The last work to appear in print before his departure was the set of piano variations on Righini's 'Venni amore' (WoO 65) which was published by Götz at Mannheim in 1791. This work, like the Joseph Cantata, justified Neefe's predictions of eight years before. Beethoven did not forget his help and encouragement. He wrote back to him from Vienna in October 1793: 'I thank you for the advice you have very often given me about making progress in my divine art. Should I ever become a great man, you too will have a share in my success.'

2

Vienna (1792–1802)

In the second week of November 1792, less than a year after Mozart's untimely death, Beethoven slipped into Vienna unobtrusively like countless other youths intent on further study of the arts or sciences: in Thayer's words, 'this small, thin, dark-complexioned, pockmarked, dark-eyed bewigged young musician of 22 years'. He immediately ran into financial trouble – 'In Bonn I counted on receiving 100 ducats here; but in vain' – yet he apparently had enough ready money to set about acquiring essentials, including lodgings and a piano. He also noted down some niceties that he deemed necessary for an entry into society, such as black silk stockings, another pair for winter, the need for a wig-maker, even the address of a dancing-master. In spite of dwindling resources and the problems of gaining a foothold in the crowded musical scene his prospects and credentials were good. There were close links between Bonn and Vienna, and some word must have circulated about his reputation as a skilled and versatile Court musician. He had the Elector's support and was a protégé of Count Waldstein, whose name guaranteed him admission into many musical circles, and he had been accepted as a pupil by Haydn. He soon exchanged his attic lodgings in the Alserstrasse for a room on the ground floor, showing a propensity for moving house that was to persist for the rest of his life. Had he been directed there by Haydn perhaps, because Prince Karl Lichnowsky had apartments in the same building?

The situation could hardly have been more propitious. Like many other aristocrats in Vienna, Lichnowsky was an enthusiastic patron of music and a good amateur pianist. He had been a pupil of Mozart and had accompanied him on his tour to Prague, Dresden, Leipzig and Berlin in 1789. At all events he was quick to recognise the newcomer's talents, inviting him into his own rooms as a house-guest and thereby introducing him to a whole round of influential musicians and music-lovers. Lichnowsky organised regular musical parties and had his own private string quartet, led by

Ignaz Schuppanzigh, who was to be associated with Beethoven's works right up to the time of the late quartets. There was Baron Nikolaus von Zmeskall, an amateur cellist who worked in the Hungarian Chancellery. He became an even closer friend, cutting Beethoven's quill-pens for him and receiving an endless stream of humorous letters in return, which he preserved and dated meticulously.

Viennese musical life owed much to individual patrons, and Lichnowsky was the first in a long list of noble benefactors whose names were to resound throughout Beethoven's future years: Lobkowitz, Browne, Rasumovsky, Kinsky, the Countess Erdödy, the Archduke Rudolph. The impression of Vienna as a city given over to the pleasures of life, from the serious cultivation of the arts to the most irresponsible of diversions, is too easily gleaned from the writings of travellers – Madame de Staël, Riesbeck, John Owen – yet the historian A.J.P. Taylor has written of a 'despairing frivolity' that lurked at the heart of the traditional Viennese gaiety. The reforms of the enlightened Joseph II, who died in 1790, were not endorsed by his successors Leopold II and Franz I. Repressions and privileges were reinstated, and a dark undercurrent of spies and surveillance already foreshadowed the police state of Metternich's time. However, for the young Beethoven, freshly arrived from the Rhineland, Vienna was at least a city at peace and must have seemed secure enough, though it was not to remain immune for long. With the advent of Napoleon, war and the threat of war were to provide an ominous backcloth to Beethoven's life and work for the next two decades.

Yet whatever the turmoil of politics, war or tyranny, the arts have long acted as a means of expression and escape and often thrived under oppression. In its nature music was the least censorable of them unless related to a 'programme' or allied with the action of an opera or the words of revolutionary or patriotic songs: note that the plots of Mozart's *Figaro* and Beethoven's *Fidelio*, each potentially subversive, were enacted in Spain for diplomatic reasons. Absolute music faced no such problems, and it is significant that the mature Classical style, as manifested in the later works of Haydn and Mozart, had prospered above all in the sonata and its parallels – the string quartet, the symphony, the concerto – which proved capable of conveying the subtlest shades of human emotion to the receptive listener. This was the musical language that Beethoven inherited, and although he had written songs and cantatas before leaving Bonn, he took most readily to the pure instrumental forms and, with few exceptions, continued to devote himself to them during his first ten years in Vienna. It was moreover as a pianist that he made the greatest impact on his new audiences. When he acknowledged his growing maturity by publishing works with opus-numbers, twenty out of the first twenty-eight were to involve the piano in some way: sonatas, chamber music, concertos.

Beethoven was never to see Bonn again, though it must have been expected that after a period of study with Haydn he would return to benefit local music with his enriched experience. He probably thought so too, for in August 1794 he wrote back to Nikolaus Simrock: 'If your daughters are now grown up, do fashion one to be my bride. For if I have to live in Bonn as a bachelor I will certainly not stay there for long.' Yet although he never lost his love for the Rhineland and his friends there, his family situation had little to hold him. His mother, whom he had loved, had died in 1787, and in December 1792, within weeks of his arrival in Vienna, he heard of his father's death, the news of which had called forth a caustic remark from the Elector about the loss to the liquor excise. Beethoven found to his dismay that Johann had misappropriated the allowance agreed for his two brothers' upkeep, and wrote in humble terms to the Elector asking for its reinstatement and for assurance of his own quarterly salary. Within two years the situation was to change radically: the Elector was forced to leave Bonn for good, the payments ceased, Beethoven became a free-lance, and his brothers found their ways independently to join him in Vienna. For centuries the Electorate of Cologne had survived wars and skirmishes with the French and the whims of its succession of electors and archbishops, but at the time of Beethoven's departure its very existence was at stake. Refugees from the Reign of Terror had descended on Bonn to the embarrassment of the culture-loving Max Franz, who strove to remain neutral even after the execution of his sister Marie Antoinette in 1793. Yet in the following year he too departed, and within a further three the Electorate itself was annexed by the new French republic – but by that time Napoleon's troops were rapidly approaching Vienna.

Meanwhile Beethoven had moved in with the Lichnowskys. His attitude to his benefactors soon developed into an alternating pattern of gratitude and stubborn independence: his concept of equality worked both ways and his pride rebelled against special favours. For example, when Lichnowsky told his servants to give precedence to the composer's needs, Beethoven hired another at his own expense. He would eat out at taverns rather than groom himself for the set meal-times of the household. Even the Princess's maternal concern for him met with resistance: 'She would have put me under a glass case' he told Schindler years later. Some writers, like Ernest Newman, have attributed his untamed manners to simple lack of breeding. Stories abound of his refusal to play if he felt he was being exploited or taken for granted, yet most of his patrons and friends came to accept his stubbornness as inseparable from his genius. His letters reveal both his touchiness and his remorse. He was to owe much to Lichnowsky's financial help and he treasured his gift of a quartet of early Italian instruments, describing him to Wegeler as his warmest friend, but then adding that 'of course we have had misunderstandings but these have only strengthened our friendship'.

Dedications of works of genius were at least enduring rewards for tangible help received. Should we remember such names as Count Rasumovsky or the Archduke Rudolph without Beethoven's music? Thus the op. 1 piano trios were aptly dedicated to Lichnowsky, at whose house they were first played; the op. 9 string trios to Count Browne, whom Beethoven called 'the foremost Maecenas of my muse'; the op. 10 piano sonatas to the Countess Browne; and the op. 18 quartets to Prince Lobkowitz. This was continuing a tradition well established by Haydn and others, though the implication of social deference was on the decline. Haydn himself received the dedication of the op. 2 piano sonatas, though Beethoven refused to add the requested words 'pupil of Haydn'.

Beethoven's success as a keyboard virtuoso centred on his gift for extempore playing, which had apparently so impressed Mozart on his brief earlier visit. The daring improviser, who would move his listeners to tears and then chide them with rough humour for not applauding, was soon feared by his rivals. When the Abbé Gelinek, a popular Viennese pianist-composer, was challenged to measure his wits against Beethoven's he said afterwards: 'Ah, he is no man, he's a devil; he'll play me and all of us to death.' In 1800 Daniel Steibelt, notorious for his facile tremolando effects, descriptive fantasies and 'prepared' improvisations, was demolished at a similar confrontation and swore never to meet Beethoven again. This flair for spontaneous invention was not however to be confused with the art of serious composition. When it came to actual composing Beethoven remained the most cautious and painstaking of artists, and his surviving sketchbooks are a permanent reminder of his powers of self-criticism. In fact he craved for discipline, and from this viewpoint his eagerly awaited lessons with Haydn were a disappointment.

It could be blamed on a conflict of temperaments and ages: Beethoven, headstrong, obstinate and mistrustful, but certainly in need of technical guidance; Haydn, already in his sixties, paternal and benevolent but set in his ways and easy-going, qualities too readily misunderstood by his pupil as condescending, possessive, even jealous. Yet he showed Beethoven many kindnesses, introduced him to the Esterházys at Eisenstadt, lent him money, and reported to the Elector at Bonn on his progress and financial needs. Unfortunately four of the five compositions sent in evidence were recognised as old ones and it seems that Beethoven had misled Haydn about the advances already paid. The Elector's curt reply that he should return to Bonn rather than run into further debt was ignored, and Haydn was in any case preoccupied with plans for his second visit to London. The possibility of taking Beethoven with him as assistant came to nothing, and though the experience of travel and of London's musical life could have been fruitful, it is hard to imagine him in the roles of valet and copyist. His remark that he never learnt anything from Haydn could hardly be taken at face value, though he undoubtedly owed far more to the composer than the teacher. He could scarcely fail to be impressed by the master's latest symphonies and quartets, one good reason for delaying his own first attempts in these important fields. This may account for the ambitious compensating scale of his op. 1 trios and op. 2 sonatas. He was annoyed at Haydn's misgivings over the publication of the third of the trios lest its originality should be misunderstood, though the motive may have been genuinely protective; and the subsequent success of the work in question, the C minor, must have added to Beethoven's suspicion of jealousy.

Haydn might criticise and advise but could scarcely 'teach' free composition, and Beethoven must have known that he would have to learn most through his own experience and experiment; but basic techniques such as strict counterpoint *could* be taught, and ironically his chief complaint with Haydn's lessons was that they were not strict enough. He told the Abbé Gelinek about his problem, and

Gelinek introduced him to Johann Schenk, who agreed to supervise and correct his contrapuntal exercises in secret. Thirty years later they laughed over the deception, though in fact Gelinek had soon fallen out with Beethoven and confessed to Haydn about the whole affair. Haydn however had made other plans for Beethoven to study during his absence with Albrechtsberger, more renowned as a pedagogue than a composer. It says much for Beethoven's thirst for discipline that he applied himself diligently to his new teacher's 'musical skeletons', graduating from simple species counterpoint to canon and fugue, and that he preserved and returned to the exercises as if aware of their long-term benefit. In his turn Albrechtsberger acknowledged Beethoven's talents but was frankly baffled by his compositions. Other teachers included Salieri, whose advice Beethoven sought on vocal declamation, certainly after the turn of the century when oratorio and opera began to absorb him. There was also Aloys Förster, a Silesian composer of quartets and quintets who settled in Vienna in 1799, but although Beethoven generously called him 'my old master' and gave his young son piano lessons, the influence of Förster's modest talents on the real master of the op. 18 quartets can only have been minimal.

Beethoven's contrapuntal studies did not impede his rapid development as a composer. The op. 1 piano trios were published by Artaria while Haydn was in London, though the first of them may have been sketched, if not completed, in Bonn. His variations for violin and piano on Mozart's 'Se vuol ballare' (WoO 40), dedicated to Eleonore von Breuning, had already appeared. He wrote to her explaining that their publication was intended to forestall the plagiarists and, in view of some special difficulties in the piano part, to confound his rivals. His own playing had, however, been largely confined to private salons, like Lichnowsky's, but in March 1795 he made his first official appearances before the Viennese public. He hurriedly completed his B flat Concerto op. 19 for a charity concert in the Burgtheater on the 29th, following it with a public extemporisation on the 30th and a Mozart concerto on the 31st, played as an interlude during a performance of *La Clemenza di Tito* organised by Mozart's widow, Constanze. Perhaps the concerto was the D minor, which Beethoven especially admired and for which he later wrote cadenzas? Later that year, on 18 December, he also played a concerto of his own in a concert celebrating Haydn's return from London and including three of his Salomon symphonies, though it is not clear whether he repeated the B flat or introduced the C major op. 15 on this occasion. If the latter, it would almost certainly have been played in an early version. He revised both works before their publication and wrote a new rondo for the B flat, which he nevertheless held back as 'not one of his best' until the C major had appeared – hence their reversed numbering with the earlier B flat as 'no. 2'. The splendour of Haydn's latest symphonies may have caused Beethoven to sketch and then to abandon a symphony in C about this time. With the concerto, on the other hand, the greatest precedents had come from Mozart and there was no direct competition from Haydn, whose keyboard concertos had been early and slight pieces by comparison.

Within three years Beethoven had gained an enviable reputation in Vienna, confirmed by these public appearances and clinched by a commission to compose the minuets and other dances for the traditional charity ball at the Redoutensaal in November 1795. He had made many new friends as well as the inevitable 'sworn enemies' among his rivals. Nor had he lost touch with old friends and relatives in Bonn. In the general exodus from the Rhineland his brothers Caspar Carl and Nikolaus Johann came to Vienna in 1794 and 1795 respectively, the former setting up as a music teacher, the latter as an apothecary. Other arrivals included Franz Gerhard Wegeler and the three von Breuning brothers. Wegeler came primarily to complete his medical studies, and although he returned to Bonn in the summer of 1796 he was able to add some important memories of Beethoven's early Vienna years to his accounts of the composer's youth. He eventually married Eleonore von Breuning and settled in Koblenz and though he and Beethoven never met again they remained friends through correspondence: it was to Wegeler that Beethoven first confided the dreaded secret of his deafness in June 1801.

In February 1796 Beethoven undertook an extended tour of Prague, Dresden and Berlin, setting out with Prince Lichnowsky just as Mozart had done seven years before. From Prague he wrote to his brother Johann: 'My art is winning me friends and renown, and what more do I want? And this time I shall make a good deal of money', adding as though from bitter experience 'I hope you will enjoy living in Vienna more and more. But do be on your guard against the whole tribe of bad women.' In Prague he composed some curiosities for mandolin and piano and the vocal scena 'Ah, perfido!' for the young Countess Josephine de Clary, though the first performance of the latter was actually given by another Czech singer, Josepha Dusek. This was his first real attempt at the operatic style, but apart from sketches from some Goethe settings the other products of the tour were instrumental. Information about his travels is scanty however, and no further letters survive from the spring and summer of 1796. He is known to have played to the Elector of Saxony in Dresden on 29 April but there is no evidence of a projected visit to Leipzig. Berlin was in any case the highlight of the tour. In deference to the cello-playing Friedrich Wilhelm II, for whom Mozart had composed his three 'Prussian' quartets, Beethoven wrote his two sonatas op. 5 and performed them with the King's resident cellist, Jean Pierre Duport, receiving in return a gold snuff-box 'fit for an ambassador' and filled with louis d'ors. It is now accepted that the cello variations on a theme from *Judas Maccabaeus* as well as those on Mozart's 'Ein Mädchen oder Weibchen' date from this visit, which was thus an important landmark in the evolution of the duo for cello and piano. In Berlin, too, he met Friedrich Himmel, the Kapellmeister, yet another to be floored by Beethoven's extemporisations, and the composer Carl Friedrich Zelter, a friend of Goethe and an early master of the German Lied. According to Czerny, Beethoven was invited to consider a permanent post there by the King, whose death in the following year put an end to any such plans.

Research also suggests that the Quintet for wind and piano op. 16 was written in Berlin and may have been inspired en route by the hearing of a group of Czech wind-players in Mozart's work for the same medium, though its first known performance was given at one of Schuppanzigh's concerts in Vienna after Beethoven's return. Meanwhile on 23 November 1796 he played at Pressburg (Bratislava) and thanked the piano-maker Johann Andreas Streicher for the excellent instrument that had been sent from Vienna. Streicher had married Nanette, daughter of the Augsburg maker Stein, whose fortepianos Mozart had admired so much on his visit there in 1777. In due course the Streichers became close friends of Beethoven's, and at a much later stage Nanette was to be a tower of strength in helping to sort out his domestic disorders during the lengthy litigation over his nephew Karl. In another letter of 1796 (the precise date is unknown) Beethoven made the following general remarks about pianos and piano-playing to Streicher:

There is no doubt that so far as the manner of playing it is concerned, the *pianoforte* is still the least studied and developed of all instruments; often one thinks that one is merely listening to a harp. And I am delighted, my dear fellow, that you are one of the few who realise and perceive that, provided one can feel the music, one can also make the pianoforte sing.

Very few letters of Beethoven's survive from the next three years, apart from his usual entertaining (and carefully preserved) notes to Zmeskall, full of cryptic comments, puns and other witticisms; but on 29 May 1797 he wrote to Wegeler, now back in Bonn, about his 'steadily improving health' as though he had been ill, perhaps seriously. His creative powers had continued to flourish, however, and more works were published by Artaria, including the recent cello sonatas. In October 1797 the solitary but splendid Piano Sonata op. 7 appeared, and, as if to prepare himself for the string quartet, he wrote several works for string trio, an exacting medium with a famous precedent in Mozart's Divertimento K. 563. Sketches for many works of this time are to be found in the 'Kafka' miscellany, a random collection of manuscripts which Beethoven preserved from his earlier period, from about 1786 to 1799. He was soon to transfer such preliminary work to actual sketchbooks, a subject revealing and fascinating enough to have called forth endless research and commentary, with Gustav Nottebohm (1817–82) as the first great pioneer. The sketches in 'Kafka' include those for another of Artaria's 1797 productions, the setting of Matthisson's 'Adelaide' which Beethoven dedicated to the poet without obtaining his approval. He eventually sent him a copy three years later, writing in an apologetic manner: 'My most ardent desire will be fulfilled if my musical setting of your heavenly Adelaide does not entirely displease you and if it inspires you soon to write another similar poem.'[1] In fact he had already set other poems by Matthisson, 'An Laura' and 'Opferlied', returning to the latter for a choral and orchestral version in the late period (1824).

It may have been on Salieri's advice that Beethoven also applied himself to some *a cappella* settings for two, three and four voices of texts by Metastasio between 1792 and 1802, but in April 1797 a vocal offering of a very different kind was precipitated by political events, the Napoleonic advance and the calling out of the Vienna Landsturm. As a patriotic song, however, Beethoven's 'Ein grosses

---

[1] Letter of 4 Aug. 1800.

deutsches Volk sind wir' to Friedelberg's words was no match for Haydn's 'Emperor's Hymn' and with the signing of the makeshift Treaty of Leoben it was soon forgotten. Within a year the arrival in Vienna of the minister of the French Directory, General Bernadotte, was to have musical as well as political significance. His party included the violinist Rodolphe Kreutzer, and Schindler maintained that it was Bernadotte who first gave Beethoven the idea of composing a 'heroic' symphony in honour of Bonaparte.

In 1798 Beethoven's many teasing letters to Zmeskall included one addressing him as 'Baron Muck-driver' and enclosing his duet for viola and cello 'with two obbligato eye-glasses' (WoO 32), a playful reference to the Baron's weak sight. More important works of the year were the three string trios op. 9 and the piano sonatas op. 10, and he also explored chamber-music forms new to him in the Trio for clarinet, cello and piano op. 11 and the three violin sonatas op. 12, surprisingly dedicated to Salieri, his mentor in vocal composition. The 'largo e mesto' in the third of the piano sonatas, the D major op. 10. no. 3, was one of his profoundest earlier slow movements. Yet he also found time to travel again, and on his return to Prague played his C major and B flat concertos, presumably in their revised forms, and some solo works including the Adagio and Rondo of the Piano Sonata op. 2 no. 2. The Bohemian composer Tomašek wrote about this: 'Beethoven's magnificent playing and particularly the daring flights in his improvisation stirred me strangely to the depths of my soul; indeed I found myself so profoundly bowed down that I did not touch my pianoforte for several days . . .[2] Tomašek, like his pupil Voříšek, is largely remembered for his groups of short piano-pieces, Eclogues and Dithyrambs, which foreshadowed the popular miniatures of the next generation, such as Schubert's *Moments musicaux* and countless works by Schumann, though Beethoven's first set of Bagatelles op. 33 came earlier still (1802). Although Tomašek called Beethoven 'the giant among piano-players' he had reservations about the compositions themselves:

> His frequent daring deviations from one motive to another, whereby the organic connection, the gradual development of idea was broken up, did not escape me. Evils of this kind frequently

---

[2] Johann Wenzel Tomašek: autobiography (1845), quoted by Thayer.

weaken his greatest compositions . . . . The singular and original seemed to be his chief aim in composition.[3]

Such remarks could of course have been levelled at Haydn, who exploited the humour of surprise even in his most serious quartets and symphonies, and had claimed that his long seclusion with the Esterházys had obliged him to be 'original'. Beethoven must have been aware too of the original genius that emanated from Haydn's *Creation*, which was first heard at a private performance in April 1798, beginning with the extraordinary 'Representation of Chaos' and its pre-echoes of Berlioz and Wagner. But apart from his 'daring deviations' Beethoven's deployment of dynamics and tonality was 'new' and therefore perplexing, above all perhaps to fellow composers like Tomašek or Albrechtsberger and not excluding Haydn himself.

Yet the 'organic connection' which eluded Tomašek was one of the strengths of Beethoven's next piano sonata, the *Pathétique* op. 13, in which main themes from all three movements can be traced back to two basic motives. Here the title, unlike the 'Moonlight' and 'Appassionata', was Beethoven's own, and the storm and stress in the outer movements stretched the medium to its limits with smouldering orchestral effects – a hint that his first symphony was soon to come? His piano-playing had been challenged and stimulated by two visiting virtuosi, Joseph Wölffl of Salzburg, who had studied with Leopold Mozart and Michael Haydn and was also a considerable composer; and Johann Baptist Cramer, who was born in Mannheim but spent his early life in England as a pupil of Clementi. Another visitor to Vienna was the double-bass virtuoso Dragonetti, who astonished Beethoven by playing the G minor Cello Sonata op. 5 no. 2 on the bass, thereby revealing the instrument's unsuspected potential. The effect on Beethoven's orchestral treatment of the double-bass had an amusing sequel twenty-five years later: when Dragonetti was engaged to play the instrumental recitatives in the first London performance of the Ninth Symphony he said he would have doubled his fee if he had seen the part beforehand.

Two further names must be mentioned for their long-term association with Beethoven: Johann Nepomuk Hummel and Carl Czerny, both destined to become famous pianist-composers. Hummel had been a child pupil of Mozart's and like Beethoven had

[3] Ibid.

continued his studies with Albrechtsberger and Salieri, reappearing before the Viennese public as a mature artist in 1799. He had travelled widely as a prodigy, but his link with Mozart became somewhat attenuated in the anachronistic cadenzas and embellishments he wrote for some of the piano concertos, in which he over-exploited the higher reaches of the extended keyboard. His relation with Beethoven was, however, sporadic: in 1814 he took part in the 'Battle Symphony' and in 1827 visited him during his last illness. Czerny, on the other hand, played to Beethoven as a child and became a favourite pupil. They were introduced by the violinist and mandolin virtuoso Wenzel Krumpholz, with whom Beethoven had been taking some violin lessons. The year was probably 1800, since in his memoirs Czerny recalled climbing the many stairs to the fifth or sixth-floor apartment in the Tiefen Graben, where Beethoven was living at the turn of the century. Although he was only about nine at the time, his recollections of that first meeting give a typical impression of Beethoven's domestic chaos:

> The room presented a most disorderly appearance: papers and articles of clothing were scattered about everywhere . . . . hardly a chair, save the wobbly one at the Walter fortepiano (then the best) . . . . Beethoven himself wore a morning coat of some longhaired dark grey material, and trousers to match, so that he at once recalled to me the picture in Campe's 'Robinson Crusoe', which I was reading at the time. His coal black hair, cut *à la Titus*, bristled shaggily about his head. His beard – he had not shaved for several days – made the lower part of his already brown face still darker. I also noticed with that visual quickness peculiar to children that he had cotton, which seemed to have been steeped in a yellowish liquid, in his ears. At that time, however, he did not give the least evidence of deafness.[4]

When asked to play, Czerny began with Mozart's C major Concerto, 'the one beginning with chords' – presumably K. 503 – and, duly encouraged, he continued with Beethoven's recently published *Sonata Pathétique* and also accompanied his father in 'Adelaide'. On the strength of all this he was immediately accepted as a pupil and told to bring C.P.E. Bach's *True Art of Keyboard Playing* to his first lesson. The incident underlines the high regard that Beethoven, like

[4] Carl Czerny's reminiscences quoted in *Beethoven: Impressions by his Contemporaries*, ed. O.G. Sonneck (New York, 1926).

Haydn and Mozart, had for the work of Bach's most influential son.

Some important new friendships date from around this time. In 1798 Beethoven met Karl Amenda, a theological student and keen violinist from Courland on the Baltic, where he later became Provost. On his visit to Vienna he acted as precentor for Prince Lobkowitz and also taught music to the family of Mozart's widow. Although he only stayed for about eighteen months, Beethoven was much taken by his amiable character. He is also associated with the first version of the F major String Quartet op. 18 no. 1, which Beethoven gave him before his departure in the late summer of 1799, though two years later he wrote to him in Courland telling him to disregard it 'since only now have I learnt to write quartets properly'. A comparison between the two versions, Amenda's and the familiar revised one with its many subtle changes of texture, is an object-lesson in self-criticism.

In 1799 Beethoven was introduced to the aristocratic Brunsvik family from Hungary, acquiring new pupils in the young countesses Therese and Josephine, for whom he wrote the exquisite song and variations for four hands, 'Ich denke dein' (WoO 74). His attachment to Josephine, who married a Count Deym but became a widow in 1804, raises the subject of his many affairs of the heart. Wegeler, who was in Vienna only from 1794 to 96, remarked that Beethoven was 'always in love' and sometimes made conquests 'that an Adonis would have found difficult if not impossible'.[5] He remained single though he often contemplated marriage. One of his known proposals during the 1790s was to the singer Magdalena Willmann, who said she refused him because 'he was ugly and half-crazy'. Yet he clearly had a fascination for women of rank and his name has been linked, rightly or wrongly, with a whole series of them, culminating in the anonymous 'Immortal Beloved' to whom he addressed, but did not send, the much discussed love-letter from Teplitz in 1812. His earlier romance with the young Countess Guicciardi, a cousin of the Brunsviks, was popularised and speculated upon through the dedication of the so-called 'Moonlight' Sonata, but a familiar pattern emerged: after flirting with Beethoven she married someone of her own station, though also a composer of sorts, called Count Gallenberg.

We know from Beethoven's sketches, as well as from his parting

[5] Wegeler and Ries: *Biographische Notizen* (Koblenz, 1838).

gift to Amenda, that work on the op. 18 string quartets was well advanced by 1799, and presumably on the First Symphony too, but apart from the op. 12 violin sonatas the publications of that year were all for piano solo. There were variations on operatic airs by Salieri, Winter and Süssmayr, and the storm-and-stress drama of the *Pathétique* had been followed by a pair of more intimate sonatas, op. 14. Schindler later gave a rhapsodic account of Beethoven's free manner of playing them, indulging in ecstatic comments such as, of the transition-theme in the first movement of op. 14 no. 2, 'the hearer could fancy he actually beheld the lover in his living form, and heard him apostrophising his obdurate mistress'.[6] It would be more constructive for the interpreter to note the cross-influences between different media. For instance, a quartet texture often looks up from the pages of the piano music, and Beethoven seemed to acknowledge this when he arranged op. 14 no. 1 *as* a string quartet.

It would be tempting to offer the year 1800 as a watershed, a convenient dividing line between the 'first' and 'second' periods, but in fact it was marked by works of consolidation rather than stylistic departures. The turn of the century was nevertheless a milestone: on 2 April 1800 Beethoven's First Symphony was played at a benefit concert in the Burgtheater. He promoted the concert himself and the programme was typically gargantuan. It included a piano concerto, probably the C major, the recent Septet op. 20, and paid deference to his forebears with a Mozart symphony (it is not known which) and an aria and duet from Haydn's *Creation*. He also threw in an improvisation, a feature of concert-giving to be inherited by the early Romantic virtuosos. Despite the importance of the occasion the Viennese critics made no comment – or did Beethoven fail to send them tickets? – but a delayed report in the Leipzig *Allgemeine Musikalische Zeitung* described it as 'truly the most interesting concert in a long time'. As expected, Beethoven had improvised 'in a masterly fashion', though there were some complaints about the over-use of the wind-players in the First Symphony and of the generally poor playing of the orchestra, which had been hired from the Italian opera. The remark that 'Beethoven's compositions are difficult to execute' may surprise one at this early stage in view of the interpretative and technical demands of the later Haydn and Mozart symphonies, but his more dynamic style already depended on au-

---

[6] Anton Schindler: *Life of Beethoven*, ed. Moscheles (London, 1841).

thoritative direction and more adequate rehearsal. No such problem beset the Septet, which was led by Schuppanzigh and soon acquired a lasting popularity – to the composer's annoyance as he embarked on the greater but less immediately accessible works of the middle period.

Another work that had an instant success was the Sonata for horn and piano op. 17, written in great haste for a concert on 18 April given by the itinerant Bohemian horn virtuoso Johann Wenzel Stich, better known as 'Giovanni Punto'. They repeated it in Budapest on 7 May but a further performance for the music-loving Vegh family was cancelled after a quarrel between Punto and the composer. Beethoven's name was not widely known in Hungary despite its nearness to Vienna – 'Who is this Bethover?' asked one Budapest critic – but his visit at least enabled him to spend some time with the Brunsviks at their country estate. It was back in Vienna that he had his improvising 'duels' with Steibelt, at the home of Count Fries. A sadder event was the arrival in exile of the former Bonn Elector Max Franz, whom Beethoven may have visited in his retirement and to whom he planned to dedicate his First Symphony. Although this was to be forestalled by the Elector's death, the eventual dedication to Baron van Swieten was fitting, in view of his close association with both Mozart and Haydn.

In 1800 Beethoven also worked at the two violin sonatas op. 23 and op. 24. The latter, the ever-popular 'Spring' Sonata, adopted a four-movement plan that was also followed in the Piano Sonata in B flat op. 22, a tidily organised work that Beethoven said 'hat sich gewaschen', i.e. was first-rate. More prophetic of his middle-period manner was the Third Piano Concerto in C minor, which had been on the stocks for some time and may have been intended for inclusion in the concert on 2 April. It was evidently completed too late but bears the date '1800', though its performance was delayed until 1803 and its publication until 1804, enabling Beethoven to utilise the extended compass of the latest pianos. His desire to keep back the C minor for his own later use was hinted at in a letter of 15 December to the Leipzig publishers Franz Anton Hoffmeister, to whom he offered his other recent works, the Septet, the First Symphony, the op. 22 Piano Sonata, and the much earlier B flat Concerto, which he sold off at half-price. His letters to Hoffmeister were shrewd over money matters. He suggested that sales of the popular Septet could be increased by arranging it for piano, or as a trio or quintet, even for flute – 'they would swarm round it and feed on it like insects' – though such arrangements were common practice. Having quoted a figure of 70 ducats for the four works, he played the innocent, calling himself 'an incompetent business man who is bad at arithmetic' and naively proposing a Utopian solution to such things: 'There ought to be in the world a *market for art* where the artist would only have to bring his works and take as much money as he needed.'

Beethoven's attitude to arrangements showed a curious ambivalence – or expediency. It was natural enough for the Horn Sonata to have an alternative cello part in view of the scarcity of horn virtuosos, just as there were to be practical reasons for the makeshift piano version of the sublime Violin Concerto. In his letter to Hoffmeister of 22 April 1801 he even praised him for issuing Mozart's sonatas as quartets – were Mozart's own quartets insufficient? – and yet wrote to Breitkopf and Härtel in the following year protesting about the unnatural mania for such transplants which should only be done, if at all, by the composer himself. Meanwhile he had told Hoffmeister to add his name and Prince Lichnowsky's to the list of subscribers for a prospective issue of Bach's works – 'the sublime and magnificent art of that original father of harmony' – and then turned to his own recent activities: 'Well, to tell you a little more about myself, I have composed a ballet.' The work in question, which had been commissioned for the Court Theatre, was *Die Geschöpfe des Prometheus*. Beethoven did not think much of the ballet-master Salvatore Vigano, though he had been widely praised for elevating a much-abused art-form into a 'new realm of beauty', but the proof was in the success of the work, which received fourteen performances in 1801 and a further nine in 1802. One Viennese critic found Beethoven's music 'too learned' for a ballet, but at least it yielded a popular overture and, in the finale, the re-use of a contre-danse theme (no. 7 from WoO 14) that was to turn up again in the 'Prometheus' Variations for piano and the last movement of the *Eroica* Symphony. An anecdote concerning Haydn and Beethoven was to play on the word-link between the former's *Creation* and the 'creations' (*Geschöpfe*) of Prometheus. After Haydn had complimented him on the ballet Beethoven, who could seldom resist a play on words, is said to have replied '. . . but it is far from being a *Creation*!' 'That is true' said Haydn, taking his former pupil's witticism at face value: 'It is not yet a *Creation* and I can scarcely believe it will ever become one.'[7] The story, authentic or not, seems to sum up the touchiness of their relationship.

From 1800 onwards Beethoven's friendly benefactor Lichnowsky granted him an annuity of 600 gulden until he should find a 'suitable appointment'. His finances were in good order, and his brother Caspar Carl, who now worked as a cashier in a bank, had been acting as his agent for better or worse. (Ferdinand Ries in his *Notizen* accused both brothers of meddling in Beethoven's affairs to their own advantage.) Beethoven also added to his income by giving private lessons to the nobility, and on 29 June 1801 was able to report to Wegeler:

> My compositions bring me in a good deal; and I may say that I am offered more commissions than it is possible for me to carry out. Moreover for every composition I can count on six or seven publishers, and even more if I want them; people no longer come to an arrangement with me, I state my price and they pay. So you see how pleasantly situated I am.

Yet a dark cloud was hanging over these prospects of worldly success:

> But that jealous demon, my wretched health, has put a nasty spoke in my wheel; and it amounts to this, that for the last three years my hearing has become weaker and weaker. The trouble is supposed to have been caused by the condition of my abdomen which, as you know, was wretched even before I left Bonn, but has become worse in Vienna.

Czerny, it will be recalled, had noticed the cotton in Beethoven's ears when he went to play to him the previous year, but this was the first intimation in the letters of his deafness, and since Wegeler was a doctor Beethoven gave details of the various treatments he had been undergoing: almond oil, cold and tepid baths, pills and infusions. Some of these had helped his chronic stomach ailments, colic and diarrhoea, but with little effect on his hearing. His latest physician, Vering, had given him guarded hope, promising improvement but not cure, and this information Beethoven underlined, continuing in a mood of despair. He contemplated visiting Wegeler at Bonn in the following spring in order to retire to the country and 'to lead the life of a peasant' for six months.

---

[7] Thayer attributed the anecdote about Haydn's *Creation* to Alois Fuchs.

Whatever the cause of Beethoven's deafness – many have attributed it to syphilis – it is generally agreed that he suffered from otosclerosis and the subsequent deterioration of the auditory nerves. The appalling psychological effect on a musician can be imagined, and Beethoven was equally aware of its social consequences, for which reason he confided first of all in two of his closest yet most distant friends, Wegeler in Bonn and Amenda in Courland, begging them to keep the news secret. In his letter to Amenda of 1 July 1801 he wrote of his unhappy life and of being 'at variance with Nature and his Creator'. Both letters are however marked by abrupt changes of mood from utter despondency to unbounded optimism about his work. 'At the moment I feel equal to anything' he told Amenda, mentioning the improvement in his piano-playing and hoping that they might go off on some tour together: 'When I am playing and composing my affliction still hampers me least; it affects me most when I am in company', for which reason he sought a congenial and understanding companion.

On 16 November he wrote to Wegeler again about Vering's grotesque remedies, such as the application of 'vesicatories' of bark to both arms [!], and asked for his opinion of galvanism, which was supposed to have effected miraculous cures in Berlin. He added that he had found some consolation in a 'dear charming girl who loves me and whom I love', presumably the young Countess Guicciardi. Unfortunately she was not of his class, and though he had dreamt of marriage he soon discarded the idea and threw himself into his work, 'for to me there is no greater pleasure than to practise and exercise my art'. Beethoven had promoted no 'academies' of his own that year, having no new orchestral works to offer, but had taken part on 30 January 1801 with some other artists in the second of two concerts organised by the singer Christine Gerhardi-Frank in aid of soldiers wounded at the battle of Hohenlinden. The first had been devoted to Haydn's *Creation*, and the advertising of the second, in which the 'famous' Frau von Frank's was the only name to appear, brought forth a sarcastic note from Beethoven: 'I fully realise that not only I, but also Punto, Simoni and Galvani will demand the same thing, namely, that the public too shall be informed of our zeal for the charitable and excellent object of this concert. If not, we must all come to the conclusion that we are useless people.'[8] He had seldom

[8] Letter to Frau Christine Gerhardi-Frank, shortly after 16 Jan. 1801.

controlled anger with such acid diplomacy. His more explosive temperament, which broke out into violent arguments with his brothers, friends and patrons, was a recurring subject in the reminiscences of Ferdinand Ries. Ferdinand, the son of Franz Ries from Bonn, was only seventeen when he came to Vienna at the end of 1801. He studied the piano with Beethoven for three years until recalled to Bonn for military service, became a prolific composer, and had a great success in London, where he lived from 1813 to 1824. During that later time they were to have important correspondence over Beethoven's dealings with the Philharmonic Society and the English editions of such works as the 'Hammerklavier' Sonata.

In 1801, after *Prometheus*, the piano again absorbed Beethoven, but his next three sonatas introduced new elements of freedom and fantasy after the Classical precision of op. 22. The funeral march 'for a hero' in op. 26 suggests that the idea of the *Eroica* was already looming; and each of the two op. 27 sonatas bore the disarming subtitle 'quasi una fantasia', though the inescapable nickname 'Moonlight' for op. 27 no. 2 was not the composer's. A work in a different genre, perhaps a by-product of the op. 18 quartets, was the String Quintet in C op. 29 with two violas; but it was after composing yet another piano sonata, the so-called 'Pastoral' op. 28, that Beethoven told Krumpholz of his dissatisfaction and his intention to strike out on a 'new path'. One outcome was the completion the following year of the op. 30 violin sonatas and the op. 31 piano sonatas. In each case the second of the group of three was in a minor key. Both the C minor for violin and piano and the D minor for piano are outstanding for their dramatic force, and though it may be thought facile to relate their tragic overtones to the crisis of Beethoven's deafness, it is tempting to do so.

Like many other Viennese, Beethoven was in the habit of spending part of his summer months in the country, and he seemed to find relaxation and inspiration in the peaceful contemplation of nature, taking sketchbooks on his walks, noting down ideas in pencil and elaborating on them when he returned home. In 1802, possibly on the advice of one of his doctors, Vering or Schmidt, or simply to shun society, he retired to the nearby village of Heiligenstadt for a longer period than usual. He was visited by Ries for his lessons and he worked, among other things, on the op. 31 piano sonatas and the Second Symphony; but Heiligenstadt was to give its name to the extraordinary document of depression and despair, in fact a Testament addressed to his two brothers, that was set down on 6 and 10 October shortly before his return to Vienna. Two interesting observations are that he left blank spaces where his brother Johann's name should have appeared; and that although the crisis was surmounted, the document was carefully preserved and, like the letter of 1812 to the 'Immortal Beloved', only discovered after Beethoven's death twenty-five years later.

The Heiligenstadt Testament is, as Maynard Solomon has said, 'the most striking confessional statement', and his general analysis of it is worth quoting:

> But the testament's emotional tone is curiously uneven, alternating between touching expressions of Beethoven's feelings of despair at his encroaching deafness and stilted, even literary formulations emphasising his adherence to virtue. There are passages of real pathos, but these are so intertwined with self-conscious dramatics that one begins to realise that this neatly written document is a carefully revised 'fair copy' which has been scrubbed clean of much of its original emotion.[9]

Although Maynard Solomon remains unpersuaded by the references to suicide – 'I would have ended my life – it was only *my art* that held me back' – the obsession with death is enough for one to sense the depths of Beethoven's despair as he described the progress of his deafness. How impossible for him, as a musician, to say to people 'Speak louder, shout, for I am deaf'; how humiliating that a companion, perhaps Ferdinand Ries, had remarked on a distant flute or a shepherd singing and *he* had heard nothing. Yet he did not wish to be remembered as a misanthrope. There seems moreover a confusion in thought between the imminence of death and its indefinite postponement: he asks for patience and hopes that his determination will remain firm. He tells his brothers that after his death they are to procure an account of his malady from Dr Schmidt 'if he is still alive', implying some hypothetical date in the distant future. Then, four days after writing the main testament, he added a postscript which, though still addressed to his brothers and with the same blank space for Johann's name, is more self-communing: he bids farewell to Heiligenstadt, where his hopes have been blighted and his high

[9] See Appendix E for complete text of the Heiligenstadt Testament.
 Maynard Solomon's comments are from his *Beethoven* (New York, 1977).

courage has disappeared, and begs Providence to grant him at last 'but one day of *pure joy*'.

It is possible to interpret the Testament as the culmination and resolution of some desperate fantasy, a kind of death-wish to be endured for the sake of a new philosophy, a new resignation, a greater will-power. One recalls the remark in his second letter to Wegeler: 'I will seize Fate by the throat; it shall certainly not bend and crush me completely.' The Heiligenstadt year had in fact been astonishingly productive, and within eight days of the Testament, after his return to Vienna, Beethoven was writing to Breitkopf and Härtel about two sets of variations for piano that he had composed. 'Both sets' he wrote 'are worked out in quite a *new manner*, and each in a *separate and different way*.[10] These were the F major op. 34, with its carefully planned circle of keys, and the 'Prometheus' set op. 35, with the unusual treatment of the bass of the theme and the climactic fugue. The 'new path' already had the *Eroica* Symphony as its goal, and rudimentary sketches for it followed Beethoven's work on the 'Prometheus' Variations in the 'Wielhorsky' sketchbook of 1802 and 1803; but they were soon shelved temporarily on account of an unexpected project, the oratorio *Christus am Oelberge* or 'The Mount of Olives'.

[10] Letter to Breitkopf and Härtel, 18 Oct. 1802.

3

The middle period (1803–12)

The division of Beethoven's creative life into the customary three periods has been justly criticised as 'simplistic', but even the most fastidious scholar will instinctively refer to a work as early, middle or late for mere convenience. In Beethoven's case 'early' is particularly misleading since its usual application covers the immense growth of mastery and style from the Dressler Variations of 1782 to the Second Symphony of 1802, the year of the Heiligenstadt Testament. By this reckoning it might be argued that Schubert, who died at thirty-one, only wrote 'early' works. Even Beethoven's op. 1 trios, though early enough in relation to the late quartets, are sufficiently mature to call for some line of demarcation shortly after his arrival in Vienna. As for the so-called 'middle period' the Heiligenstadt crisis and the astonishing break-through of the *Eroica* justify the marking off of a new phase from around 1802 to 1803 up to the end of 1812, which saw the completion of the Seventh and Eighth symphonies and was followed by a notable lull in creativity.

Surprise is often expressed that the Heiligenstadt year (1802) should have yielded such a radiant and untroubled work as the Second Symphony. The relation between art and life is a subtle affair, for the true artist creates out of his total experience, a point made by Deryck Cooke in *The Language of Music* on the great contrasts in character and emotion of Mozart's last three symphonies. The nature of a work may however be dictated by a commission or an occasion. Early in 1803 Beethoven took up lodgings in the Theater an der Wien as a result of a request for an opera from its director Emanuel Schikaneder, librettist of *The Magic Flute*. The availability of an orchestra and chorus called for an immediate concert, and on 5 April Beethoven introduced his new oratorio *Christus am Oelberge*, specially written for the event, in another generous programme that also included the first two symphonies and the long-awaited Third Piano Concerto.

Beethoven had not written a large-scale choral work since the cantatas of 1790, and although *Christus* had a moderate success during his lifetime it has not stayed in the repertory. He half-blamed its rushed composition, though copious sketches survive, but in any case its importance as an interim work should not be underrated. His interest in a religious topic may have been kindled by his recent crisis and was also shown in his hymnlike settings of Gellert poems op. 48, but despite his growing experience as a vocal composer he was well aware of his shortcomings. The discussions with Salieri had been supplemented by a study of Sulzer's *Allgemeine Theorie*, which quoted liberal examples of recitatives from the Italian operas of Carl Heinrich Graun, a younger contemporary of Bach and Handel. Graun's influence has been traced in the recitatives in *Christus* and also in the first version of *Leonore* of two years later, a further reason for relating Beethoven's oratorio to his entry into the world of opera. The entry was however to be perilous and protracted, and Beethoven found a welcome diversion in composing the fieriest and most ambitious of all his violin sonatas, the 'Kreutzer', for the visit of a mulatto virtuoso called George Bridgetower. Meanwhile the proposed opera for Schikaneder, *Vestas Feuer*, proceeded slowly and was eventually abandoned, the libretto having little appeal for him, as he explained in a letter to Johann Rochlitz of Leipzig: 'Just picture to yourself a Roman subject (of which I had been told neither the scheme nor anything else whatever) and language and verses such as could proceed only out of the mouths of our Viennese *apple-women*.'[1] Rochlitz had also sent a libretto which Beethoven rejected, though more reluctantly, because it dealt with magic, 'in which the public is no longer interested'. The truth of the matter was that the Viennese audiences, and Beethoven himself, had been captivated by the influx of new French operas by Cherubini and Méhul, with their up-to-date plots of heroism, rescue and escape; and it was to a French libretto that Beethoven now turned, Bouilly's *Leonore ou l'amour conjugal*. Schikaneder had meanwhile left the theatre, the original contract was suspended, and Beethoven was obliged to move lodgings, sharing rooms for a time with his old friend Stephan von Breuning. He found a new librettist in Joseph Sonnleithner, who became secretary to the Court Theatres in February 1804. By the autumn he had quarrelled with Stephan but sent a typical letter of repentance, putting the blame on to anonymous outsiders:

[1] Letter to Johann Friedrich Rochlitz, 4 Jan. 1804.

It was not *malice* which was surging within me against you, no, for in that case I should no longer have been worthy of your friendship. It was passion, both *in your heart* and *in mine*. – But distrust of you began to stir within me – People interfered between us – people who are far from being worthy of *you* or of *me* . . . .

Beethoven enclosed a portrait of himself, and their friendly relations were sufficiently restored for him to call on Stephan's help in revising Sonnleithner's *Leonore* libretto after the failure of its first performances.

The year spent in the Theater an der Wien, with *Vestas Feuer* literally hanging fire, had been fruitful in another direction, the *Eroica*, though much of the work may have been done in Beethoven's summer retreat at Oberdöbling. His approach to this monumental conception can be studied in progressive detail in the sketchbook of 1803 known as 'Landsberg 6', which was the subject of Nottebohm's most famous commentary. The account of Beethoven's furious destruction of the dedication to Bonaparte when he proclaimed himself Emperor is well known, but his attitude to the fallen hero was to fluctuate. He even considered leaving Vienna for Paris in the summer or autumn of 1804, in which case the restoration of the title would have been expedient, to say the least; but, as it turned out, the 'hero' of the symphony became anonymous. In another sense it could be claimed as Beethoven himself. For its date and its unprecedented time-scale the *Eroica* continues to astonish for its architectural certainty, the more so when one observes its laborious gestation in the sketches, with fragmented and apparently unrelated ideas gradually merging into a continuous whole. Yet it is easy to understand the perplexity and even the hostility with which it was received in some quarters. The man who shouted from the gallery 'I'll give another kreutzer if only the thing will stop' had after all been confronted with a symphony twice as long as usual, not to mention its violent contrasts, vehement reiterations and cross-accents, and its passages of themeless, almost timeless suspense. Even Ferdinand Ries was misled by the 'false' horn entry halfway through the first movement and incurred Beethoven's wrath for saying that the player had come in wrongly.

The first public performance of the *Eroica* was given on 7 April 1805, though there had been a private run-through at Prince Lobkowitz's in the previous December. The new French 'revolutionary' style, touched on with reference to *Leonore*, did not only leave its mark on opera: its influence can be felt on a good deal of Beethoven's instrumental music, even the three Marches for piano duet op. 45 that he wrote in 1802 and 1803. It showed expectedly in a work originally intended for Bonaparte: in the rousing martial tuttis of the *Eroica*, in the fanfare of horns in the trio of the scherzo, and the apotheosis of the opening theme itself, far transcending its amusing kinship with the overture to Mozart's youthful *Bastien und Bastienne*. Beethoven's other orchestral work of 1804 was a hybrid that has won its way back into the repertory only after a long neglect: the Triple Concerto for piano, violin and cello op. 56. Like the oratorio *Christus* it was an important stepping-stone and contained structural features that affected his three remaining concertos. Meanwhile the piano sonatas reflected the grand manner of the *Eroica*. Sketches for the 'Waldstein' followed in its wake, and the 'Appassionata', though not published until 1807, was its stormy minor-key counterpart. There are however plenty of examples of the great middle-period architect taking smaller forms in his stride – the Bagetelles op. 33, the Marches op. 45, and the strange two-movement Piano Sonata in F op. 54. In 1803 Beethoven also began a long correspondence with George Thomson of Edinburgh, for whom he later arranged numerous Scottish, Irish and Welsh folksongs with accompaniment for piano trio, carrying on a tradition already established by Haydn and other Viennese composers.

Two extra-musical matters must be mentioned, the one private, the other decidedly public: the Deym affair, and the Napoleonic advance on Vienna. Beethoven's friendship with the Countess Josephine Deym, née Brunsvik, whose first husband died in 1804, led to an emotional exchange of letters lasting until the autumn of 1807. Once again he had fallen violently in love with an aristocratic pupil, but in spite of her devotion to him as an artist she kept him at bay, using her too recent widowhood and her concern for her young family as excuses. By the time of her second marriage to Baron von Stackelberg in 1810 Beethoven's affections had drifted elsewhere, to his physician's niece Therese Malfatti, who became the object of yet another unsuccessful proposal. His continuing list of amorous obsessions was as usual counterbalanced by absorption in his work, and the earlier stages of the Deym affair (1804–5) coincided with his increasing devotion to his one operatic heroine, the 'ideal feminine' and faithful wife Leonore, whose enterprise and courage saved her wrongfully imprisoned husband Florestan from death at the hands of the tyrant Pizarro. The first performances of *Leonore* were however fraught with hazards, delayed by censorship problems, and finally confounded by the arrival of the Napoleonic troops, who filled the theatre at the premiere on 20 November 1805. Vienna having fallen to the French, most of Beethoven's influential friends had fled or otherwise failed to attend, and those that did had serious reservations about the opera, which survived for only three nights. When plans were made to revive it in the spring of 1806 Beethoven was reluctantly persuaded to make drastic cuts and revisions, reducing its three acts to two; but even with Stephan von Breuning's help the second version failed also. Beethoven complained bitterly about the standard of the production, demanded extra rehearsals and withdrew the score after only two performances. He had already given his opinion of the orchestral playing to Sebastian Mayer, Mozart's brother-in-law, who had sung – and protested about! – the part of Pizarro in the ill-fated 1805 production:

> I shall not say anything about the wind instruments but – that all the *pianissimos* and crescendos, all the decrescendos and all fortes and *fortissimos* should have been deleted from my opera! In any case they are not all observed. All desire to compose anything more ceases completely if I have to hear my work performed *like that*![2]

Only eight years later did Beethoven achieve the opera's definitive form as *Fidelio*, though he always preferred the title *Leonore*; but the earlier versions afford some interesting comparisons and yielded two magnificent overtures, *Leonore* nos 2 and 3, which proved too overwhelming for the opening scenes and were discarded from the opera-house in favour of the much shorter and lighter *Fidelio* overture of 1814.

Although the greatness of *Fidelio* is not in doubt, its protracted history betrays Beethoven's problems in dealing with the voice, the stage, librettists and outmoded conventions. After the initial failure in 1805 he turned again to his indisputable and unfettered mastery in the instrumental forms, and the years 1806 to 1808 were especially productive. He had been commissioned to write three more string quartets by the Russian ambassador, Count Rasumovsky, an amateur violinist who had studied with Haydn and may have seen Beethoven's op. 18 set as a new landmark in the quartet's develop-

[2] Letter to Friedrich Sebastian Mayer, probably 8 Apr. 1806.

ment. He fulfilled the Count's wishes by incorporating Russian themes in the first two of the 'Rasumovsky' quartets, but the three works showed how far his style had developed in the five or six years since op. 18 appeared. Both listeners and players were bewildered, including Schuppanzigh himself, who probably thought back to the easy-going Septet of 1800. However the impression that Beethoven was writing for a future age showed his confidence in his powers, and among the sketches for the third quartet he made the curious personal note: 'Let your deafness no longer be a secret – not even in art.'

Beethoven seemed to be coming to terms with his affliction and found himself more able to mix in society without fear or embarrassment. In the summer of 1806 he travelled more widely than usual, visiting the Brunsviks in Hungary and going on to stay at the country estates of Prince Lichnowsky and Count Oppersdorff in Silesia. His ambivalent attitude to his patrons had not changed and an incident that autumn illustrated his recalcitrant nature when principles were at stake. Lichnowsky was entertaining some French officers and asked Beethoven to play for them, but this, despite repeated entreaties, he would not do. Not only that: he left the castle that night and trudged in the rain to the nearest town clutching, it is said, the manuscript of the 'Appassionata' Sonata, and later vented his wrath by smashing a bust of his patron. His remark about Lichnowsky may have been arrogant and ungrateful, but it was true enough: 'There have been, and will be, thousands of princes; there is only one Beethoven.'[3]

Whereas the damp-stained autograph of the 'Appassionata' symbolised the turbulent side of Beethoven's nature, in music as in life, his next orchestral works breathed a more serene confidence: the Violin Concerto, the G major Piano Concerto, and the Fourth Symphony. Since the Violin Concerto is regarded by so many as the supreme work of its kind, it is a shock to learn of the conditions of its first performance, but as often happened the work was only ready at the last moment. The occasion was a benefit concert at the Theater an der Wien on 23 December 1806, at which the leader of the orchestra, Franz Clement, more or less sight-read the solo part and interpolated some violinistic acrobatics of his own between the

---

[3] This famous remark, though hard to verify, has been much quoted and paraphrased.

movements. The piano concerto and the symphony were introduced at Lobkowitz's palace in the following March, and the Prince must have noted the relaxed manner of both works after the titanic experience of the *Eroica*; but Beethoven, with sketches for the Fifth Symphony well advanced, offered his stormier C minor mood in the overture to Collin's *Coriolan*, which was also heard for the first time.

Beethoven's fame had spread abroad and although he never managed to visit London like the child Mozart and the sixty-year-old Haydn he showed an increasing interest in the British market, hardly to be satisfied by the prospect of arranging folksongs for George Thomson of Edinburgh. He therefore welcomed a visit from Muzio Clementi in April 1807 to discuss English publication of some of his recent works. Clementi's long career was a varied one: though born in Rome he settled in England in his early teens and from about 1770, the year of Beethoven's birth, produced a steady output of piano sonatas that were influential in their idiomatic treatment of the instrument and the development of a genuinely pianistic technique. He later turned to piano-making and publishing and wrote an amusing account to his partner Collard about his meeting with Beethoven, whom he called 'that haughty beauty':

> 'Are you engaged with any publisher in London?' – 'No' says he. 'Suppose then that you prefer *me*?' – 'With all my heart.' 'Done. What have you ready?' – 'I'll bring you a list.' In short I agree to take in MSS three quartets, a symphony, an overture and a concerto for violin, which is beautiful and which at my request he will adapt for the pianoforte . . . and a concerto for the piano, for *all* of which we are to pay him two hundred pounds sterling.[4]

Clementi was on tour at the time, and it was not until 1810 that the works were published and payment received. Beethoven's associations with England thrived however. As early as 1793 William Gardiner of Leicester had enthused over the String Trio in E flat op. 3, which had arrived in manuscript with the Abbé Dobbeler, the Elector of Cologne's refugee chaplain; and, looking ahead, the Philharmonic Society, founded in 1813, was to play all nine of the symphonies in its first twelve seasons. Beethoven was astute enough about money to seek simultaneous contracts for the same works in different countries, with Simrock in Bonn, Pleyel in Paris, and so forth. In these dealings he was assisted by Baron Ignaz von Gleichen-

---

[4] Letter to Collard, 22 Apr. 1807.

stein, amateur cellist and secretary to the War Department, whom he repaid with the dedication of the A major Cello Sonata op. 69; and also his brother Nikolaus Johann with whom he fell out, typically, over the repayment of a loan he had made him to set up as a chemist in Linz.

In 1807 Beethoven was invited to follow in Haydn's footsteps and to produce a mass for Prince Nikolaus Esterházy to celebrate his wife's nameday. He had not written a mass setting before and the work proceeded slowly, with illness as an additional excuse, but it was ready in time and in September he went to Eisenstadt to direct the performance. Unfortunately the Prince was scornful about it, no doubt drawing invidious comparisons with Haydn's last six masses, and the presence of Hummel as the resident Kapellmeister added to Beethoven's feeling of humiliation. The work was the Mass in C and he nevertheless thought well enough of it himself to commend it to several publishers and made no mention of its poor reception when writing to Josephine Deym on his return. The Deym affair was drawing to a close, sadly for Beethoven, but he was soon preoccupied with two of his most important middle-period works, the completion of the Fifth Symphony and the creation of the Sixth, the *Pastoral*, on which he worked during the summer of 1808. In each case there was a chamber-music bonus: the A major Cello Sonata and the two piano trios op. 70. The renewed orchestral activity called for a concert, and bearing in mind his vain attempts to obtain a commission for an opera a year [!], his considerable services to charity, and his veiled threat to leave Vienna if his request was not met, he was granted the use of the Theater an der Wien for his own benefit on 22 December 1808.

His works had already been featured that season in a series of concerts given by some enthusiasts known as the Liebhaber or 'Dilettanten', but the December affair must surely rank as one of the most fantastic displays of new music ever put on by a single composer. With the length of the programme, the limited rehearsal time and the coldness of the hall, one can imagine the roughness of the performances; and, as with the Violin Concerto two years before, it seems ironic that so much great music should have been first heard in such adverse conditions. The concert included the first performances of the Fifth and Sixth symphonies, numbered in reverse order with the *Pastoral* as 'no. 5'; the first public performance of the Fourth Piano Concerto; movements from the Mass in C, new to

Vienna; and, since a chorus was available, a grand finale hurriedly written for the occasion, the Fantasy for piano, orchestra and chorus op. 80. Beethoven improvised the introduction to the Fantasy, having already given a separate extemporisation, and also revived a much earlier work, the aria 'Ah, perfido!', which was poorly sung by a last-minute substitute. It is not surprising that the orchestra broke down in the Fantasy and that Beethoven cut the long 'da capo' in the scherzo of the C minor Symphony, as the surviving band-parts show, leaving posterity in doubt about his ultimate intentions for this movement.

The profits from this historic benefit concert are not known, but it is clear that Beethoven, in spite of his earlier letter to Wegeler, was obsessed with the problem of financial security. His annuity from Prince Lichnowsky, dating from 1800, had presumably ceased, but his earnings as a free-lance must still have been considerable. Though he was haunted by the idea of marriage he remained single, and if he seemed hopeless in his dealings with servants, honest or dishonest, he could always count on the hospitality of his well-to-do friends. Yet the notion of a permanent appointment appealed to him, even the antiquated title and status of Kapellmeister, in which childhood memories of his grandfather's prestige and his father's failure may have played a part. He retained a wavering attitude to Napoleon, despite his adamant refusal to play for Lichnowsky's French officers; and two months before the famous benefit concert he was offered the post of Kapellmeister at Kassel in the service of Napoleon's brother Jerome, who had been created 'King' of Westphalia in the new Revolutionary empire. He took the invitation seriously enough to inform the publishers Breitkopf and Härtel that he would be calling at Leipzig on his way to Kassel: 'At last' he wrote 'I have been forced by intrigues, cabals and underhanded dealings of all sorts to leave the only surviving German fatherland.'

In the end he never went to Kassel, despite his vituperations against the Viennese, but was able to use the terms of the appointment, equivalent to about 3400 Austrian florins a year, as a bargaining-point with his patrons. His negotiators included the Countess Erdödy, with whom he had been sharing lodgings, and his cellist friend and part-time agent Gleichenstein. The outcome was a guaranteed annuity in excess of the Kassel offer, namely 4000 florins, with the proviso that he should remain in Austria and forfeit the salary if he should ever obtain a comparably paid appointment.

The guarantors and signatories to this agreement, dated 1 March 1809, were the Archduke Rudolph, Prince Lobkowitz and Prince Kinsky; but even with these generous terms Beethoven was a hard bargainer and requested further conditions that he later waived, such as the annual use of the Theater an der Wien for a benefit concert and the still coveted title of Imperial Kapellmeister. There were to be problems in maintaining the agreed annuity, partly due to the wartime inflation that followed the French occupation; and the deaths of Kinsky in 1812 and Lobkowitz in 1816 led to much argument with their heirs and agents; but a basic security was assured, and the Archduke Rudolph lived to receive in return a number of important dedications, including those of the 'Hammerklavier' Sonata and the *Missa Solemnis*. His chief claim to immortality was however through the 'Archduke' Trio op. 97 of 1811, and his prowess as a pianist seemed to have been reflected in the earlier dedications of the Fifth and so-called 'Emperor' Concerto and the 'Lebewohl' Sonata op. 81a, both dating from 1809, the year of the agreement.

The Archduke, youngest brother of the Emperor and always addressed deferentially as 'Your Imperial Highness' or 'YIH' by Beethoven, had first come to him for piano lessons in 1803 or 1804, and it says much for his musicality that Beethoven also helped him with composition. The 'Lebewohl' Sonata was an affectionate tribute occasioned by Rudolph's enforced departure from Vienna during the 1809 occupation and was the only really programmatic sonata Beethoven ever wrote. Its three movements expressed the emotions of farewell, absence and reunion, and their appeal reaches out far beyond this personal localised incident. Beethoven remained in Vienna meanwhile to endure the French invasion but nevertheless completed some other things: the 'Harp' String Quartet op. 74, some songs, and a strange mixture of shorter piano works – the improvisatory Fantasy op. 77, the miniature but forward-looking Sonata in F sharp op. 78 and the far simpler one in G major op. 79. The one orchestral work of the year, the E flat Piano Concerto, was in the same key as the Quartet and the 'Lebewohl' Sonata and proved to be a farewell of a different kind. It was the last and grandest of his concertos and its cadenza-like opening may have owed something to the piano introduction in the Choral Fantasy that preceded it.

Beethoven's deafness had by now made his public exposure as a pianist more and more of a trial, and the first performance of the E flat Concerto was given not by him but by Friedrich Schneider at Leipzig in 1811, leaving Carl Czerny to introduce it to Vienna in the following year, when the splendours of the work seemed to pass without much comment. Posterity has made ample amends, though the nickname 'Emperor', attributed to J.B. Cramer, has an ironic ring about it, bearing in mind the title-page of the *Eroica* and with Napoleon's armies once more at the gates of Vienna. As Beethoven buried his head in pillows at his brother Caspar Carl's house during the bombardment of the city on 12 May 1809 he may have recalled a remark he had made to Wenzel Krumpholz after the Battle of Jena three years before: that if only he understood the art of war as well as he did that of music he would certainly have defeated Napoleon.

The French occupation lasted only two months but left a trail of disruption. Beethoven wrote to Breitkopf on 26 July: 'The existence I had built up only a short time ago rests on shaky foundations. . . What a destructive disorderly life I see and hear around me: nothing but drums, cannons, and human misery in every form.' 1809 had been a year of paradoxes for Beethoven. It produced the contract for the annuity and, in music, the grand optimistic manner of the 'Emperor' Concerto, some of which overflowed into the finale of the 'Lebewohl' Sonata. After the invasion he appeared to abandon the heroic style for a while and, as already noted, adopted more intimate forms, in turn tenderly expressive and humorously laconic. Two deaths must have affected him deeply: his physician Johann Schmidt, who had taken over from Dr Vering at the time of Heiligenstadt, died in February; and on 31 May a whole musical epoch ended with the death of Haydn, who more than any other composer had bridged the gap between the first glimmerings of the Classical style and its glorious fulfilment. Haydn had lived long enough to have been able to hear the *Eroica* and the 'Rasumovsky' Quartets, and even the recent December 'Akademie' that included the Fifth and *Pastoral* symphonies, but there is no indication that he did so. Beethoven, on the other hand, had attended the performance of *The Creation* given on 27 March 1808 to celebrate its composer's 76th birthday and, according to Geiringer, 'knelt down before Haydn and fervently kissed the hands and forehead of his old teacher'. The earlier problems of their pupil-teacher relationship had evaporated, and in a letter to a young admirer four years later Beethoven was able to write: 'Do not rob Handel, Haydn and Mozart of their laurel wreaths. They are entitled to theirs but I am not yet entitled to one.'[5]

If 1809 had been Beethoven's E flat year, 1810 was his F minor one, since it produced the music for Goethe's *Egmont* and the strikingly dramatic but concise Quartet op. 95, his last string quartet until he returned to the form for the late series from op. 127 onwards. He described the Quartet as 'serioso' and the incidental music for *Egmont* was also a serious undertaking in that it partly compensated for his lack of further opera commissions or, more to the point, suitable libretti. The story of *Egmont* was of heroism and self-sacrifice, dealing with the martyrdom of the Flemish nobleman who predicted the triumph of the Netherlanders over their Spanish oppressors; and the 'Symphony of Victory' in which F minor yields to an overwhelming burst of F major is well known to concertgoers from its use in the coda of the overture. *Egmont* brought Beethoven into personal touch with Goethe, whom he had long admired from afar, and here the intermediary was Bettina Brentano from Frankfurt, whose warm friendship helped to distract him from his rejection by Therese Malfatti. Yet he still suffered severe bouts of depression, as shown in his letters fo Wegeler and Zmeskall. This was the first time he had written to Wegeler since the Heiligenstadt crisis and he stressed similar feelings of despair and isolation:

> Yet I should be happy, perhaps one of the happiest of mortals, if that fiend had not settled in my ears – If I had not read somewhere that a man should not voluntarily quit this life so long as he can still perform a good deed, I would have left this earth long ago – and, what is more, by my own hand. Oh, this life is indeed beautiful, but for me it is poisoned for ever.[6]

None the less it may have been renewed thoughts of marriage that led him to ask Wegeler to acquire his baptismal certificate from Bonn.

Apart from *Egmont* and the F minor Quartet Beethoven's 'good deed' of 1810 had been the work on his last and greatest piano trio, the B flat op. 97, dedicated to the Archduke Rudolph, who had by now become his closest patron and pupil and for whom he had prepared a detailed course of study. The Trio was not completed until the following spring, but Beethoven was otherwise occupied with publishers and proof-reading. He wrote to Breitkopf about his

[5] Letter to Emilie M. at H. (Hamburg?), from Teplitz, 17 July 1812.
[6] Letter to Wegeler, 2 May 1810.

continuing search for opera libretti and complained bitterly about the careless engraving of some of his recent works. On 6 May 1811 he began his letter to them, 'Mistakes – mistakes – you yourself are a unique mistake' and went on: 'Apparently the tribunal of music at Leipzig can't produce one single efficient proof-reader; and to make matters worse, you send out the works before you receive the corrected proofs . . .' One setback to his operatic ambitions was the death of Heinrich von Collin, for whose play he had written the *Coriolan* overture; another was the forestalling of a French melodrama setting, *Les Ruines de Babylone*, by an unexpected production of the original play at the Theater auf der Wieden. In the summer of 1811 he did however write overtures and incidental music for Kotzebue's *Ruins of Athens* and *King Stephen* to celebrate the opening of a new theatre in Pest, though the overtures have never matched his earlier ones in popular esteem. He spent this summer at Teplitz, a Bohemian spa renowned for its 'cure' and, during the Napoleonic upheaval, its neutrality as a meeting-place for diplomats and other dignitaries.

Beethoven had gone to Teplitz on the advice of Dr Malfatti and the change and cure evidently benefitted him, for on returning to Vienna he launched into the vigorously exultant Seventh Symphony, working on it throughout the winter and making a note in his sketches about 'a second symphony in D minor'. A further symphony, the Eighth, was in fact completed the following year and was decidedly not in a minor key but in F major, carrying over some of the vitality of the Seventh though on a more compact scale; but the memo about yet another 'in D minor' reappeared, and he had already informed Breitkopf of his intention to compose *three* new symphonies. No third symphony was forthcoming however – until the Ninth of twelve years later. Was this already stirring in Beethoven's mind, with or without Schiller's 'Ode to Joy', when he made this long-term prophecy about its key? Meanwhile, before completing the scoring of the Eighth Symphony, he returned to Teplitz for a more eventful visit in July 1812. He met and talked with Goethe but was disturbed that such a great man should defer so much to his mere social superiors. Goethe's impression of Beethoven was to be expected: 'His talent amazed me but he is an utterly untamed personality, who is not altogether in the wrong in holding the world to be detestable . . . He is easily excused, on the other hand, and much to be pitied, as his hearing is leaving him, which perhaps mars the musical part of his nature less than the social.'[7]

The return to Teplitz is however associated with a very different matter: Beethoven's impassioned love-letter to the 'Immortal Beloved' (see Appendix F). The mystery surrounding this document, which was addressed to an unnamed person and never posted, has taxed biographers ever since its discovery after his death. The letter bears no place-name and no year and was written in three instalments, on the morning and evening of 6 July and the morning of 7 July; but the addition of 'Monday' to the evening one narrows down the possible years, assuming that Beethoven had not mistaken the day of the week. Schindler, in his confident and unreliable manner, assumed that the beloved must have been the Countess Guicciardi and had the effrontery to add the date '1806' without having checked that she was married and living in Naples at that time; he then suggested 1803, though in neither year did 6 July fall on a Monday. A later biographer, Ludwig Nohl, proposed 1801 and kept to the idea of Giulietta, bearing in mind Beethoven's rapturous account of her in his second letter to Wegeler that year. The matter was reopened by the indefatigable Thayer who, having calculated that the only applicable years were 1795, 1801, 1807, 1812 and 1818, returned to 1806, blamed the composer for an error of one day, and offered the Countess Therese von Brunsvik. Other theories were propounded towards the end of the nineteenth century, mostly based on scanty evidence and wishful thinking, and it was not until Thomas San-Galli's book of 1909 that an accurate sifting of information, including Beethoven's references to his journey, the times of posts and so forth, confirmed Teplitz as the place and 1812 as the year beyond reasonable doubt. In that case the abbreviation 'K' for the beloved's temporary residence may be taken as Karlsbad, and a research into the police records of arriving and departing visitors restricts the potential candidates further. Moreover if the letter is taken at face value it seems evident that Beethoven had met his beloved recently, probably in Prague, where he is known to have stayed on his way to Teplitz.

For these and other circumstantial reasons Maynard Solomon has made a strong case for Antonie Brentano, despite the fact that she was married to Bettina Brentano's half-brother Franz and had a young musical daughter Maximiliane, for whom Beethoven was

[7] Letter to Zelter from Karlsbad, 2 Sept. 1812.

shortly to compose an 'easy' piano trio in one movement (WoO 39). Many other contenders had been put forward from the long list of his known or conjectured attachments: Amalie Sebald, Bettina Brentano, Marie Bigot, Dorothea von Ertmann, the Countess Erdödy, and even Magdalena Willmann and Therese Malfatti, both of whom are known to have rejected his proposals; but Solomon's claim for Antonie Brentano is the most convincing. Beethoven's closeness to the whole family and his stated disapproval of such extra-marital affairs do not rule it out. It is known that Antonie was estranged from her husband over her reluctance to return to their home in Frankfurt, and her devotion to Beethoven was to be reciprocated in the dedication of one of his most important and intellectually challenging late piano works, the Diabelli Variations. The unique and uninhibited nature of the letter and the fact that it was never sent may lead some to regard it as a fantasy, and if Antonie was indeed its object this did not prevent Beethoven from joining the whole Brentano family in Karlsbad a week or two later.

Beethoven's travels in the autumn of 1812 also included a visit to Linz, where his brother Nikolaus Johann's business as an apothecary had thrived rather than suffered as a result of the Napoleonic wars. A word is called for about his strained relationships with both his brothers, which seemed to be afflicted with common mistrust and mutual interference. The elder, Caspar Carl, who worked as a cashier in Vienna, had married in 1806. His wife Johanna was pregnant at the time, and Beethoven's disapproval of the whole affair may have some bearing on a note he made among the sketches for the melancholic Adagio of the first 'Rasumovsky' Quartet: 'A weeping willow or acacia tree on my brother's grave.' Their son Karl was to play a tragic role in Beethoven's life after Caspar Carl's death in 1815, when a lengthy battle was to wage over the guardianship of the child; but they had been on good enough terms for him to seek refuge at their home during the Napoleonic bombardment in 1809. His sudden arrival at Linz in 1812 had been prompted by uncannily similar circumstances, as though his own lack of success in achieving a lasting relationship with a woman forced him to intervene in the private affairs of others. If, as is now thought, his passionate letter to the 'Immortal Beloved' had in fact been addressed to a married woman, it seems pathetically incongruous on moral grounds that he should try to break up a liaison between his other brother and his housekeeper Therese Obermeyer. His drastic attempts, including the acquisition of an eviction order for Therese and a visit to the local bishop, were foiled: Nikolaus Johann married her on 8 November and Beethoven departed, though it is not known whether he returned directly to Vienna. In the light of all this it is surprising that he found the time and the mood to complete the scoring of the Eighth Symphony and to compose his three *Equali* for trombones at Linz; and that he should produce by the end of the year the last and most subtly expressive of his violin sonatas, the G major op. 96, for a performance by the visiting French violinist Pierre Rode and the Archduke Rudolph.

After the emotional turmoil and the artistic productivity of 1812, which had seen the completion of both the Seventh and Eighth symphonies, Beethoven again entered a period of deep depression, to which other factors may have contributed: the serious illness of Caspar Carl, during which Beethoven persuaded him to sign the fateful document concerning the future guardianship of his son; and financial anxiety over disruptions in the payment of his annuity. His three benefactors had agreed in principle to combat inflation by increasing their contributions, but Prince Kinsky had been killed in a riding accident in November 1812, and Lobkowitz's payments had been frozen owing to his own financial straits, leaving the Archduke's the only regular source of income during a crucial period. After much legal wrangling with Kinsky's heirs the agreed amount was restored, but not until the spring of 1815.

4

Years of crisis and new horizons (1813–20)

It is significant, though tragic and ironic, that the rich decade of Beethoven's 'middle period' should have been ushered in and out by such crises of intense personal despair; but whereas Heiligenstadt had intensified and certainly not disrupted his creative energy, the year 1813 was practically barren. Yet his last work, the Violin Sonata op. 96 of December 1812, had shown no sign of a falling-off. On the contrary, its tenderly resigned character seemed to presage a new style, another 'new path'. Perhaps it is too easy in retrospect to see or hear it as a harbinger of the third period, in which such introspection abounds, but one is tempted to ask, in view of his impending silence: was Beethoven not yet ready to pursue this path further and to turn his back on the more heroic style that had even characterised much of his 'little' Eighth Symphony? The gentle manner of op. 96 had however been partly influenced by the violinist's wishes, and especially the final variations. Beethoven had written to the Archduke a few days before the performance: 'I have not hurried unduly to compose the last movement merely for the sake of being punctual, the more so as in view of Rode's playing I have had to give more thought to the composition of this movement. In our Finales we like to have fairly noisy passages but R does not care for them – and so I have been rather hampered.'[1] Other letters to Rudolph refer to his depression: 'I have been ailing, although mentally, it is true, more than physically'; and in January 1813: 'As for my health, it is pretty much the same, the more so as moral factors are affecting it and these apparently are not very speedily removed.'

Moral factors? Beethoven wrote in May 1813 about being driven into a state 'bordering on mental confusion' and made entries in his diary or *Tagebuch* that hark back to the short-lived but obsessive 'Immortal Beloved' affair: 'O terrible circumstances, which do not suppress my longing for domesticity, but its realisation.

---

[1] Letter written shortly before 29 Dec. 1812.

O God, God, look down upon the unhappy B., do not let it continue for longer.' This *Tagebuch*, which he kept from 1812 to 1818, is an extraordinary miscellany of trivial day-to-day memoranda, proverbs and prayers, profound self-communings, and lengthy transcripts from poetic, philosophical and religious writings. His faith, though always personal and undogmatic, was strengthened in such times of emotional crisis, but although he had often found consolation in his work and wrote repeatedly about 'living for his art', even this was of little avail in 1813. Somehow he managed to keep up with correspondence during that spring and summer: the letters to the Archduke, to Zmeskall, and to Joseph von Varena about performances of his works at a convent in Graz; and on 19 February a lengthy reply to George Thomson in Edinburgh, copied into French by another hand, about payments for his recent folksong elaborations.

He ruminated in the *Tagebuch* about moral scruples, and his letters to Zmeskall make several veiled references to prostitutes, such as: 'Keep away from rotten fortresses, for an attack from them is more deadly than one from well-preserved ones'; and in excuse or remorse he wrote in the *Tagebuch* that 'the weaknesses of nature are given by nature herself'. Whether he seriously considered suicide in the first months of 1813 is hard to prove, though Schindler said that his close friends knew of one such attempt; but in the summer at Baden he was found by the Streichers 'in the most deplorable condition' and so ill-kept and unhygienic that guests at an inn avoided sitting near him. The concern shown by his friends helped to restore him to society, and towards the end of the year an unexpected event was to revive his creativity in a bizarre, mundane sort of way. In November, back in Vienna, he wrote to Zmeskall: 'I am dining today with Maelzel.'

Johann Nepomuk Maelzel, famous for his metronome, was an inventor and an opportunist. If his mechanical trumpeter was a sensation, his automatic Panharmonicon, which imitated most of the sounds of a full orchestra, was more so. He now sought Beethoven's help in concocting a piece of programme music to celebrate Wellington's victory over Napoleon at Vittoria. The resultant 'Battle Symphony' was orchestrated by Beethoven for more normal use, and his own hand is abundantly clear in the fugal treatment of 'God save the King' at the end. Although the musical world has generally written it off as a professional frolic, if not the downright nadir of his career, its success with the Viennese was stupendous. It received four performances in quick succession that winter, brought Beethoven considerable financial gain, and inevitably led to a bitter quarrel with Maelzel over the future rights of the work. Plans were afoot for Beethoven to take it to England, where further successes seemed assured; but Vienna had other proposals for him, and the first performances of his two recent real symphonies, especially the Seventh, helped in this sudden upsurge in popularity. The wave of patriotism that had greeted the 'Battle Symphony', and the Napoleonic defeats, called for other occasional works, the chorus 'Germania' and two cantatas, *Ihr weisen Gründer* and *Der glorreiche Augenblick*; but Beethoven's main preoccupation during the spring of 1814 was the revival of *Fidelio*, alias *Leonore*, which he reworked completely with the aid of yet another librettist, Georg Friedrich Treitschke.

At last his opera was a success, and after its reappearance on 23 May it was heard repeatedly, thereby making an appropriate contribution to the spirit and festivities of the Congress of Vienna. Two piano works also brought Beethoven back to a familiar medium after a long absence: the Polonaise in C op. 89 was written for the Empress of Russia, one of the many crowned heads attending the Congress; and the short but important two-movement Sonata in E minor op. 90, dedicated to Lichnowsky's brother Moritz, who was offered an informal 'programme' for the music, relating it to his forthcoming marriage to a singer. On the subject of the piano, however, the tragic decline in Beethoven's own playing was evident when he took part in the 'Archduke' Trio in April and about which Ludwig Spohr wrote:

> On account of his deafness there was scarcely anything left of the virtuosity which had formerly been so greatly admired. In *forte* passages the poor man pounded on the keys till the strings jangled, and in *piano* he played so softly that whole groups of notes were omitted, so that the music was unintelligible.[2]

If this signalled the last throes of his playing career, his activity as a composer had at least been aroused again, yet he must have been aware that his recent works, apart from the op. 90 Sonata and the new *Fidelio*, were of slight or ephemeral worth. He had taken a somewhat malevolent delight in 'thrashing the Viennese' with the 'Battle Symphony', but even during the Congress his sudden new popularity began to decline. The 'sworn enemies' were still at work, and a report

[2] Spohr's autobiography, quoted by Thayer.

to the secret police on 30 November 1814 claimed that his adversaries 'formed an overwhelming majority of connoisseurs who refuse absolutely to listen to his works hereafter'. Not to the *Pathétique*, the 'Moonlight', the Fifth and the *Pastoral* – or even the Septet? Yet even his loyal admirers cannot have been encouraged by the occasional works he continued to produce in the spring of 1815: the Overture *Namensfeier* in honour of the Kaiser; and incidental music for another drama of female heroism called *Leonore Prohaska*, which was in any case banned by the censor. Two young admirers however became closely associated with him at this time: the pianist and composer Ignaz Moscheles, who arranged the vocal score of *Fidelio*; and the law student and violinist Anton Schindler, who became the master's general factotum and his far from trustworthy biographer.

When Moscheles signed the completed vocal score of *Fidelio* with the pious words 'finished with God's help' he brought forth a rejoinder from Beethoven: 'O Man, help thyself!' The pleasantry had serious overtones: his attitude to religion was like that to his work, in short, that rewards, material or spiritual, can only accrue through continuous mental application. In that case the material success of the Maelzel affair must be considered a windfall in circumstances not likely to recur; and it is amusingly ironic to find Beethoven offering the 'Battle of Vittoria' score to Sir George Smart for publication in London on the same terms as the Seventh Symphony and at almost twice the price of another absolute masterpiece, the Eighth. Other financial problems had dragged on. Early in 1815 he pursued his claim on the Kinsky estate through the Prague lawyer Nepomuk Kanka, insisting on the late Prince's undertaking to pay his portion of the annuity in redemption bonds. Although the matter was eventually resolved, there seemed little sign of Beethoven recovering his serious creative powers. There was the brief setting of Rupprecht's 'Merkenstein' and there were touches of his old genius in the choral work based on Goethe's 'Calm Sea and Prosperous Voyage'. The success of *Fidelio* had rekindled his interest in new libretti, but the prospect of working with Treitschke on another opera, *Romulus*, came to nothing. In fact if some fell disaster, illness or suicide, had cut short his life during the winter of 1814–15, his closest friends would have been justified in thinking that he had after all written himself out or succumbed to his growing deafness, and posterity could have regarded the final rewriting of *Fidelio* as a fitting conclusion to his life's work.

Yet the brief op. 90 Piano Sonata of 1814, like the earlier op. 96 with violin, had shown signs of a new growth, concentrated but sensitive, intellectual but spiritual, and with an increasing integration of subtle contrapuntal textures. In the summer of 1815 there was to be a decisive sequel in the two cello sonatas of op. 102, felt by many to be the first real manifestation of Beethoven's 'third period' manner. They were brought about by a strange sequence of events, including Beethoven's reconciliation with the Countess Erdödy after one of his customary but protracted misunderstandings, but their creation also hinges on a disaster, for early on New Year's Eve 1814 the palace of another of his patrons, Count Rasumovsky, had been destroyed by fire. One result was the dispersal of his resident quartet and the engagement of the cellist Joseph Linke as musical tutor to the Erdödy family. Hence the reason and the request for the sonatas, which also produced a characteristic pun from Beethoven about the cellist starting to play on the left bank of the Danube, 'Linke' being German for 'left'. The next important move in this new direction was the Piano Sonata in A op. 101, which he worked on during the following summer of 1816, and which adopted the closely-woven four-movement scheme of the cello sonatas and something of their fugal propensities.

This productivity, vital but sporadic, was to be hampered by a further crisis. On 15 November 1815 Beethoven's brother Caspar Carl died, thereby opening up a new and agonising chapter in the composer's life. Having been cajoled into appointing Beethoven as sole guardian of his son Karl, Caspar Carl had added a codicil to his will pressing for a joint guardianship with his widow Johanna: 'inasmuch as the best of harmony does not exist between my brother and my wife I have found it necessary to add to my will that I by no means desire that my son be taken away from his mother . . . . I recommend *compliance* to my wife and more *moderation* to my brother.' But could one imagine Beethoven exercising moderation in such a situation? His immediate response was to ignore his brother's wishes. Since they had been upheld by the Landrecht of Upper Austria his only chance of gaining custody of the child was by proving the widow's unsuitability as a parent. In desperation he dragged up a four-year-old charge of embezzlement. After various legal arguments he won his case, took the official oath on 19 January 1816, and was granted the right to remove Karl from his mother. Yet it was obvious that Beethoven, for all his pathological possessiveness, could hardly have understood or catered for the needs of a child of nine in his own lodgings and with his way of life. He immediately looked out for a boarding-school on the outskirts of Vienna where Karl would be reasonably safe from his mother's attempts to see or abduct him. This grotesque situation, in which Beethoven saw himself as a kind of Sarastro fighting against the evil machinations of the Queen of the Night, his favourite term for Johanna, was to continue almost to the end of his life, bewildering and tormenting the unhappy nephew to the verge of suicide, and leading his mother to a whole series of deceptions and intrigues. On 6 February he wrote to Antonie Brentano in Frankfurt, sending her a copper engraving of himself in the care of Charles Neate, who was on his way back to London after negotiating some performances of Beethoven's works by the recently formed Philharmonic Society. He made a passing reference to the Karl crisis: 'In the meantime I have fought a battle for the purpose of wresting a poor unhappy child from the clutches of his unworthy mother, and I have won the day – Te Deum laudamus – He is the source of many cares, but *cares which are sweet to me.*'

The whole subject of Beethoven and his nephew has been exhaustively debated and analysed, related to his own internal conflicts and supposed complexes, frustrations and inhibitions, and traced back to the turbulent family background of his childhood, the death of his mother, the drunkenness of his father, and the household responsibilities that had been thrust upon him while still in his teens. His longing for companionship and for a child of his own became an obsession that he regarded in Karl's case as a right; and his ambivalent attitude to Johanna has been seen as an expression of jealousy, guilt or even, a favourite last resort of analysts, his latent homosexual tendencies. Out of the extensive literature mention must be made of the controversial study by Richard and Editha Sterba (1954) and a more recent reappraisal by Maynard Solomon (1977). Critics of the Sterbas have included K.R. Eissler, who sought to justify the unhappy truth by describing the irrationality, even the rudeness and brutality of Beethoven's everyday life as a prerequisite of his creative genius: 'A mastered emotion would never have led to those musical compositions we admire.' Yet paradoxically the preoccupation with Karl, in its earlier stages, had a cramping effect on his creativity.

The only really lasting works of the years 1815 to 1817 had been intimate ones: the three sonatas already mentioned, and the equally intimate song-cycle *An die ferne Geliebte*, with shades of

1 Ludwig van Beethoven, Beethoven's grandfather.
Portrait in oils by Leopold Radoux.

2 Beethoven *c.* 1786.
Silhouette by Joseph Neesen.

3 Beethoven. Engraving by
Johann Neidl from a drawing
by Von Treuberg, 1800,
published by Cappi.

4 Prince Karl Lichnowsky. Anonymous portrait in oils.

5 Ignaz Schuppanzigh. Lithograph by von Schrötter.

7 Josephine Deym. Anonymous miniature, pencil, highlighted with white, on dark paper.

6 Giulietta Guicciardi. Anonymous miniature on ivory.

8 Prince Rasumovsky. Miniature on ivory by J. Le Gros, 1820.

9 Archduke Rudolph von Habsburg. Portrait in oils by J. Baptist the Elder, 1805.

10 Countess Erdödy. Miniature on ivory.

11 Antonie von Brentano. Anonymous miniature.

12 Beethoven. Engraving by Blasius Höfel, from a pencil drawing
by Louis Letronne, 1814.

13 Beethoven. Portrait in oils by Ferdinand Schimon, *c.* 1818.

14 Prince Galitzin. Lithograph by
Georg Christian Hahn and Franz Seraph
Hanfstaengl.

15 Karl van Beethoven. Unsigned
miniature, original lost.

16 Beethoven. Portrait in oils by Ferdinand Georg Waldmüller,
1823.

17 Piano Sonata Op. 27 No. 2, the 'Moonlight'. Autograph of the
first page of the Finale.

Teplitz and the Immortal Beloved maybe, but dedicated to his dying friend and patron Prince Lobkowitz. Otherwise he produced a few canons, songs, a march for military band, a fugue for string quintet, and a quintet arrangement of his early C minor Piano Trio op. 1 no. 3; and he continued to arrange Scottish and Welsh airs for George Thomson. There were sketches for a piano concerto and a symphony, but nothing to add to the glorious line of orchestral and other public music that had culminated in the Seventh and Eighth symphonies and the 1814 version of *Fidelio*. When Charles Neate visited Vienna he was offered three 'new' overtures for the Philharmonic Society in London. They turned out to be *The Ruins of Athens*, *King Stephen* and *Namensfeier*, hardly to be welcomed by a Society that expected something comparable with the symphonies and concertos. The lack of important orchestral and other large-scale activity eventually found compensation in the colossal 'Hammerklavier' Sonata op. 106, which was completed in 1818, and the supreme effort seemed to spur him on in other directions. While working at the *Missa Solemnis* and the Ninth Symphony he composed his last three piano sonatas and the monumental Diabelli Variations; and the unforeseen world of the late string quartets was to follow.

This is looking ahead, however: we must return to the beginning of 1816 and continue the history of Beethoven's relations with Karl and his mother from the time he was granted sole custody of the child. The school he chose for him was run by its founder, the Spanish-sounding Cajetan Giannatasio del Rio, and at the end of January Beethoven wrote to him about his plans for Karl:

> In any case it will certainly be best to remove him later on from Vienna and send him to Mölk or somewhere else. There he will neither see nor hear anything more of his beastly mother; and where everything about him is strange he will have fewer people to lean upon and will be able solely by his own efforts to win for himself love and respect.

The measures were certainly tough for a nine-year-old and Beethoven soon made concessions, with the approval of the Landrecht, that Johanna should be allowed to see the child on controlled occasions; but this compromise was soon undermined by suspicions about abuses and secret visits to the school. His opinion of her morals was not improved by the rumour that she had offered herself 'for hire' at an Artists' Ball in February 1816. He wrote to del Rio:

'And to such hands are we to entrust our precious treasure even for one moment? No, certainly not.'

Whatever the truth about Johanna's behaviour, Beethoven's denigration of her was a diplomatic necessity and ran rife in his imagination. He even alleged that she had poisoned her husband until medical evidence to the contrary was produced, and then developed a fantasy that he was in fact Karl's physical father. This emphasised his ambivalent attitude to Johanna: at times he tried to prevent all contact between her and the child, but on other occasions he became cooperative, took her to see Karl himself or arranged meetings at his lodgings. In the summer of 1816 however he made abortive plans to remove him from Giannatasio's in order to have closer control over him, but agreed that he should remain there while recovering from a hernia operation. In preparation he sought Zmeskall's advice about servants and engaged a married couple whom he immediately suspected of theft. To the eternal servant problem was added the difficulty of finding a suitable tutor for Karl. By November, as he told Giannatasio, his household threatened to look like a shipwreck. So Karl after all continued at the school for a further year but paid regular visits to Beethoven for his musical upbringing. He had piano lessons from Czerny, to whom Beethoven wrote urging 'patience and loving consideration' and giving sensible advice on teaching methods:

> I beg that once he has acquired the correct fingering and can play in time and reads the notes with reasonable correctness, you then direct his attention to the matter of interpretation; and when you have got *that far* don't stop him *because of trifling mistakes* but point them out after he has finished the piece.[3]

It says much for Beethoven's respect for Czerny that he entrusted his 'precious treasure' to his guidance, though this had not prevented him from criticising Czerny in public for his playing in the Quintet op. 16 for piano and wind at a farewell concert for Schuppanzigh in February 1816. Czerny had apparently amplified the original piano part to make use of the extended keyboard, and although Beethoven wrote to apologise for his outburst, he added a remark that should be taken to heart by all interpreters of his music: 'But you must forgive a composer who would rather have heard his work performed exactly as it was written.'

[3] Letter of 1817.

The year 1816 had opened stormily for Beethoven with the legal dispute over Karl, and it ended on a sad note with the death on 15 December of Prince Lobkowitz. Although the only new works of importance had been the op. 101 Piano Sonata and the song-cycle for Lobkowitz, there had been some publications of earlier masterpieces by Steiner: the F minor Quartet op. 95, the Violin Sonata op. 96, the 'Archduke' Trio, and the Seventh Symphony. The following year was even less productive, though it did involve preliminary work on the 'Hammerklavier' Sonata op. 106 and indeed on the far more distant project of the Ninth Symphony. The familiar title of op. 106 is concerned not with character but with language. In a wave of chauvinism, presumably anti-Napoleonic, Beethoven wrote to Steiner on 23 January 1817: 'Instead of pianoforte, Hammerklavier – this is to be clearly understood once and for all', but the order was only carried out in print on the title-pages of op. 101, op. 106 and op. 109, surviving on the second of them as a nickname and producing some occasional German tempo-marks elsewhere, as with the earlier op. 90 Sonata.

Some personal memories of the composer at this time were related by Albrechtsberger's grandson Carl Friedrich Hirsch to whom, remembering the past, Beethoven gave free tuition in harmony during the winter and spring of 1816 and 1817. In spite of his advanced deafness Beethoven would recoil in anger if any mistakes, such as parallel fifths, were made, carefully watching his pupil's hands at the keyboard. Hirsch described Beethoven's appearance:

> Of powerful build, his face was a healthy red, his eyebrows very thick and his brow low. His nose was very big and broad, especially the nostrils which were finely shaped. His bushy thick hair was already partly gray and stood up from his face. His hands were coarse and stout, his fingers short, the veins on the back of his hands thick, and the nails cut short.[4]

The composer lodged, or gave lessons, at the hotel 'zum Römischen Kaiser', yet 'in his rooms there was the greatest disorder, notes, sheets, books lying partly on the desk, partly on the floor'. Hirsch also remarked that 'in his whole dress Beethoven was very slovenly', though he worked at home in a flowery dressing-gown.

Other impressions were recorded by Giannatasio's daughter Fanny, who developed a great affection for Beethoven despite the

[4] Hirsch, quoted in Thayer-Forbes, p. 664.

usual routine of misunderstandings and angry moods. It is hard, too, to imagine him surviving his domestic shipwrecks without the reappearance of his old friends Johann and Nanette Streicher. Nanette, it may be recalled, was the piano-maker Stein's daughter whom Mozart had heard as a young prodigy at Augsburg in 1777; but Beethoven's lengthy correspondence with her in 1817 and 1818 was mostly confined to mundane matters: lodgings, servants, house-keepers, cooks, washerwomen and suchlike. She also advised him on finance, so that by the end of 1817 he was impelled to write to her: 'I am in so many respects your debtor that when I think of it I am frequently overcome by a feeling of shame.' One important musical event had been the publication in February 1817 of the op. 101 Piano Sonata with its surprise dedication to Baroness Dorothea Ertmann, whose sensitive playing and interpretative gifts had done much for the prestige of the earlier sonatas in Vienna. In writing to her Beethoven also referred to his ill-health: he had been suffering from colic and from a catarrhal complaint that had plagued him through-out the winter. There was the ever-present shadow of Johanna, who had however agreed to contribute towards Karl's education and living expenses; but in August Beethoven was still complaining to Giannatasio about her malicious gossip and insisting that she should only see her son twice a year and never in private.

Beethoven hoped that travel might improve his health, but a plan to visit the Countess Erdödy did not materialise, and he had to content himself by spending that summer and autumn at Heiligen-stadt and Nussdorf. The idea of London arose again. In June 1817 he had an invitation from Ferdinand Ries to compose two symphonies for the Philharmonic Society and to appear there in person the following January, and this he accepted gladly, simply quibbling about expenses and his need for a travelling companion. Although he later waived this in his keenness to go, the project once again fell through, and the prospect of composing two new symphonies in six months had been optimistic, to say the least. Instead he finally decided to take Karl under his own roof, removing him from the school on 24 January 1818 but sending a cautionary request in his warm letter of thanks to Giannatasio: 'Let me remind you that on account of his mother I should not like it to be too widely known that my nephew is now living with me.' The Queen of the Night, however, was to formulate her own plans for Karl's future.

As though in compensation for the cancellation of his visit to

England, Beethoven received the gift of a six-octave grand piano from the London firm of John Broadwood and Sons, which was despatched at the end of December 1817, sent by the long route via Trieste and Vienna, and eventually delivered to him in Mödling, where he spent the following summer with Karl. By chance he was visited there by Cipriani Potter, an English pianist and composer who had been studying with Förster in Vienna and was better equipped than the Viennese to demonstrate the Broadwood's qualities and its heavier action. When Potter remarked that it was badly out of tune, Beethoven replied naively that to tune it would spoil it, a tragic reflection on his deafness. As for Karl's education at Mödling, he studied for a time with a priest named Fröhlich, who dismissed him for unruly conduct and for reviling his mother, a habit no doubt encouraged by Beethoven himself. On returning to Vienna, a tutor still had to be found to prepare him for the entrance examination to the Academic Gymnasium, where Beethoven hoped to send him; but by this time Johanna had taken her own action with the legal advice of Jacob Hotschevar, a distant relation and a government clerk. In September she applied to the Landrecht for permission to send Karl as a boarder to the Royal Imperial *Konvikt*. This tussle between the co-guardians, a mother of dubious reputation and an eccentric genius of an uncle, would have been problematic enough for any court of law; but after an adjournment to enable Beethoven to produce Karl's entrance examination report the case was again decided in his favour.

Karl accordingly entered the Gymnasium in November 1818 but on 3 December ran away to his mother. Although he was promptly returned by the police the incident was enough to provoke Johanna into making a further petition, aided and abetted by Hotschevar, claiming that she had been illegally deprived of her rights and that Karl was likely to suffer irreparable physical and moral harm if left solely in Beethoven's care, which was in any case contrary to her late husband's wishes. This time the evidence went against Beethoven. When questioned about Karl's education he let slip the unfortunate remark: 'if he were but of noble birth . . . .', which immediately drew attention to his own nobility fantasy and the confusion between the Flemish 'van' and the German 'von'. Since he was quite unable to prove such a status, except by maintaining his much-quoted claim that his nobility lay in his heart and his head, the case was promptly transferred from the Landrecht to the commoners' Magistrat, to Beethoven's great humiliation and, as it transpired, to Johanna's advantage. Early in 1819 she was granted temporary custody and in the following June sent Karl to a school run by Joseph Blöchlinger, though even the court ruling did not deter Beethoven, who did his best to influence Blöchlinger against Johanna and tried to persuade the authorities to have Karl sent abroad to study. This was of no avail, and on 17 September the Magistrat confirmed that the guardianship should be shared by Johanna and a municipal official called Leopold Nussböck.

Beethoven remained as tenacious as ever. His letters to the journalist Karl Bernard from the summer of 1819 onwards are obsessed with his nephew, and from February that year he also enlisted the support of the lawyer Johann Baptist Bach. In October a counter-petition to the Magistrat was rejected in favour of Johanna, and as a last resort Beethoven brought all possible pressure to bear on the Court of Appeal, preparing a lengthy memorandum, presenting it to two of the judges in advance, and calling on the influence of powerful friends like the Archduke Rudolph. Faced with such overwhelming odds the Court yielded to Beethoven in April 1820 and appointed him and Karl Peters as guardians. Johanna made a further desperate but unsuccessful appeal to the Emperor, and on 24 July, after four-and-a-half years of turmoil, intrigue and litigation, the case was declared closed.

Needless to say there had been many references to the Karl crisis in the *Tagebuch*:

> God help me. Thou seest me forsaken by all Mankind, because I do not want to commit an injustice; hear my plea to be together with my Karl, but only in the future, as there does not appear to be any possibility of that now. O harsh Fate, O cruel destiny, no, no, my miserable state will never end.

Yet at times he obviously felt some sympathy for the much-abused Johanna, especially when she had agreed to contribute to Karl's upkeep: 'How it pains me to have to make somebody suffer through my good works for my dear Karl!!!' Although the ultimate legal issue was no more than a Pyrrhic victory and the troubles with Karl were far from over, by 1820 Beethoven's creative powers seemed fully restored. Other entries in the *Tagebuch* had already referred to his working habits – 'Always study from half-past five until breakfast' – and to the increasing interest in counterpoint so characteristic of his later works – 'the best opening phrases in canons are built around harmonies.'

5

The last years (1820–7)

In 1818 Beethoven had closed his *Tagebuch* with quotations from the Odyssey and from Christoph Christian Sturm, a Lutheran clergyman he admired for his radical writings on the compatibility of science and religion. Immediately preceding these was a memorandum relating to his impending work on the *Missa Solemnis*: 'In order to write true church music go through all the Gregorian chants etc. Also look there for the stanzas in the most correct translations along with the most perfect prosody of all Christian-Catholic psalms and hymns in general.' He had decided to write the great mass for the Archduke Rudolph's elevation as archbishop of Olmütz in March 1820, though it was not completed until three years later; but his study of the earlier church styles from Gregorian chant to Palestrina and Bach left its mark on other late works too, including parts of the Ninth Symphony and the last string quartets. Work on the symphony proceeded alongside that on the *Missa* and the Ninth itself appeared to emerge from a confluence of ideas: the long-planned symphony in D minor as a sequel to the Seventh and Eighth and presumably purely instrumental; a later desire to compose one incorporating 'a pious song in the ancient modes'; and the much older but still unfulfilled wish to set Schiller's 'Ode to Joy'. The prospect of composing two symphonies, one with voices, may have been encouraged by the London invitation of 1817, but in the end the various ideas were merged into a single work, the Ninth as we know it, a symphony in D minor with Schiller's 'Ode' as finale, and this was not ready until 1824. Considering the colossal proportions of the Ninth and the *Missa Solemnis* the renewal of creative energy was remarkable, bearing in mind that between 1820 and 1823 Beethoven also produced his last three piano sonatas, the Diabelli Variations, and the Overture *Die Weihe des Hauses* ('The Consecration of the House').

An important source of information about the later years was a direct result of Beethoven's deafness: the Conversation Books. They are tantalising in that they record the written remarks and questions of others and not Beethoven's spoken replies, though the gist of these can often be deduced from the context; but they are valuable enough for the topics raised, whether politics, philosophy, literature, personalities, other composers, or the interpretation of Beethoven's own works. A more serious obstacle was the interference of Schindler, who destroyed a large number of the books after the composer's death, leaving only about a third of the four hundred known to have existed. Like the sketchbooks their value for posterity may not have been fully foreseen, and Schindler was notorious for his zeal in suppressing details that he thought injurious to Beethoven or himself. It has been remarked that Beethoven's sudden popularity during the Congress of Vienna waned just as suddenly, and this has been blamed on a general public apathy following the end of the Napoleonic wars and on his own lack of new works; but during the fallow years from 1815 onwards he never lost his esteem in select musical circles. His sonatas and other chamber works were played regularly at the informal parties given by Czerny or the Streichers, and on occasion he would even improvise with a semblance of his earlier powers. Although deafness had forced him to give up playing in public, he continued to direct performances of his symphonies at charity or benefit concerts, until a disastrous rehearsal of *Fidelio* in 1822 put an end to his conducting activities too.

There is little doubt that his personal eccentricities increased during the Karl crisis. Even in his twenties Magdalena Willmann described him as 'half crazy'; now, in his late forties and fifties, the impression of a 'mad genius' became widespread, from the urchins who mocked at the dishevelled figure stamping and singing round the streets of Vienna, to Metternich's secret police who benevolently tolerated or ignored his outspoken blasphemies against the state. A more balanced and perceptive account of him was given by Friedrich Rochlitz, editor of the Leipzig *Allgemeine Musikalische Zeitung*, who visited him in the summer of 1822:

> His talk and his actions were one long chain of eccentricities, some of them most peculiar. Yet they all radiated a truly childlike amiability, carelessness and confidence in all who approached him. Even his barking tirades, such as those against his Viennese contemporaries, were only explosions of his fanciful imagination and his momentary excitement. They were uttered without any haughtiness, without any feeling of bitterness or resentment,

simply blustered out lightly and good-humouredly . . . He often showed . . . that to the person who had grievously injured him, or whom he had just most violently denounced, he would be willing to give his last thaler, should that person need it.[1]

Of the many portraits dating from these later years, by Heckel, von Klöber, Schimon, Stieler, Waldmüller, and the well-known out-of-door sketches by Lyser, Schindler considered the oil painting by Schimon the most true to life:

> From an artistic point of view Schimon's is not a distinguished work of art, yet full of characteristic truth. In the rendering of that particular look, the majestic forehead, this dwelling-place of mighty, sublime ideas, of hues in the drawing of the firmly shut mouth and the chin shaped like a shell, it is truer to nature than any other picture.[2]

The contrast between the 'dwelling-place of mighty, sublime ideas' and the unkempt Beethoven mistakenly arrested by the police as a tramp is bizarre enough, but such was the case. Even the musical side of his nature had its paradoxes. In March 1819 he had sent Ferdinand Ries in London two lengthy lists of misprints in the copies that had been sent of the 'Hammerklavier' Sonata and the quintet version of the Piano Trio op. 1 no. 3, excusing his aging copyist Schlemmer; yet he seemed only too willing for Ries to omit or rearrange the movements of the Sonata should it not be suitable for the English market:

> . . . or you could also omit the Largo and begin straight away with the Fugue, which is the last movement; or you could use the first movement and then the Adagio, and then for the third movement the Scherzo – and omit entirely no. 4 . . . or you could take just the first movement and the Scherzo and let them form the whole sonata. I leave it to you to do as you think best.

So we meet another anomaly: the meticulous musical craftsman who was prepared on occasion to accept any compromise to sell his wares. Certainly the difficulties of the work placed it well beyond the reach of the vast majority of pianists: in his words it was a sonata 'for fifty years' time'. Was it these thoughts that enabled him to propose such an arbitrary pragmatic solution to Ries? In the end the Regent's

[1] Quoted in Thayer-Forbes, p. 803.
[2] Thayer-Forbes, p. 742.

Harmonic Institution in London published it complete, but in two instalments, leaving it to appear as a single entity from Artaria in Vienna.

Despite the contradictions in his outward aspect and manner it says much for his essential character that Beethoven was seldom short of faithful devotees; but by 1820 many of his earlier friends and patrons had died, like Kinsky, Lobkowitz and Karl Lichnowsky, or moved away, like Waldstein. The Archduke remained, and Beethoven's many letters to him retained a deliberate formality, even when congratulating him on his set of piano variations on a song of Beethoven's own, 'O Hoffnung'. With publishers like Diabelli and Steiner he was on intimate and jesting terms, and his close circle of friends included former pupils like Czerny and, during the time of the last quartets, string-players such as Karl Holz, Linke and Schuppanzigh. Schuppanzigh, a friend of over thirty years' standing, had left for Russia after the disbandment of Rasumovsky's quartet in 1816 but returned to Vienna in 1823. There were those who had befriended him during the lawsuit, the Streichers, Karl Bernard and Johann Baptist Bach; Hofrat Karl Peters, tutor to the Lobkowitz family and Karl's co-guardian; Franz Oliva, who figures in the Conversation Books and gave Beethoven a graphic account of the maltreatment of the Fifth Symphony by the Vienna Dilettanten; and the persistent but unreliable Schindler, who become his amanuensis after Oliva's departure in 1820. Women played a decreasing part in his life and letters, though he must have considered the desirability of marriage again during the Karl affair. Fanny Giannatasio overheard a conversation between Beethoven and her father in 1816:

> My father thought that B. could rescue himself from his unfortunate domestic conditions only by marriage, did he know anybody, etc. Now our long foreboding was confirmed: he was unhappy in love! Five years ago he had made the acquaintance of a person, a union with whom he would have considered the greatest happiness of his life. It was not to be thought of, almost an impossibility, a chimera – 'nevertheless it is now as on the first day'.[3]

Was this still harking back to the 'Immortal Beloved', perhaps to Antonie Brentano, who was then apparently living happily with her husband and family in Frankfurt-am-Main?

---

[3] Fanny Giannatasio's diary, Thayer-Forbes, p. 646.

The Brentanos were still in Beethoven's mind when he composed his last important piano works: the Diabelli Variations were dedicated to Antonie and the op. 109 Sonata to their musical daughter Maximiliane. The three sonatas, op. 109 to op. 111, far more concise and intimate than the colossal 'Hammerklavier', occupied him from 1820 to 1822, and the possible influence of Diabelli's theme on the C major Arietta and variations of op. 111 is worth noting. In 1819 Anton Diabelli, publisher and composer, had circulated a waltz-tune of his own among fifty or more composers in and around Vienna, inviting each to contribute a single variation to a composite work under the grandiose title of *Vaterländische Künstlerverein*, literally 'a union of artists of the fatherland'. Beethoven, having scorned the waltz as a 'cobbler's patch' on account of its commonplace sequences, took it up as a challenge and wrote not one but thirty-three variations, producing a formidable masterpiece that Diabelli hailed as a worthy successor to Bach's 'Goldberg' Variations and published as a separate work. The contributors to the original scheme included Czerny, Hummel, Moscheles and many lesser and long-forgotten names. The Archduke Rudolph submitted a workmanlike fugue, but variations of genius came, as might be expected, from Schubert and Liszt, who was announced as 'a child of eleven, born in Hungary'. Beethoven's work took him until 1823, and in that same year, according to Ludwig Nohl, he heard the young Liszt play and afterwards 'lifted up the prodigy and kissed him'.

The previous year, 1822, had been largely spent on the *Missa Solemnis*. Beethoven wrote numerous letters inviting subscriptions for manuscript copies and bargaining with several publishers simultaneously over the work he considered 'perhaps the greatest' he had ever written. He aimed high, and in March 1823 wrote to Cherubini in Paris asking him to use his influence with Louis XVIII, who became a subscriber and sent Beethoven a gold medal, though Cherubini told Schindler later that he had never received the letter. Cherubini had once described Beethoven as 'an unlicked bear', but there is no reason to doubt the latter's great admiration for him as a composer of opera, a field in which he had found such difficulty himself. He told Holz too that he preferred Cherubini's Requiem to Mozart's. Beethoven's visitors often asked his opinions of other composers. To Johann Andreas Stumpff he said he considered Handel the greatest of all, 'before whom he bowed his knee'; Mozart remained 'good and admirable'; and Sebastian Bach only suffered neglect because people lacked time to study him. Yet Bach was wrongly named, he told Karl Freudenberg, who became organist at Breslau, for in German 'Bach' means 'brook', whereas the composer was no less than the ocean in his 'infinite and inexhaustible wealth'. Spohr he found too richly chromatic, but he praised Rossini for his productivity and melodiousness, so suited to the frivolous spirit of the time, and Spontini for his understanding of theatrical effects and 'the musical noises of warfare'.

Beethoven's general health, like his deafness, had deteriorated. Early in 1821 he had written to Simrock at Bonn saying that he had been confined to bed for six weeks, reputedly with rheumatic fever; and later that summer he suffered from jaundice, a symptom already of the liver complaint that contributed to his final illness. Although alcoholism is often blamed for cirrhosis he hardly inherited the weaknesses of his father and grandmother in this respect. Thayer's researches suggest that he drank a good deal of wine, but Karl Holz, who knew him only in his later years, said that he normally restricted himself to one bottle a meal, even if he sometimes overstepped the mark in company. An unexpected turn of events in the summer of 1822 was the attempt at a reconciliation with his surviving brother Nikolaus Johann, the pharmacist from Linz, who also had rooms in Vienna and only three years before had taken Johanna's side in the dispute over Karl. 'God grant that the most natural bond, the bond between brothers, may not again be broken in an unnatural way', Beethoven wrote from Oberdöbling, but trouble soon flared up between him and Johann's wife Therese, and having taken neighbouring lodgings he soon moved out.

It was during that summer that he was visited by Rochlitz from Leipzig, and he also received Rossini, whose operas had taken Vienna by storm. Although he told others that the Viennese were suffering from a surfeit of raisins (*Rosinen*), he contented himself by thanking his visitor for *The Barber*, which he much admired, but advised him against attempting opera seria, which despite its long tradition he felt unsuited to the Italian temperament. Two events in the autumn renewed his own association with the stage. In September he adapted his earlier music for *The Ruins of Athens* to celebrate the opening of the Josephstadt Theatre and composed a splendid new overture in contrapuntal style, *Die Weihe des Hauses*. Then on 3 November *Fidelio* was revived, with the 17-year-old Wilhelmine Schröder as Leonore, but this was the occasion of the tragic dress rehearsal that the deaf Beethoven tried vainly to conduct. When he was made to realise that the orchestra had broken down completely he called for Schindler, who begged him to abandon the attempt and to return home, and who wrote: 'Once there he threw himself on the sofa, covered his face with his hands and remained thus until we sat down to eat. During the meal not a word passed his lips . . .'

Within a week, on 9 November 1822, a letter of great significance arrived from Prince Nikolas Galitzin – or Golitsin – of St Petersburg, inviting Beethoven to write 'one or two quartets' and to quote his own fee. The idea of returning to the string quartet, however, cannot be entirely ascribed to Galitzin, since Beethoven had already promised a still unwritten one to Peters in June, but the generous commission was an added incentive. His reply that he hoped to have the first of these new works ready in a month was once again typically optimistic, with the *Missa Solemnis* and the Ninth Symphony still in progress, and it was not until March 1825 that Galitzin received the Quartet in E flat op. 127. Other proposals had come Beethoven's way. The London Philharmonic Society offered fifty pounds for a new symphony, and in Vienna the Kärnthnerthor Theatre, encouraged by the successful revival of *Fidelio*, commissioned another opera. Neither of these materialised, though the operatic project brought Beethoven in touch with the poet Franz Grillparzer, who was proposed as the somewhat reluctant librettist, and various subjects were considered, including *Macbeth*, *Romeo and Juliet*, and the Bohemian legend *Dragomira*. At last *Melusine* was decided upon, but although Grillparzer visited Beethoven at Hetzendorf, where he spent part of the summer of 1823, the enthusiasm waned, and as with all his operatic ventures – save one – it came to nothing.

The Kärnthnerthor was, however, to be the venue for the historic concert on 7 May 1824 at which the Ninth Symphony was first heard, along with the Kyrie, Credo and Agnus Dei of the *Missa Solemnis* and the Overture *Die Weihe des Hauses*. It had leaked out that Beethoven was considering taking his new works abroad, perhaps to Berlin, because of his disillusionment with the Viennese, but a pressing appeal signed by thirty musicians and music-lovers caused him to change his mind:

> Do not withhold longer from the popular enjoyment, do not keep
> longer from the oppressed sense of that which is great and perfect,

a performance of the latest masterworks of your hand ... We
know that a new flower glows in the garland of your glorious still
unequalled symphonies ... Do not longer disappoint the general
expectations! [4]

Although such florid wording was indeed persuasive, there were to
be difficulties in finding a suitable hall for the concert; and Beethoven, despite encouragement from the singer Henriette Sontag, was
justly apprehensive about the reaction of the Viennese to the Ninth,
more so since its great difficulties, and those of the extracts from the
Missa, had to be dealt with in only two full rehearsals. 'Nevertheless'
a Leipzig critic reported, 'strange as the music must have sounded to
the audience, the impression which it made was profound and the
applause which it elicited enthusiastic to a degree.' At rehearsal there
had been the usual complaints about the vocal demands – especially,
no doubt, from those more used to singing Rossini – but Beethoven
refused to yield, except in the case of the high F sharp in the opening
baritone recitative. In the performance the singers who were unable
to take the high notes simply omitted them, but Beethoven, listening
only with his imagination, was oblivious of all this. Neither was he
aware, of course, of the applause that followed the dramatic timpani
entries in the scherzo. The pianist Thalberg, who was present,
recalled that the contralto Fräulein Unger had turned Beethoven
round after that movement to witness the ovation he was unable to
hear, though Unger herself maintained that this only happened at the
end of the whole symphony.

For the composer's benefit Schindler wrote a detailed and
glowing account of the concert and its reception in a Conversation
Book. Ironically the financial outcome, so important to Beethoven,
was disappointing owing to the heavy expenses involved. He had
ordered an opulent meal for his friends at a restaurant in the Prater,
but it broke up after a violent outburst in which he accused Schindler
and the management of cheating him, even when assured that the
accounts were in order. His brother Johann, who was jealous of
Schindler, may have planted these suspicions in order to cool off
Beethoven's relations with him. If so, he succeeded. Although
Schindler had defended his honesty, Beethoven wrote to him: 'As for
friendship, that is a difficult thing in your case; in no event would I
like to entrust my welfare to you since you lack judgment and act

---

[4] Open letter to Beethoven, Thayer-Forbes, pp. 897–8.

arbitrarily . . .' A second concert on 23 May was held at midday in the Grosser Redoutensaal and included a repeat performance of the Ninth Symphony; but it was poorly attended on account of the fine weather and the time of day, and this only increased Beethoven's despondency.

Meanwhile he spent much of the summer of 1824 at Penzing and Baden Gutenbrunn. He continued to write to publishers about the *Missa Solemnis* and the Ninth, with the added promise of the op. 127 Quartet on which he was still working. On 7 August Diabelli wrote asking for 'a grand sonata for four hands' and agreed to Beethoven's proposed fee of 80 gold ducats, but unfortunately it was never written. Although he seldom travelled far from Vienna, Beethoven's prestige abroad continued to flourish. Earlier that year, on 7 April, the enterprising Prince Galitzin who had commissioned the quartets gave the first complete performance of the *Missa Solemnis* in St Petersburg a month before the extracts had been introduced to Vienna. London also kept up its interest in Beethoven's latest works: in December Neate wrote acknowledging the safe arrival of the score of the Ninth, which was to be performed by the Philharmonic Society on 21 March 1825. The conductor, Sir George Smart, hoped that Beethoven would turn up in person but once again he called off the journey. Instead Smart visited him in Vienna and Baden the following September, discussing among other things the tempi of the symphony. He was assured that the Vienna performance had taken less than three-quarters of an hour [!], which he deemed 'totally impossible', but learnt with interest that the difficult cello-and-bass recitatives had been confined to a small group of select players. Smart also had the privilege of hearing two rehearsals of the second Galitzin quartet, the A minor op. 132, and gave a valuable, if amusingly naive, account of this in his diary:

> This Quartette is 3/4 of an hour in length – they played it twice. The 4 Performers were Schuppanzigh, Holtz, Weitz [Weiss] and Linke. *Most chromatic*, a slow movement subtitled – *praise for the recovery of an invalid* – Beethoven intended to allude to himself I suppose – he presided, took off his coat, and to express the staccato passages, took Mr Holtz's Violin and played this passage un peu hors de tone. I looked over the Score during the Performance – all paid him the greatest attention. About 14 were present . . .[5]

[5] Papers of Sir George Smart, quoted in Percy M. Young's *Beethoven: A Victorian Tribute* (London, 1976).

Smart's allusion to the Lydian Hymn as 'most chromatic', though wide of the mark, presumably referred to its modal flavour. Meanwhile Schuppanzigh and his colleagues had given the first performance of the op. 127 Quartet in the previous March, though a later and more successful one was by Joseph Böhm's quartet.

Beethoven's nephew Karl was present at the meetings with Smart and joined in the discussions, though the relationship with his uncle was still hazardous. Since the end of the legal battle in 1820 his education, first at Blöchlinger's school and after 1823 at the University, had revealed his powers of application. From time to time he helped Beethoven with messages and accounts, staying with him at Baden in the summer of 1823 and in Vienna during his University studies. In the spring of 1825, however, he entered the Polytechnic Institute and moved to independent lodgings. Though storm-tossed and bewildered by conflicting allegiances, aggravated by the enforced separation from his mother, he seems to have tried hard to placate his uncle; and on 1 August 1824 Beethoven notified his lawyer friend Bach of his intention to leave all his property to Karl, except for his Erard grand piano, which as a gesture was to go to his brother Johann. Yet the situation worsened during 1825 and 1826 as a result of Karl's independence: Beethoven became more and more demanding, jealous and suspicious, and it was even rumoured that he used his young violinist friend Holz to spy on his nephew. His many letters to him waver in confusion between recrimination and reconciliation, and are laboriously signed 'your sincere and faithful father' or with some such phrase.

The climax came on 30 July 1826 when Karl, faced with unresolvable conflicts and probably in debt too, went to one of Beethoven's favourite country retreats, the Helenenthal, and tried to commit suicide by shooting himself in the head. Although he survived and his injuries were soon remedied, the effect on Beethoven was shattering. The disgrace, the ingratitude, the 'crime' of suicide, which he himself had resisted, were more than he could bear. The thought that he might have been partly and unwittingly responsible may never have occurred to him. When Karl was discharged from hospital the decision was made for him to join the army. It accorded with Karl's own wishes and was helped by Stephan von Breuning, with whom Beethoven had renewed his old friendship and who was now a councillor in the War Department. Through his influence Karl was accepted as a cadet in Field Marshal von Stutterheim's regiment, joining it on 2 January 1827: and the Field Marshal might have been surprised to learn that his name would be handed down for generations in the dedication of the great C sharp minor Quartet op. 131, recently completed, as a mark of the composer's gratitude and relief.

In the interim Beethoven took Karl to his brother's new estate at Gneixendorf to recuperate, where despite inevitable tensions and quarrels there appear to have been genuine attempts at friendship on all sides, even between Beethoven and his sister-in-law Therese. Though far from well, he was able to enjoy the countryside that made him nostalgic for the Rhineland he had not seen since his youth. He composed his last quartet, the F major op. 135, and a new finale for the B flat op. 130 to replace the controversial 'Grosse Fuge', which had been criticised as too overwhelming for its context. One may read into these very last works the rediscovery of an earlier Classicism, a renewed simplicity and tranquillity, partly a reaction from the grander scale of op. 131, and possibly related subjectively to the resolving of the recent crisis.

Trouble brewed again, however, when Beethoven tried to persuade his brother to make over his will in Karl's favour, and on 1 December 1826 he left hurriedly for Vienna with Karl, in an open coach and freezing weather, taking to bed with a severe chill on arrival home. Unfortunately Karl did not view the matter seriously enough to send for a doctor, but after three days Holz produced a Dr Wawruch, who diagnosed and treated Beethoven for pneumonia. His condition improved a little only to deteriorate again through his chronic liver complaint and stomach pains. Other doctors were called in, including his old friend Malfatti, whom Beethoven hopefully regarded as a Messiah, but the advent of dropsy led to a series of tappings, and by the middle of January all hopes of a cure had dwindled away.

Some comforts, like Malfatti's prescription of iced punch, brought temporary relief. Beethoven had also been overjoyed at receiving the 'royal gift' of Samuel Arnold's edition of Handel, sent from London by Johann Andreas Stumpff. In thanking Stumpff, Beethoven referred to the threatened poverty caused by his illness and hoped the Philharmonic Society might fulfil its earlier intention of giving a benefit concert for him. He also wrote to Smart and Moscheles on the same lines. The Society, without waiting to organise a concert, sent him an outright gift of a hundred pounds, a gesture which he told Moscheles had touched him to the innermost depths of his soul. Yet he begged the Philharmonic not to abandon the idea of a benefit concert, but to go ahead and deduct the gift from the proceeds, undertaking to compose a new symphony or overture in return. Schindler later wrote to Smart:

> He requested me, when he should be no more, to offer his warmest and most grateful thanks to you and Mr Strumpff, and thro' your medium to the Philharmonic Society and the whole English nation for the attentions and friendships shown to him during his life, and more especially towards the close . . .[6]

Sketches for a tenth symphony, Beethoven had said, were already in his desk; and he had hoped that he would soon be restored to health. Alas, the money from the Philharmonic was used to pay for his own funeral.

In February Diabelli had given Beethoven a picture of Haydn's birthplace in Rohrau, a humble cottage and yet 'such a great man was born in it', as he remarked to Stephan von Breuning's son Gerhard. Thoughts of his own childhood must have returned to him when he wrote to Schotts at Mainz on 22 February asking for some Rhine or Moselle wine which Dr Malfatti had prescribed. The bottles did not arrive until 24 March. 'Pity, pity, too late!' he commented. Two days later there was a snow-storm with thunder and lightning, during which Beethoven, who had been in a coma, suddenly opened his eyes, raised his right arm and clenched his fist, as though still defying the forces of nature. It was his last and most typical gesture.

This dramatic account of his death was given by Schubert's friend Anselm Hüttenbrenner, and though friends and admirers had flocked to his bedside during those last days, it seems that the only other actual witness was Johanna, the Queen of the Night. Thus Fate played its part to the very end. He had already received the last rites on 24 March despite his mistrust of ceremony, and made his moving but ambiguous remark to Schindler and Stephan von Breuning: 'Plaudite, amici, comoedia finita est.' On 29 March 1827, three days after his death, an estimated twenty thousand people crowded into the square in front of his last lodgings in the Schwarzspanierhaus. The funeral, so different from Mozart's, was commensurate with the immense fame he had acquired in his lifetime. Hummel was one of

[6] Letter from Schindler to Smart, 2 Apr. 1827, ibid.

the pall-bearers, and the torch-bearers included Czerny, Grillparzer, Schubert and Schuppanzigh. An eloquent oration, written by Grillparzer, was read by the actor Anschütz at the gates of the cemetery in Währing where Beethoven was buried. Over sixty years later, in 1888, his remains were removed to the Zentral Friedhof in Vienna.

6

Piano music

In view of the vast gulf that lies between Beethoven's early and late piano works it is all too easy to regard the op. 2 sonatas as a starting-point. In that case their maturity must come as a constant surprise: he was in fact twenty-five when they appeared and no newcomer to keyboard writing. Several of his much earlier Bonn compositions are of value and interest, if only as stepping-stones. Most were announced as for the 'clavecin' (harpsichord), and the expedient proviso 'for pianoforte or harpsichord' was to linger as an anachronism even up to the op. 31 sonatas of 1802, which would have made nonsense on the older instrument. Although Beethoven played the harpsichord (and the organ) as part of his duties at Bonn, it soon became clear that his keyboard style demanded the piano, and like Mozart at Augsburg he would doubtless have preferred it for his earlier works too. The first of these, the Dressler Variations WoO 63, would, however, not come amiss on the harpsichord, with the crossed-hand dialogues in the sixth variation and the crisply brilliant major-key ending; and at the age of twelve Beethoven can hardly be blamed for relying on basic scale and arpeggio figures when not actually harking back to Dressler's humdrum little march. Within a year, in 1783, Beethoven produced his more ambitious 'Electoral' sonatas WoO 47, in which the expected touches of Mozart in the first two, and perhaps of Haydn in the minuet and finale of the third, do not rule out other possible models such as C.P.E. Bach, or even his teacher Neefe's sonatas of the previous decade. One formal feature was the recurring slow introduction to no. 2 in F minor, a unifying device to be employed in the *Pathétique* sixteen years later.

Two separate rondos date from around the same time, the A major WoO 49 turning from a decidedly Mozartian poise to an already Beethovenish outburst in C major for the first episode. The influence of his Bach studies is more apparent in the F minor Prelude WoO 55, and fugal textures abound in the pair of modulating

Preludes, each moving through the whole cycle of major keys, to be misleadingly published in 1803 as 'op. 39'. Here the alternative instrument was the organ, for which he also left a solitary early Fugue in D major WoO 31. Other slight or fragmentary works included short two-movement sonatas in F and C, WoO 50 and 51, the latter completed by Ferdinand Ries, but more substantial projects may have been sketched or even finished and taken on by Beethoven to Vienna. One impressive work of 1790 deserves special mention for its advance in technique and invention: the 24 Variations on Righini's 'Venni amore' WoO 65, which Beethoven played and elaborated upon to the Abbé Sterkel the following year. They already show in miniature the resource of dealing with a simple text that was to characterise the great Diabelli Variations of over thirty years later; though no known copies survive from the original edition and they may have been revised considerably for their republication in 1802. The vogue for such variations on operatic and other popular airs led to nine further keyboard sets between 1792 and 1799 on themes by Dittersdorf, Grétry, Salieri and others. Before leaving Bonn Beethoven also composed some for four hands on a theme by Count Waldstein, WoO 67, which were published there by Simrock in 1794 though somewhat to the composer's displeasure. By that time he had far more important things in the offing: the op. 1 trios and the op. 2 piano sonatas.

Despite the immense journey ahead the op. 2 sonatas need no condescension for being first in the accepted series of thirty-two: their scope and variety already illustrate Beethoven's all-embracing qualities. Like the trios, they adopted a grander four-movement plan instead of the usual three, as though to compensate for his delayed attention to the quartet and symphony, in which there was more formidable rivalry from Haydn. Op. 2 no. 1 in F minor is the most compact of the three, and any likeness between its opening 'Mannheim rocket' and the finale of Mozart's great G minor Symphony is soon forgotten in Beethoven's brusque treatment of it and abrupt dynamic changes. To compare the first movement's exposition with a rambling sketch for it quoted by Nottebohm is to witness Beethoven's critical powers and instinct for unity at work, in which the reshaping of the second subject into a free but purposeful inversion of the first is but one example (see Ex.1).

The Adagio re-used and enhanced a theme from the third of his youthful piano quartets WoO 36, owing something to Mozart in its

Ex.1

(sketch)   (Op.2, No.1)

graceful melodic line – compare the slow movement of his D major
Sonata K. 576 – and to Haydn in the later variants of the opening
phrase. The 'extra' movements in these earlier sonatas tend to sit on
the fence between minuet and scherzo – see also op. 7, op. 10 no. 3,
op. 22 and the 'Moonlight' op. 27 no. 2 – and op. 2 no. 1's 'minuet' is
a solemn-faced Allegretto with a smoothly flowing trio in the major.
Its finale is more prophetic: a stormscape foreshadowing those in the
'Moonlight' and 'Appassionata', though unlike its successors it finds
relaxation with a long-breathed cantilena in place of a development.

   The more spacious time-scale of op. 2 no. 2 in A seems at first
belied by its terse opening quips and a tendency to break into
scurrying triplet scales, but not least of Beethoven's gifts was his
ability to evolve long paragraphs from short motifs. This happens
with the modulating sequences in the second subject and the close
canons in the development with their taxing right-hand skips. The
Largo, unusually marked 'appassionato', is both deeply expressive
and imaginatively scored, beginning with sustained chords over a
quasi-pizzicato bass, a texture also found in the slow movements of
op. 7 and op. 28. Both the scherzo, now so called, and the final rondo
open gently but leave no doubt as to their reserves of strength,
though the sonata chooses to end on a gracious intimate note. For
more extrovert brilliance one has only to turn to the last of this
group, op. 2 no. 3 in C. Its attractions for the virtuoso are obvious:
the thirds in the opening subject, the chains of broken octaves, the
acrobatic leaps in the scherzo and the flights of sixths in the finale.
Such technical features had already been exploited by Clementi and
Dussek, but Beethoven's structural certainty outstrips any possible
models. Moreover the whole work demands insight as well as
precision from the player, from the string-quartet texture of the
opening to the thundering out of the E major slow movement theme
in C major, the sonata's home key. Bravura is however granted the
bonus of a brief written-in cadenza in the first movement; and its
minor-key transition theme, like the Adagio of op. 2 no. 1, was
borrowed from an early piano quartet.

Several shorter piano works are now known, or thought, to derive from this early Vienna period of the 1790s in spite of their higher opus-numbers: the two slight sonatas op. 49, familiar to beginners, of which no. 2 in G major lent its minuet theme to the Septet of 1800; the C major Rondo op. 51 no. 1; and the Rondo a capriccio op. 129. This last, subtitled 'The Rage over the lost penny, vented in a Caprice', extracts lengthy developments from a trivial theme in an improvisatory manner akin to that in Haydn's entertaining Fantasy in C (Hob.XVII/4) of 1789. Its opus-number led to an illusion that it was a late work, but the autograph, the sketches, and the compass of the piano writing place it clearly in the first period. Like Mozart, Beethoven was restricted to a five-octave keyboard until he acquired an Erard grand with extended compass in 1803. Some passages were hampered by the limitation, especially parallel ones recurring in a higher key, a point Mozart so often turned to artistic purpose; but the richly varied sonorities of the next sonata, op. 7 in E flat, seemed to thrive within the resources.

Beethoven's op. 7 was dedicated to his pupil the Countess Babette von Keglevics and once nicknamed 'Die Verliebte'. Czerny suggested that it was composed in an 'impassioned' mood, borne out by the urgent sweep of the first movement which carries a wealth of material on a swift tide of six-eight quavers, living up to the 'Grande Sonate' of the title-page. The Largo, unexpectedly in C major, is a profoundly expressive movement in which the measured silences in the opening theme are as eloquent as sound, until a moving bass fills in the rests and marvellously enriches the harmony in the closing bars. Once again the third movement is a cross between minuet and scherzo, tenderly melodic and firmly rhythmic in turn, offset by the smouldering triplets of its minor-key trio. The finale, like that of op. 2 no. 2, is gentle-paced with a warmly lyrical rondo-theme mostly poised on dominant harmony. The influence of Clementi's op. 2 no. 2 on the stormy middle episode has been cited, but the strong offbeat accents are pure Beethoven and so is its translation from C minor to E flat major in the coda, after an inspired distant modulation in the rondo-theme's last appearance.

At the time of op. 7 (1796–7) Beethoven also worked on the three sonatas of op. 10. The first two revert to three movements, and no. 1 in C minor invites comparison with Mozart's Sonata in that key, K. 457. A few parallels in the first movement are striking: the rising arpeggios followed by sudden *pianos* at the start, the leap into

C major for the development and its quick turning aside into F minor. Beethoven's form here is far looser than Mozart's tautly-held one, and he was soon to pursue his C minor daemon with greater cogency in the *Pathétique*. The Adagio, in A flat, is a long sonata-form movement without development and far more conventional in expression than the Largo of op. 7; and as if in compensation the finale pursues its full sonata-form course in a breathless prestissimo, with urgent quaver figures hinting at still later C minor works, the Fifth Symphony and the *Coriolan* Overture. The strength of key-associations is also noticeable in parts of the very different F major Sonata op. 10 no. 2. Here the wit and good humour of the music suggest Haydn, and emotional depths are reserved for the F minor Allegretto that replaces a slow movement. Schubert, one imagines, would have admired the D flat section with its left-hand accents, similar in texture to the trio in the scherzo of his own B flat Sonata D. 960. If the finale with its mock-fugal opening and drone-bass cadence-theme conjures up visions of a rustic wind-band, it also reminds one that F major was to be the relaxed open-air key of the *Pastoral* Symphony. Its monothematicism was another Haydnish trait.

The last of this group, op. 10 no. 3 in D, is on a grander scale and again in four movements. Its opening octave theme is immediately arresting and the first four notes, no more than half a downward scale, are used with immense resource, appearing immediately in harmonised sequences and broken sixths, building up long paragraphs in the second group or serving, as at the end of the exposition, to beckon back the whole subject. The marking 'presto', unusual in a first movement, gives a new vitality to the standard accompanying patterns; but the slow movement, marked 'largo e mesto', is the heart of the work. Here the key is D minor, 'mesto' means sad or gloomy, and the overwhelming pathos and sustained tension have prompted thoughts of extra-musical influences: perhaps the memory of his mother's death, possibly the first onset of his deafness. The rest of the sonata is optimistic, even humorous. The finale, for example, makes great play with a three-note fragment that was noted down in an odd corner of the 'Kafka' sketches with the words 'for the rondo'.

Beethoven's output of piano sonatas continued unabated, and in 1799 he completed the *Pathétique* op. 13 and the pair of more intimate ones op. 14. The *Pathétique* soon acquired a widespread popularity both for its unbridled C minor 'Sturm und Drang' and, even more, for its consoling Adagio cantabile, which exploited the piano's singing quality with one of Beethoven's best-loved themes and in simple rondo form. An unusual feature of the first movement was the dramatic slow introduction that returns twice during the succeeding Allegro. Opinions differ as to whether it should be included in the exposition repeat, but the pause in the 'first time bar' and the overall balance seem to call for it. A sketch for the end of the finale suggests that it at least may have been conceived for violin, either as part of a duo sonata or maybe the C minor String Trio op. 9 no. 3 on which he was working at the time. Yet the three movements of the *Pathétique* form an impressive unity and abound in thematic connections, consciously or not on the composer's part. The relation between the E flat minor second subject in the first movement and the finale's rondo-theme is clear enough, but a melodic sequence of falling fifths is more subtly pervasive, as three brief quotations will show:

Ex. 2

The interval of a diminished fifth is also outlined in many of the sonata's downward swooping scales, from the fourth bar of the introduction to the abrupt ending of the finale. One need not go to the lengths of Rudolph Reti, in his analysis of Beethoven's 'thematic patterns', to appreciate the thread or *filo*, as Leopold Mozart called it, that so often binds together the material in the mature Classical style.

Many composers have turned from a powerfully dramatic work to a more relaxed one, and it was typical of Beethoven to follow the *Pathétique* with the gentler op. 14 sonatas. Schindler's account of Beethoven's playing of them has already been mentioned (p. 27), and so has the composer's adaptation of op. 14 no. 1 as a string quartet. In the process he also transposed it up a semitone from E to F in order to place the low dominant, C within the cello's reach. The opening of this sonata and the following E minor Allegretto invited quartet treatment almost verbatim, but the accompaniment to the finale's rondo-theme and its later episode of pianistic arpeggios needed radical reshaping in the string version. Meanwhile op. 14 no. 2 in G had introduced variation-form for the first time in the sonatas: a miniature set on a march-like theme, placed between a tenderly lyrical Allegro and an unusual scherzo-finale beset with capricious cross-rhythms and in straight rondo-form. There is no room in either work for a reflective slow movement, but the next sonata, op. 22 in B flat, returned to a grander manner and a four-movement plan. The year was 1800, the time of the First Symphony, the Septet, and the near-completion of the Op. 18 quartets.

This was the sonata that Beethoven had recommended so highly for its decorum, though its very respectability led to a certain predictability in form and mood. The first movement's energy derives from an opening snatch of a motif, but although much of the passage-work is conventional there are sonorous doublings in thirds, sixths and octaves in the second-group themes. The punctuality of this well-behaved movement even sacrificed the expected Beethoven coda. There are, however, some arresting harmonic complexes in the development of the slow movement's Italianate aria; and the remaining movements alternate geniality of manner with sterner material, in the second part of the minuet, in its trio, and in the middle episode of the rondo. Yet, all in all, op. 22 is a work of consolidation rather than adventure, gathering strength from convention and in marked contrast to its neighbours on either side.

The next four sonatas, all completed in 1801, form a heterogeneous group. Op. 26 in A flat opens, like Mozart's A major Sonata K. 331, with a leisurely set of variations and continues with the fieriest scherzo in the sonatas so far. Then comes the Funeral March 'on the death of a hero' in A flat minor – was it already Bonaparte? – and this is notable for its low-lying theme in an insistent dotted rhythm, its enharmonic modulations to B minor and

D major, and in the middle section its vivid evocation of drumrolls and salvoes. Czerny detected the influence of Cramer on the finale, which flows along with apparent detachment in its context and in almost unbroken semiquavers: its patterns, and its many exchanges between the hands, give it added bonus as a study, though it ends on a gently poetic note.

Both the op. 27 sonatas carry the subtitle 'quasi una fantasia' as if to disarm criticism of their unorthodox procedures. The four movements of no. 1 in E flat, for instance, are to be played without a break; apart from this, the serene and childlike opening Andante is interrupted by a scurrying six-eight Allegro in the alien key of C major, though that chord had in fact been dwelt upon in the first section, and the later slow movement's theme returns in the coda of the finale. Schubert was also to use the term 'fantasy' for through-composed works of this type: the 'Wanderer' for piano, the C major for violin and piano, the F minor for piano duet. Beethoven's op. 27 no. 2 in C sharp minor is a more regular sonata, and here the subtitle presumably refers to the unique nature of the opening Adagio sostenuto, probably the most famous single movement he ever wrote. There may have been a hidden programme to the work, taking in the brief Allegretto and the tempestuous finale as well, and although Rellstab's title of 'Moonlight' was bestowed on it after Beethoven's death it is apt enough for the nocturnal calm of the first movement, which is incidentally in clear sonata form. So is the finale, its urgent drama demanding the dominant minor instead of the 'consoling' relative major for the second group.

The remaining sonata of 1801, op. 28 in D, also acquired a nickname, the 'Pastoral', which appeared in an early English edition long before its adoption by the publisher Cranz. It is easy to sense pastoral elements in the outer movements, both of which begin with themes hovering over a repeated tonic pedal, and the drastically naive humour of the scherzo may also be thought rustic. Yet there is great intellectual strength in the development of the first movement, with so much arising from the closing figure of the ten-bar opening phrase; and its spacious climax on F sharp major harmony is related to the mediant wanderings in the exposition, a tonal feature shared with the Second Symphony, also D major, which was completed in the following year. Czerny maintained that Beethoven's favourite movement was the D minor Andante, a plaintive song sustained over a staccato bass and later decorated; and here any 'pastoral' associations, intended or not, would seem confined to the dance-like major-key section.

If Beethoven's remark about following 'a new path' is taken seriously, the three op. 31 sonatas of 1802 may be regarded as a conscious departure, though the novel features in the first and third are apt to be overshadowed by the drama, pathos and originality of the D minor op. 31 no 2. No. 1 in G major, though emotionally detached, has however its interesting structural features, and two points in the first movement anticipate the 'Waldstein': the immediate restatement of the opening a tone lower, and the shifting of the second subject from the expected D major to the mediant, B major. It is tempting to describe the major-minor alternations at the end of the exposition as Schubertian, but such a prophecy could also apply to the spaciousness of the other two movements, the highly decorative Adagio grazioso and the Rondo, with its final fragmentation of the theme and presto coda, a process reproduced by Schubert at the end of his A major Sonata D.959. The 'Kessler' sketchbook of 1801 includes a fragment scored for quartet and based on the syncopated chords featured in the first movement of op. 31 no. 1. Such changes of medium in the early stages of sketching were not uncommon, but it is hard to imagine the next sonata, the D minor, conceived except as piano music. A rough outline of the whole first movement also appears in 'Kessler', in which the idea of alternating slow and fast tempi, and of the recitatives in the recapitulation, was established, though a major-key ending was rejected.

The D minor Sonata opens with a quiet, slowly rising arpeggio which returns from time to time, often on an unexpected harmony, breathing an air of mystery into an otherwise headlong movement; and in fact the most defiant subject in the Allegro is a simple speeding-up of this Largo idea. Bearing in mind the violent dynamic changes and the limitations of the instruments of the time, the Beethovenish comment that 'the piano must break!' seems appropriate. Limitations may, however, be strength in disguise, and no one will regret the fierce dissonances that arise in the recapitulation, where the shorter keyboard prevented him from taking a phrase upwards in octaves. It was earlier, at the moment of return itself, that the Largo arpeggios were expanded into the recitatives that 'should arise like a voice from a tomb-vault', enhanced by the veiled effect of Beethoven's long pedal-marks, which may be modified but certainly not ignored on more modern instruments:

Ex. 3

Whereas the outer movements of op. 31 no. 2 pursue minor keys with scarcely a glimmer of 'consolation', the Adagio, in B flat major, has a brooding solemnity behind its outward calm. The lower reaches of the keyboard, in fact, exert a kind of magnetic pull on the wide 'vocal leaps' of the opening subject; and there is a striking contrast between the sonorous transition theme and the stark drum-like figure accompanying it. One curious sidelight from the sketches is the derivation of the haunted, and haunting, moto perpetuo finale from a grotesque waltz in E flat major with humorous two-octave one-finger leaps in the left hand. The idea of the leap was preserved and refined in the sonata, producing an inner pedal-note in the theme's opening bars. Beethoven's remark 'read Shakespeare's *Tempest*', which according to Schindler referred to both op. 31 no. 2 and op. 57, once again led to speculation about a 'programme'. If taken literally, one might read Prospero into the mysterious Largo sections of the first movement, and perhaps Miranda into the feminine grace of the Adagio's second subject, but the finale can surely only express a more general mood of alternating pathos and turbulence. Its obsession with its initial motif recalls the rondo of Mozart's A minor Sonata K.310, though while Mozart's Presto ends in a gesture of strength the final climax of Beethoven's Allegretto subsides, like the first movement, into a passage of quiet exhaustion or resignation.

The third of the op. 31 sonatas, in E flat, is far removed from the tragic overtones of the D minor. Its first movement might be described as conventionally brilliant were it not for the oblique and strangely hesitant harmonic progression that characterises the first subject and its returns. Of the four movements none is a truly slow one, though the third is for once a moderately paced minuet, richly melodic and with a chordal trio that was borrowed by Saint-Saëns for a set of two-piano variations. In compensation the previous movement had opened up its own 'new path', a lively scherzo in two-four with a lightness of touch Mendelssohn must have admired; and the finale was to add fire and zest to the 'hunting' six-eight so often associated by Mozart with the key of E flat.

Next in the book come the two miniature sonatas op. 49, already mentioned for their misleading opus-number and probably dating from around 1797. They prompt a retrospective glance at some of Beethoven's other piano music of the intervening period. The two rondos op. 51 are also earlier works and hardly intended as a pair: no. 1 in C major, with its mixture of Mozartian clichés and wayward modulations, was written in 1797, whereas its successor in G, probably of the following year, is a maturer and more extensive sonata-rondo. Its lyrical unfolding, with much attention to the graceful flourish in bar 2 of the theme, is interrupted by a more rapid six-eight episode in E major, a submediant key-relation to be exploited in many later works. Among the many shorter pieces, from isolated fragments to sets of minuets and other dances, one must mention the Seven Bagatelles op. 33, completed in 1802 but probably gathered from various dates. The word 'bagatelle', literally a trifle or *Kleinigkeit*, was used for other occasional pieces and especially in two much later sets; but many of Beethoven's said much within their brevity, like the intimately communing no. 6 from op. 33, while others – nos 2, 5 and 7 – were playful, brilliant or explosive scherzi. Even the childlike no. 3 in F has the true Beethoven hallmark in its surprise change of key and dynamics:

Ex. 4

Variation-form continued to occupy him. Having dealt mostly with other composers' themes, operatic or otherwise, he produced a set of six 'easy' variations in 1800 on an original theme, WoO 77, which may have been a by-product from his work on the G major Quartet op. 18 no. 2. Their freshness is appealing but they were soon to be eclipsed by the two important sets of 1802, each 'in a new manner' as Beethoven told Breitkopf. Both were on original themes, though the F major, op. 34 has been overshadowed by the grandeur and virtuosic appeal of the 'Prometheus' set of op. 35. The former deserves more attention than it gets: the theme, a slow one, is static and hardly distinguished but the six variations are uniquely varied and colourful, descending by thirds through the keys of D, B flat, G, E flat and C minor with as many changes in tempo and time-signature. When C minor turns to C major it provides a natural way back to the home-key for the sixth variation, followed by a lavishly embellished return of the theme.

In contrast with this intimate set, the 'Prometheus' Variations are challenging from the start. Several features were to be adopted in the *Eroica* finale: the use of the bass as a variation-subject before the arrival of the theme itself; the fugal treatment of the bass and its inversion; and the ultimate glorification of the theme in slow tempo. In the symphony the hybrid nature of the finale permitted some dramatic key-contrasts not usually acceptable in straight variation-form, and in op. 35 Beethoven seemed anxious to re-establish the norm after the tonal adventures of op. 34. He kept to the home-key of E flat throughout, never straying far from the basic harmony of the subject, apart from a sideways glance at C minor in variation 6, a dramatic semitonal lift in the second half of variation 10, and one variation, no. 14, in the tonic minor. The fugue, as part of the coda, was legitimately free, but as with the much later Diabelli Variations it closed into a further 'strict' variation, extended for the sake of finality. The simple harmonisation of the theme, mostly tonic and dominant, threatened a monotony that Beethoven circumvented with a wide range of character and texture: ebullience in variations 2, 9 and 13; humour in nos. 3 and 11; pensiveness in nos. 5, 8 and 14. No. 15, the slow variation preceding the fugue, may be felt too contrived with its increasingly elaborate subdivisions, though it was a masterstroke to follow it with a postlude recalling the C minor-F minor manoeuvres of the sixth variation as a foil to the E flat opening of the fugue.

After the grand manner of the 'Prometheus' Variations Beethoven produced two short sets in 1803 on 'God save the King', WoO

78, and 'Rule, Britannia', WoO 79, a curiously anti-Napoleonic gesture in view of his work on the *Eroica*, but maybe influenced by the increasing British interest in his music. In the same year he wrote the third of his Three Marches for piano duet op. 45. Their military character is obvious: in the prevalent dotted rhythms, in the secondo player's percussive contributions to the trio of no. 2, and the unison fanfare that opens no. 3. This calls for a few words about Beethoven's other four-hand duets, a medium in which he had less to say than Mozart and far less than Schubert. One of the last products of his Bonn years had been the 'Waldstein' Variations WoO 67. Although ingeniously decorative, with a fair sharing between treble and bass, they were somewhat hampered by the Count's prosaic moves from C major to minor and back, leading Beethoven to indulge a more improvisatory manner in a final Capriccio. In 1797 his only duet sonata appeared as op. 6, in no way matching Mozart's mature ones, but a pleasantly tidy two-movement work opening with an amusing prediction of the Fifth Symphony, albeit in D major. In that key he was also to produce his most perfect work for the medium, the Six Variations on 'Ich denke dein' WoO 74, based on a song to words by Goethe and written in the autograph book of the Brunsvik sisters Josephine and Therese. Though slight in scale the variations were composed in two instalments, four in 1799 and a further two, nos 3 and 4, in 1803 or 1804. The theme itself is of surpassing beauty, with two eloquent six-bar phrases crowned by a four-bar postlude. Beethoven wrote no more for four hands and nothing whatever for two pianos. A request from Diabelli for another duet sonata in the late period (1824) came to nothing; and the authentic four-hand version of the *Grosse Fuge*, published as op. 134, can hardly count as a duet in the true sense.

The expansion of form in the *Eroica* Symphony was to be reflected in the grandeur of his two most famous middle-period sonatas, the 'Waldstein' and the 'Appassionata', and sketches for the former, the Sonata in C op. 53, followed soon after those for the symphony in the 'Landsberg 6' sketchbook. Meanwhile some interim sketches had included drafts for keyboard exercises, scales in tenths, contrary motion etc, as if flexing the muscles in preparation for the C major brilliance of the sonata to come. Yet virtuoso pianists might also note that the most common dynamic mark in the 'Waldstein' is *pp*: all three movements begin quietly, and it was probably the hushed, veiled opening of the rondo that gave the work a former nickname, 'L'Aurore'. To complain that the 'Waldstein' indulges in long stretches of tonic and dominant harmony is to ignore the splendour of its long-term key relations. The move to E major for the second subject of the first movement is an example, but its tonal adventures begin in the opening bars. In fact the stability of the E major theme and the triplet patterns that flow from it is all the more welcome, and it is left for the development to pursue the figures of both main subjects in turn through a wide range of keys and with unremitting energy. The coda too, by setting off in the remote region of D flat, throws the eventual triumph of C major into strong relief; and here Beethoven, having acquired an Erard grand in 1803, was able to enjoy the higher reaches of the extended keyboard for the first time in the sonatas.

The sketches reveal the chequered history of the rest of the 'Waldstein'. An Andante was planned in E major and completed in F major, but meanwhile the conception of the finale as a lively three-eight movement changed to the most spacious of rondos in two-four time. In this new context the original slow movement was rejected, though it was published separately and became known as the 'Andante favori' WoO 57. It was replaced by the shorter but more mysterious and profound Introduzione, which forms a fitting contrast to the serenely diatonic rondo-theme. Although the theme of the rondo sounds simple enough, the sketches once again show the pains it cost in the making. One feature, the low bass C, to be held with the pedal, was the only surviving remnant from the earlier three-eight idea:

Ex. 5

(sketches for 'Waldstein' finale)

The first three notes of the final version provided a rhythmic motif that particularly dominates the latter part of the movement, including the Prestissimo coda. From the purely pianistic angle there are demands and rewards in plenty: in the brilliant semiquaver-triplet passages of the episodes; in the right-hand trills that underpin the climaxes of the rondo-theme and its further development in the coda; in the quasi-glissando octave scales, hard to bring off as true glissandi quietly and in rhythm on a modern piano; and, conversely, the passages of subdued mystery, like the pianissimo wanderings in the second episode.

Between the 'Waldstein' and the 'Appassionata' there lurks a strange and neglected two-movement work, the Sonata in F op. 54. Yet as an example of Beethoven at his most capricious it deserves hearing and repays study: a stately minuet-style first movement beset by storming passages in double octaves, thirds and sixths; and a moto perpetuo finale, reminiscent of op. 26, that runs in and out of a whole gamut of keys with irrepressible energy and humour.

The Sonata in F minor op. 57 acquired its indelible title 'Appassionata' from the publisher Cranz, but for once it is fully appropriate. The work's character, alternately tempestuous and compassionate, has become almost synonymous with the term 'Beethovenish', and its domination by minor keys makes it a perfect counterpart to the C major brilliance of the 'Waldstein'. The sketches show that the first movement was conceived in common time until the continuous undercurrent of triplet quavers, incorporating the famous 'fate' motif, persuaded it into twelve-eight. Apart from an increase of explosive dynamic marks, the pathos of the music is enhanced by frequent Neapolitan inflections, already inherent in the quiet move from F minor to G flat harmony at the outset. There is a clear kinship between the rhythm of this opening and the one 'consoling' subject in the second group; and the movement's two overwhelming climaxes, one leading to the recapitulation and the other preceding the 'più allegro' of the coda, spread arpeggio figures over the entire keyboard to achieve the maximum sonority possible.

The Andante, a calm between two storms, is a set of four variations on a chordal theme firmly rooted to the key of D flat. Its second and third variations engender a certain excitement by ascending in octaves and introducing quicker note-values, but the climax subsides abruptly to make way for the final variation, which restores the original mood until interrupted by a mysterious diminished-seventh arpeggio. After a moment of suspense it is taken up vociferously, thereby releasing the torrent of the finale which, like the rondo of the 'Waldstein', follows without a break. Much of the torrent of semiquavers is subdued, giving added point to the sudden fortes and climaxes as they arrive; and as with the first movement the Neapolitan harmony, stressing the chord of G flat in F minor or D flat in relation to C, is a continuing and unifying feature. An unusual formal detail is that Beethoven asked for the latter part of this sonata-form finale, and not the exposition, to be repeated, thus increasing the cumulative effect and, by delaying it, the shattering impact of the coda.

After the 'Appassionata', which was completed in 1805 but not published until 1807, Beethoven gave the piano sonata a rest for over four years. He wrote a few slight works, such as the Six Ecossaises WoO 83 with their amusing common refrain; but an exception was the set of 32 Variations in C minor WoO 80, probably dating from 1806 and which he is said to have disowned later. This is surprising, for they are strikingly compact, rich in textural invention, and clearly from the same stable as the 'Appassionata'. Both rhythmically and structurally they look back to Bach's violin Chaconne, which Beethoven probably never knew, and forward to the passacaglia of Brahms's Fourth Symphony. The eight-bar harmonic progression of the subject, and the placing and character of the central group of major-key variations, are common factors in all three cases. It is curious to turn from these closely-knit variations to the improvisatory Fantasia op. 77 of 1809, though this probably gives a fair idea of Beethoven's extempore playing and links up with the long piano preamble in the Choral Fantasy of the year before. The Fantasia, having arrested attention with a downward rush of scales in G minor, proceeds to try out a series of ideas and keys before settling down to some variations in B major. In this improvising frame of mind he also wrote down cadenzas for his first four piano concertos and the piano version of his Violin Concerto, having disposed of the optional cadenza 'problem' in his most recent E flat Concerto, the so-called 'Emperor'. These were done for his pupil the Archduke Rudolph, whose departure from Vienna occasioned the 'Lebewohl' Sonata op. 81a.

The two previous sonatas of 1809 had offered a strange juxtaposition of styles. Op. 78, in the rare key of F sharp major, is a short but concentrated two-movement work that Beethoven rated more highly, he said, than the ever-popular 'Moonlight'. A four-bar slow introduction establishes a warmly intimate manner which is carried over into the first subject of the Allegro. There are presages here of the late period, especially in the coda, with its fragmentation of the subject over a flowing left-hand counterpoint; yet it restored the earlier tradition of repeating the longer second 'half' as well as the first, thus stressing the binary origin of sonata form. The second movement of op. 78 is capricious in tonality, phrase-length and dynamics, making great play with pairs of short-slurred semiquavers, sometimes crossing hands and demanding fastidious precision from the player. In great contrast the G major Sonata op. 79 is a deliberate throw-back in style, being labelled 'Sonata facile' in the sketches and 'Sonatina' in the first edition, though the opening Presto with its leaping octaves is far from a beginner's piece. The marking 'alla Tedesca', in the manner of a German dance, was used again for the fourth movement of the late B flat Quartet op. 130, which actually adopted an inversion of the sonata's opening figure and in the same key of G major.

The Archduke's 'Lebewohl' Sonata in E flat op. 81a, sometimes called 'Les Adieux', resumed Beethoven's grander middle-period manner, and some passages in its six-eight finale could have come straight from the florid episodes in the rondo of the 'Emperor' Concerto. The emotions involved in the movements are explicit in the subtitles – farewell, absence and return – and the word 'Lebewohl' (farewell) is spelt out over the opening motif of the introduction, scored as for a pair of horns and recurring in various guises during the first Allegro. As it turned out, op. 81a was to be Beethoven's own farewell to the piano sonata for another five years, but again one or two isolated pieces deserve mention. In 1809 he also composed the Six Variations op. 76 for his newly-found young friend Franz Oliva on an original theme that became better known as the Turkish March from *The Ruins of Athens*; and in the following year he wrote the popular miniature, in fact a Bagatelle, called 'Für Elise', though it is thought that 'Elise' may have been a misreading of 'Therese', and presumably the Therese Malfatti he had hoped to marry at that time. No further piano music is known until 1814, when Beethoven presented the Russian Empress with his Polonaise in C op. 89 during the Congress of Vienna, an attractive piece with a genuine Chopinesque polonaise rhythm in its rondo-theme, and beginning with a cadenza-like flourish; but the Sonata in E minor op. 90, dedicated to Count Moritz Lichnowsky, was far more significant.

Op. 90 stands on the threshold of Beethoven's third-period

style, and its two movements, E minor followed by E major, make an unusually satisfying whole: Hans von Bülow likened their contrast to speech and song, while others have suggested prose and poetry. Beethoven offered a more specific programme to the Count, who was about to re-marry: for the first movement 'a struggle between the heart and the head'; for the second, 'conversation with the beloved.' There is in fact plenty of brain-work in the first movement, of which the re-emergence of the opening subject out of the decorative semiquavers of the development by a process of changing note-values is a classic example, but its more lyrical sequel (the heart?) has the last word, paving the way for the major-key second movement. This rondo, with its German instruction 'sehr singbar vorzutragen' is a piece Mendelssohn would have been proud to call a 'song without words'; and after running a rich but leisurely course it glorifies its theme in the tenor register, like Schubert in his A major Rondo for four hands, and closes with the most delicately wrought of all sonata endings.

Something of this intimate manner may be felt in the opening movement of the next piano sonata, the A major op. 101 of 1816, though its compact four-movement scheme seems a more direct offspring from the C major Cello Sonata op. 102 no. 1 of the previous year. They both alternate slow and fast movements, and in each case the opening theme is recalled before the advent of the finale; and there is a further parallel in the vigorous dotted rhythms of the second movements. The dedication of op. 101 to the Baroness Dorothea Ertmann has some bearing on the work's character, since she was renowned for her sensitive playing of Beethoven's sonatas. The tender restraint of the first and third movements, which Beethoven described as 'reveries', is however offset by the vigorous Alla Marcia in F major, where the persistent dotted rhythm may have left its mark on Schumann – the middle movement of the Fantasy op. 17 for example – and by the jubilant finale with its fully-worked fugal development. Counterpoint is however more generally abundant: the subject of the finale is itself in double counterpoint, while the Alla Marcia's quartet texture abounds in imitative ripostes, with strict and sparse canonic two-part writing in the middle section or 'trio'. There are shades of the Baroque, and especially J.S. Bach, in the profound calm of the third movement, just as in the chorale-like Adagio of the Cello Sonata op. 102 no. 2; but the renewed absorption in counterpoint was to have more cataclysmic results in the next piano sonata, the 'Hammerklavier' op. 106 in B flat.

The slow gestation of some of Beethoven's later works, such as the 'Hammerklavier', the Diabelli Variations, the Ninth Symphony and the *Missa Solemnis*, has sometimes been attributed to the lull in creativity that followed his second 'crisis' year of 1813, to his domestic upheavals, and the endless litigation over his nephew Karl. Yet such works as op. 106 also involved 'unprecedented creative struggles', as William. S. Newman remarks in his commentaries on the Classical Sonata. Op. 106 (the 'Hammerklavier') was Beethoven's main preoccupation from the autumn of 1817 to the late autumn of 1818 and could claim to be 'the greatest of all Classical sonatas', not only on account of its time – 45 minutes on average – but because of its expressive, spiritual and intellectual range. It enlarged the four-movement plan to an epic scale without resorting to the easy cross-references and retrospects that had been hinted at in op. 101, op. 81a, even op. 27 no. 1, and were to become a commonplace in the Romantic age. The 'Hammerklavier' has far subtler internal unities, including the pattern of a rising and falling third, already inherent in the opening bars:

Ex. 6

This pattern can be seen easily enough on paper as the starting-points of the scherzo and slow movement, but the tremendous opening affirmation of the chord of B flat can be related elsewhere, to sketches for a choral greeting to the Archduke to whom the work was dedicated – 'vivat, vivat Rudolphus' – giving a clue to its vociferous character and rhythmic impetus. After the warmly lyrical response has reached its own climax and subsided, the opening returns but with an abrupt change of harmony to D major, leading naturally enough to G major for the long flowing paragraphs of the second group, an exotic key-relationship already explored in the

'Archduke' Trio op. 97. The richness of this exposition was un-paralleled: at its heart lies a cantabile theme with an elusive mixture of major and minor tonality, which also haunts the development and coda. Its texture, with a prolonged internal trill, had been fore-shadowed in the rondo of the 'Waldstein' and was to be carried further in the variations of two later sonatas, op. 109 and op. 111.

The second movement of op. 106 is the scherzo, deriving from a one-bar motif, lightly scored but prone to quirks and alarms, with occasional touches of modal harmony and a darker but widely-spaced trio. A theory that it should come after and not before the slow movement was supported by the pianist André Tchaikowsky on logical grounds and internal evidence, including the added intro-ductory bar of the Adagio which seems designed to follow the first movement and not the scherzo; and the fact that the prolonging of the mood of the Adagio into the 'gradual awakening' of the finale was quite untypical. The issue was confused by Beethoven's letters to Ries about possible abridgments for the English market, such as 'you could use the first movement and then the Adagio and then for the third movement the Scherzo' – was the extra bar envisaged in this context? – but his later letter of 16 April 1819 would seem to clinch the accepted order of events.

The Adagio of the 'Hammerklavier', in whatever context, must impress as one of the greatest of all slow movements. Its length is in proportion to the breadth of its themes, which are worked out in the fullest sonata form and the richest range of textures. Mozart also chose the remote key of F sharp minor for the gravely beautiful slow movement of his A major Concerto K.488, and Beethoven's opening theme, with its darkly contemplative mood, turns to the Neapolitan harmony of G major at a parallel place. The long transition to the second group contains some exquisitely wrought fioritura; and since the development concentrates on the first subject the recapitulation is disguised in an elaborate variation, saving the simpler form for the coda. The ending in F sharp major at last establishes a link with the sonata's main key, since A sharp is the enharmonic of B flat; and the relationship is clarified when F sharp falls to F natural in the introduction to the finale, following a procedure in the 'Emperor' Concerto and providing a counter-argument in favour of the printed order of movements. The expected resolution is however delayed by a lengthy exploration of a whole network of keys, over a bass falling in an apparently endless cycle of thirds, major or minor, with occasional pauses for orientation and brief toccata-like interludes. The elusive F natural is eventually touched upon and passed over, but recognised and regained, and a three-part fugue 'con alcune licenze' set in motion.

To describe the fugue as a challenge for both player and listener would be an understatement. Its energetic but angular counterpoint involves the subject in augmentation, inversion and cancrizans (retrograde motion); and like the *Grosse Fuge* for string quartet it stretches the medium to the utmost, sharing its obsession with trills:

Ex. 7

There is some relief in a serene D major episode with measured crotchets, and one marvels at the mastery that reveals them as a latent counterpoint to the original fugue-subject. When the conductor Felix Weingartner made the experiment of orchestrating the 'Hammerklavier' he dispersed and alleviated its severer technical demands, but also removed the sense of superhuman effort that seems so essential to the character of this colossus of sonatas.

In the wake of the 'Hammerklavier', and while working on the *Missa Solemnis* and the Ninth Symphony, Beethoven composed his last three piano sonatas. The Sonata in E major op. 109 illustrates a renewed intimacy and flexibility of form, following two brief but strongly contrasted sonata-form movements with an Andante and variations that last twice as long as the other two taken together. It was unorthodox to end with a slow movement, though op. 111 was to do likewise; but it was just as unusual to begin with a dual-tempo one which has barely established its first subject before the dramatic intervention of the second, an Adagio espressivo of the most free and rhapsodic nature. The opening Vivace, based on a regular pattern of Bach-like figurations, has the development to itself and returns in the coda, where the figures coalesce into pure harmony for a few bars, producing a touching emotional effect through their very restraint. An E minor Prestissimo follows without a break, serving the purpose of a scherzo but through-composed and hard driving in its concise sonata form, and resourceful in its later development and elevation of the initial bass line. Then come the variations on a heartfelt theme to be played 'with innermost feeling', the variations making their points through widely contrasted textures in which counterpoint plays an increasing role. After the sixth variation has generated a great climax over a prolonged internal trill, the original theme returns enhanced in the light of these experiences.

The Sonata in A flat op. 110 is also a law unto itself, though it opens with a more normal sonata-form movement, whose warm-hearted character is epitomised in the markings 'Moderato canta-bile, molto espressivo' and 'con amabilità'. Although much of the writing is in a quartet texture, the fluttering arpeggios of the transi-tion are purely pianistic, but show their allegiance to the first subject by combining with it in the recapitulation. The relation between the contours of the opening and the rising fourths of the last-movement fugue is borne out by their juxtaposition in the sketches. As with op. 109 the second movement is a scherzo substitute, now in F minor and two-four time and in the customary, though slightly varied 'da capo' form, with a trio section marked by upward crotchet leaps and perilous quaver descents. At the end F minor yields to F major, preparing for the finale, a complex movement involving recitative, arioso and fugue. The sequence of events is profoundly subjective, and one thinks forward to the 'Heiliger Dankgesang' of the op. 132 Quartet: the pathos of the Arioso dolente (A flat minor) is relieved by the confident steps of the first fugue (A flat major) but returns in broken phrases, scarcely articulate and marked *ermattet* or 'ex-hausted' (G minor), until a reiterated major chord leads to a resump-tion of the fugue, at first tentatively and with the subject inverted (G major). It gradually gathers new life – Beethoven's words – and finds its way back through a maze of complexities to its original form and key, at last shedding its contrapuntal texture in the melodic and harmonic triumph of the last page.

Each of these late sonatas is unique in form, and in the last of all, op. 111 in C minor, Beethoven returned to the two-movement scheme that had served well for some shorter works – op. 54, op. 78, op. 90 – but had never before carried such weight and significance.

Was this, then, the final answer in a medium that had become increasingly personal: the resolving in one movement of the conflicts of the other? In op. 111 the contrasts are complete: the fieriest of allegros and most serene of adagios, sonata form versus variations, the material world and the spiritual, C minor and C major. First of all the scale is set in a *maestoso* introduction with a double-dotted rhythm that might be traced back to the manner and purpose of the old French Overture, though Beethoven's boldly modulating steps had a further purpose, that of projecting his C minor-major drama against the widest tonal backcloth. This involved a stabilising process over a long dominant pedal before the launching of the Allegro, its stormy character emphasised by the marking 'con brio ed appassionato'. The powerful three-note motif C – E flat – B natural can be traced back to a sketch of twenty years before, in F sharp minor and marked 'andante', possibly intended for the slow movement of the A major Violin Sonata op. 30 no. 1. In its new character Beethoven seized at once on its fugal possibilities: the transitions and development are based entirely on first-subject material, much of it in stark two-part counterpoint. On the contrary the main theme of the second group is astonishingly free: its six bars of cantabile, held back in tempo, convey a glorious sense of relaxation. In the recapitulation, however, they are expanded and drawn back into the storm, which having reached a shattering climax in C minor gives way to the major key in the coda as if preparing for the Arietta and its variations.

The C major Arietta has become a touchstone for the interpreter. Beethoven asks for 'semplice' and 'cantabile', and few have approached Schnabel here. A further task is to convey a feeling of natural growth through the increasing subdivisions of the variations; and in fact the mood of celestial calm has given way to ecstatic exultation by the time variation three is reached, after which a double variation explores the lower and higher reaches of the keyboard with a magic alternation of darkness and ethereal lightness. The variations then break off for some freer writing including a modulatory episode of trills, but the remaining coda is vast enough to encompass a complete apotheosis of the original theme, now extended to a climax, and the essence of a still further variation transfigured with trills. The sublimity of the ending is unique in piano literature and it is hard not to sense a valedictory note; but although op. 111 was Beethoven's last piano sonata he had not yet forsaken the keyboard for good. There were the Diabelli Variations to complete and, as if to prove that in his case the greater included the lesser, there were also the two sets of Bagatelles op. 119 and op. 126.

The Eleven Bagatelles op. 119 make an odd collection of miniatures, some early, some late, yet they somehow hold together as a set. Nos 1 to 5 probably date back to 1802 or earlier, No. 3 (D major) appearing in the 'Wielhorsky' sketchbook of 1802–3, complete with the 8va signs which would have put the opening figure out of reach on Beethoven's piano at that time; and a sketch for no. 5 (C minor) occurs in the 'Kessler' sketchbook of 1801 among others for the Violin Sonata op. 30 no. 2 in the same key. Nos 7 to 11 were published in Starke's 'Wiener Pianoforte-Schule' in 1821, but no. 6 is the first to show signs of a later style, beginning with a brief preamble that seems to quote from a piano-piece in B flat WoO 60 of 1818. Some of the op. 119 set are in a simple binary form with repeats (nos 4 and 8) or ternary (no. 1) while one or two make their own form, such as no. 7 with its persistent trills and explosive ending, or the amusingly brief no. 10. The last, no. 11 in B flat, is such a perfect miniature and so intimate in expression that one regrets Max Reger's elaboration of it in some two-piano variations. A twelfth Bagatelle, adapted from the piano part of the early song 'An Laura', appeared in a later edition but hardly follows well after the profounder thoughts of no. 11.

There is more evidence that Beethoven intended his next set, the Six Bagatelles op. 126, to be played as a group. The words 'Ciclus von Kleinigkeiten' appear in the sketches, and there is a definite key-scheme: after the first two, in G major and minor, the series descends by major thirds or the enharmonic equivalent – E flat, B minor, G major, E flat. No. 1 suggests string-writing and has some wide spacings between the hands, while nos 2 and 4 are fiery minor-key outbursts, though the latter has a long and musette-like trio in the major that returns to end it. No. 3 is a richly sonorous Andante and the most pianistically rewarding, and no. 6 (also E flat) is again warmly expressive but begins and ends with a humorously brusque Presto. Although the op. 126 pieces are more substantial than the op. 119 set, apart from the light-weight fifth Bagatelle, they still make a remarkable contrast with Beethoven's colossal undertakings of the time, including his final work on the Ninth Symphony. Miniatures of a different kind may however contribute to large-scale enterprises, and earlier in 1823 he completed his longest and greatest set of piano variations, the thirty-three on a Waltz by Diabelli.

Diabelli's plan for a composite work by a host of different composers, as outlined in the previous chapter, did not appeal to Beethoven; but although he is said to have dismissed the waltz as a *Schusterfleck* or 'cobbler's patch' he soon took it up as the text for a complete work of his own. In February 1820 he was already writing to Simrock at Bonn about some 'grand variations on a well-known German waltz' but warned him that they were far from ready. He noted down some ideas in pencil for seven variations, but the work was interrupted by more pressing matters, the *Missa Solemnis*, the Ninth Symphony, and the last three piano sonatas. Variations, like fugue, had attracted Beethoven in his late period as a discipline in a wider context, and it is here that possible cross-influences between the Diabelli Variations and the Arietta of op. 111 become absorbing: the sharing of variation form and of the key of C major; and the common thematic feature of a falling fourth (C to G) answered by a falling fifth (D to G). Since these intervals, so important in the Arietta, do not appear in the earlier sketches for it, is it not feasible that the work on Diabelli's 'cobbler's patch' helped in the shaping of that sublime theme? On the contrary it seems certain that the transfigured ending of op. 111 left its mark on the ethereal final variation of the Diabelli, which was not finished until after the completion of the sonatas.

In the very first variation Beethoven established the grandeur of his undertaking by replacing the waltz-rhythm with a majestic four-four, then returning to three-four for a series of progressive variations that reach an exciting climax in nos 6 and 7. Yet already in no. 1, while preserving the general outline of the theme and its sequences, he avoided the obvious by subtle harmonic inflections. One could even say that throughout the fifty-or-more minutes of the work Beethoven was to give the subject-matter thirty-three lessons in composition, with never a predictable or untended repetition – except for the repeats in the binary form itself, and even these were sometimes omitted or varied, as in the 'double' variation 10. The gradual expansion of the harmonic horizon is remarkable. In no. 8, for example, Beethoven replaced Diabelli's dominant harmony in bars 5 to 8 with the supertonic, and to magic effect. In tempo and texture the variations cover almost every available mood and style. Nos 9 and 11 in their different ways find resource in the mere upbeat of the waltz, complete with grace-note, and carry it as a pattern over the whole framework. No. 9 is in the tonic minor, and makes a dramatic move by transposing most of its second half up a semitone, a device Brahms emulated in the ninth of his Handel Variations.

Variations on such a scale will tend to fall into groups, as with nos 2 to 7, or pairs, nos 11 and 12, 16 and 17, 26 and 27. Their characters range from the grave or profound, nos 14 or 20, to the scintillating or humorous, nos 10 or 22: in fact no. 22 caricatures Leporello's 'Notte e giorno faticar' from *Don Giovanni* – was this a reminder to Diabelli of Beethoven's own endless labours? Of the first twenty-eight variations only one, no. 9, had been in the minor key; but nos 29 to 31 bring back C minor for a far deeper purpose, culminating in the expressive Largo of no. 31 with its florid and Bach-like melodic line. No. 24 had been a tenderly shaped Fughetta, in which the landmarks of the fourths and fifths were featured in the subject and its tonal answer. At the end of no. 31 a fugue of very different character breaks in dramatically and in the key of E flat, taking the same intervals for its subject and answer, with a counter-subject derived from the sequences of the original theme; and like the 'Prometheus' fugue of 1802 it abandons the variation technique in order to storm freely towards its climax. In the case of the Diabelli, the aftermath is even more shattering, as the music evaporates in a bleak but awe-inspiring harmonic progression to restore the home-key for the final variation:

Ex. 8

It was a masterstroke to follow the material climax with an ethereal and moderate-paced minuet, already mentioned in relation to the ending of the op. 111 Sonata. Beethoven extends it beyond its allotted time and introduces even more delicate filigree-work. Then, typically, with one *forte* chord he closes the book.

7

Chamber music with piano

Two particular developments during the mid-eighteenth century had enriched the resources and affected the media of chamber music in general. One was the growing success of the piano, or fortepiano, which could discourse on more equal expressive terms with strings or wind than the harpsichord; and the other, conversely, was the emergence of independent strings, and especially the string quartet, freed from the traditional keyboard support or 'continuo'. Yet one would have thought the bringing together of piano and quartet a tempting enough proposition for special occasions, but although Mozart may have played some of his earlier piano concertos this way, no official quintet of this type survives in the repertory before Schumann's op. 44 of 1842. Even Schubert's 'Trout' Quintet had used an irregular quartet with double-bass and without second violin, and Mozart's only piano quintet had been with wind instruments, K.452. Quartets for piano and string trio were also rare, though Mozart wrote two masterpieces in this form, in G minor and E flat. This was however the medium chosen by the fourteen-year-old Beethoven, and his three early piano quartets WoO 36 actually pre-dated Mozart's by a few months. They were presumably composed for his colleagues in the Bonn Hofkapelle and he may have played the viola in them himself, but the keyboard parts dominate, and the autograph still specifies 'clavecin' or harpsichord at this stage (1785). A Mozartian style is most noticeable in the C major, which was intended as the first of the set but printed as 'no 3', and two ideas in the op. 2 piano sonatas of a decade later derived from it.

It is easier to suspect the influence of C.P.E. Bach in the other two quartets, especially the E flat; but even here the unusual procedure of following an opening Adagio with an Allegro in the tonic minor had a precedent in Mozart's G major Violin Sonata K.379, published in 1781, and in fact Beethoven's first phrase bears a striking resemblance to Mozart's. The E flat minor movement is however clearly related to a sketch in C minor marked 'Sinfonia'. No such ambitious aspirations were followed up, but there were good wind-players in the Bonn orchestra and Beethoven's next chamber work was probably the Trio in G, WoO 37, for oboe, bassoon and piano. Wind enthusiasts may revive it for its unusual medium, for which there is also a sketch for a one-movement Romance, but it was soon to be eclipsed by Beethoven's works for wind alone and by his attention to the more usual piano trio with violin and cello. Key associations seemed strong here, for the two completed trios from his later days in Bonn were in E flat, which was also to be the key of his first 'mature' trio op. 1 no 1.

The E flat Piano Trio WoO 38 stressed this by having all three movements in the tonic; and a set of fourteen variations on an amusingly spare theme in stalking quavers, published later as op. 44, traditionally remained in the home-key, major or minor. Here the two minor-key variations are slow and expressive, and the return of the second of them in the coda is effective, and earlier on Beethoven had underlined the equality of the players by giving the second variation to the piano alone, highlighting the violin in no. 3 and the cello in no. 4. WoO 38 is also notable for its independent cello writing, following Mozart rather than Haydn, and the first movement is rich in thematic predictions – of the op. 2 no. 1 Sonata and the rondo of the C major Piano Concerto, for example.

Parts of the eventual op. 1 trios may also have been sketched, or even completed, at Bonn, for they appear to have been ready in little over a year after his arrival in Vienna despite the time given to his contrapuntal studies. Considering their importance and their dedication to Lichnowsky they were probably played more than once at his musical gatherings and revised in the interim, though it is now thought that Haydn's qualms about the C minor were raised on his second return from London and after their publication. Beethoven's decision to grant them his first opus-number was fully justified. Like the op. 2 piano sonatas all three are in four movements, with scherzos in the first two and a minuet in the third. The first movement of op. 1 no. 1 in E flat already shows a Mozartian sense of proportion and deceptive ease, beginning with a crisply rhythmic and fruitful rising arpeggio and blossoming into a second group with long melodic paragraphs. Even the simple exchanges shown in Ex.9 are the essence of real trio writing. The vigorous cadences and the overflowing of second-subject material into a sizeable coda are thoroughly Beethovenish; and so is the strangely ambiguous

Ex. 9

opening of the scherzo, first heard as a modulation from the A flat of the slow movement back to the home-key. As for the brilliant wit of the finale, one might call it Haydnish, or was Haydn himself influenced by his pupil's amusing excursion into E major towards the end, when he made similar moves in his last Piano Sonata in E flat, Hob. XVI/52, a year or so later?

The G major Trio op. 1 no. 2 has more definite Haydnish traits, including a slow introduction that hints at the opening figure of the Allegro, which arrives as though in mid-flight, poised on the dominant as in Haydn's 'Oxford' Symphony. The choice of E major for the slow movement was again more typical of Haydn than Mozart, and the return of this key in the development of the finale is worth noting. A haunting feature of the Largo is the pair of undulating sequences in its first theme, though these are never given to the cello, which has less than its normal share here. Once again the finale is good entertainment, with a splendidly prepared sonata-form return through a passage in smooth quavers that goes with, or against, the lively semiquavers of the first subject. Yet for all the felicities in the first two trios, no. 3 in C minor outstrips them in dramatic force and originality, one reason no doubt for Haydn's misgivings. There are however no barnstorming preludings to sway the gullible listener: it opens, like Mozart's C minor Piano Concerto, with a quiet unison theme; and its precipitate finale, having slipped down mysteriously into B minor, ends in a hushed C major with deliberate inconclusion and no hint of triumph. All the op. 1 finales are in sonata form, not rondo, and the C minor's main subject, after an initial call to attention, was a much speeded-up version of a sketch marked 'Andante'. For the slow movement Beethoven had reverted to varia-tion form, once again in E flat, on a dignified hymnlike theme that was to have many successors in his later works. It is harmonised richly in the coda,·which ends with a curious foretaste of the conversational little Bagatelle op. 119 no. 2. Taken as a whole the drama of op. 1 no. 3 did not find a parallel in the chamber music until the C minor Violin Sonata op. 30 no. 2 of 1802, for not even the op. 18 no. 4 Quartet in that key is as well-planned or consistent in workmanship.

The next chamber works with piano broke new ground: in 1796 Beethoven composed the two cello sonatas op. 5 for his visit to Berlin. They are important in the repertory for being the first real duos for cello and piano, a medium untouched by Haydn and Mozart. At the same time they are rewarding showpieces for the cello, as befitting the occasion, exploiting its sonority as a bass instrument as well as its high melodic 'King of Prussia' register. Their shared form is unusual, basically two movements with a slow introduction to the first in each case, though the opening of the G minor op. 5 no. 2 is the more expansive, alternating contrasting ideas on a scale comparable with that in the Seventh Symphony. The problem of tonal monotony was solved by beginning both finales with themes that approach the home-key obliquely, and the C major leanings in the capricious G major finale of op. 5 no. 2 had later sequels in the Fourth Piano Concerto and, more drastically, in the E minor Quartet op. 59 no. 2. This spacious but witty finale, and the minor-key turbulence and drive of the main first movement have tended to overshadow the companion sonata, op. 5 no. 1 in F, which is effective enough in its more conventional moods. With these first cello sonatas it is convenient to mention Beethoven's three sets of variations for cello and piano, two on themes from *Die Zauberflöte*, his favourite Mozart opera, probably dating from 1796 and 1801 (op. 66 and WoO 46); and the 'Conquering Hero' variations on a theme from *Judas Maccabaeus* WoO 45, now also ascribed to the Berlin visit, in which he expressed his devotion to Handel on a grander scale and perhaps with deference to his cello-playing monarch.

Three other works with piano involved wind instruments. The Quintet in E flat for piano and wind op. 16 invites comparison with Mozart's K. 452 – which may have inspired it – and the slight likeness of the slow movement theme to 'Batti, batti' from *Don Giovanni* suggests a conscious debt. It is, however, invidious to compare mature but still early Beethoven with a work the fully mature Mozart considered 'his best', and the pleasures of op. 16 may be felt to sprawl in the process. As with the op. 5 cello sonatas there is a lengthy introduction in which a unison fanfare in double-dotted rhythm gives way to some milder soloistic writing, and in the light of op. 5 no. 2 a pleasant but plain-sailing Allegro. Beethoven later arranged the work as a piano quartet with strings, his only return to his first chamber-music medium. The reshaping of the horn solo in the Andante for viola is worth studying, and the strings sometimes play where the wind had been silent; but strings are less suited to the introduction and to the six-eight 'hunting' finale, so redolent of Mozart's horn concertos and, with wind cooperation, of some of his piano concerto finales, such as K.450, K.456 or K.482.

A possible offshoot from the Quintet was the Trio in B flat op. 11 for piano, clarinet and cello. Beethoven may not have divined the soul of the clarinet with the unerring instinct of Mozart, but the version with violin is far less colourful and one is surprised that Marion Scott wrote off the original as 'near being a dud'. The unison opening is arresting, and the approach to the second group by way of D major and G minor is also striking, even though it recalls Haydn's procedure in his Symphony no. 102, also in B flat. The Adagio highlights the cello in a reflective theme that seems related to the minuet of the Piano Sonata op. 49 no. 2 and its own near-relation in the Septet of 1800. For the finale Beethoven wrote a set of lively variations on a popular air by Joseph Weigl, 'Pria ch'io l'impegno', which gave the work its nickname as the 'Gassenhauer' or 'Street

Song' Trio. Variation 1 is for piano solo, no. 2 is a duo for clarinet and cello, and at the end there is an amusing diversion from B flat to G major and from common time to six-eight. The situation is saved and the original tempo regained in the nick of time, but such surprise codas were soon to be put to far stronger architectural purpose.

In 1800 Beethoven wrote the Sonata in F op. 17 for horn and piano, which like the cello sonatas is the earliest repertory work of its kind. Again it loses much in its inevitable arrangement for cello. The solo opening at once proclaims the range and quality of the natural horn, and though normally played on a valve-horn today there is loss as well as gain here too, as in the 'stopped' effect of the chromatic notes that characterise the first subject:

Ex. 10

Other idiomatic features are the use of low pedal-notes as a bass to the piano and the agile arpeggios at the end of the first and last movements. The slow movement, no more than an introduction to the last, makes no attempt to explore the horn's melodic abilities, but amends are made in the D minor episode of the finale, where the players expand their customary repartee into a more extended dialogue.

Whereas the Horn Sonata was a rarity, sonatas for violin and piano were plentiful, with Mozart as the most obvious precedent. Beethoven's first works for this medium were not sonatas however. There were the Variations on Mozart's 'Se vuol ballare' from *Figaro*, about which he had written to Eleonore von Breuning in 1794, sending her also the playful Rondo in G, WoO 41, later to be transformed into a popular but sentimental 'Rondino' by Fritz Kreisler; and a set of six Allemandes WoO 42, dating from 1795 and 6. His first three violin sonatas op. 12, of far greater importance, were completed in 1798 and dedicated to Salieri. Unlike the continuo sonatas of the Baroque period, with Bach as a notable exception, the sharing of interest was now a first essential, though Beethoven's textures were already more robust and less delicately poised than Mozart's, and the scent of battle never far away. Yet it was also typical that the character and variety of the works should be established in the very first bars. Op. 12 no. 1 in D major, for example, has a resolute unison opening; no. 2 in A major shows that if the piano may often 'accompany' the violin, the violin may also 'accompany' the piano; while in the E flat, which is brilliant pianistically, the violin hardly accompanies but *reinforces* the opening phrases.

It is hard to understand how contemporary criticism could find 'forced modulations' and 'hostile entanglements' in these op. 12 sonatas, which still owe so much to Mozartian models – in the slow movement's variations and the six-eight finale of no. 1, for example. In no. 2 the wit of the first movement, which extracts so much from a two-note tag, is balanced by the tender pathos of a slow movement in the tonic minor and a gentle-paced minuet-like finale. In the third sonata the pianist takes more than a fair share of initiative, partly because the key of E flat lends itself more readily to keyboard than violinistic brilliance; but in the C major slow movement, an unusual key-relation shared with the op. 7 Piano Sonata, the piano yields repeatedly to the melodic genius of the violin.

Two more violin and piano sonatas followed in 1801. The A minor op. 23 shows at once how far Beethoven had travelled musically since op. 12, and his work on the op. 18 quartets may have some bearing on the terseness, drive and economy of texture in the first movement. There is in fact a prevalence of three-part as well as four-part writing, with the violin often taking a middle voice between the pianist's two hands; and the piano prefers the austerity of octaves to harmonic thickening in *forte* passages. One may even sense a foretaste here of the driving E minor Prestissimo in the op. 109 Piano Sonata of nineteen years later, and in this context the 'scherzoso' second movement in the tonic major is a surprise. The simple opening suggests a theme and variations, but sonata form is confirmed when a fugato intervenes and leads to the dominant for a group of still more scherzoso themes and a pure Mozartian cadence. In the finale it is easy to see the 'Kreutzer' in embryo as the agitated A minor theme flares up from time to time. Another splendid moment occurs when both episodes are recalled in quick succession, and the sudden quiet ending, like that of the first movement, underlines the work's personal nature.

It is a pity that op. 23 has been overshadowed by its more relaxed neighbour, but the great popularity of op. 24 in F major is easy to understand, along with its nickname, the 'Spring' Sonata, which used to be applied far less aptly to the autumnal G major Sonata op. 96. F major was to be the open-air key of Beethoven's *Pastoral* Symphony, with B flat for the 'Scene by the Brook'. Being wise after the event it is not hard to detect bird-song in the B flat Adagio of the Sonata:

Ex. 11

The lyrical opening of the first movement is so instantly appealing that sketches for it have a special interest: the eloquent undulations from the third bar, for example, appear to have derived from an inanimate sequence of crotchets and minims. The sketches tell us much more about op. 24: that the vivacious scherzo with its offbeat violin imitations began life as a staid minuet, and that the rondo-theme was noted down earlier not in F major but in F sharp minor, perhaps intended as a separate piano-piece. Only three of the ten violin sonatas include scherzos, op. 24, op. 30 no. 2 and op. 96. Beethoven contemplated removing them, probably because he felt the 'da capo' form less suited to the antiphony of a duo sonata, but fortunately he let them stay. Op. 24's is over in a trice, but it adds a touch of athletic energy to separate the serene Adagio from the more carefree ambling music of the Rondo with its happily varied returns.

The medium continued to attract Beethoven, for in 1802 he produced another group of three violin sonatas op. 30 and within a further year the solitary but brilliant 'Kreutzer' Sonata. Growing maturity may however show itself more subtly, and the opening of op. 30 no. 1 is a case in point. As with an intimate conversation it seems to resume rather than announce a topic, and technically it shows a new-found freedom in phrase-length, a feature in Haydn that Beethoven had at last made his own. This amiable opening, with its important semiquaver figure in the bass, soon blossoms and proliferates, with the figure taking ever-new forms until it ends the movement quietly on the violin. In the Adagio the expression deepens with a rich cantilena intensified by offbeat stresses, an effect the piano can hardly match; but the compensating decorations and touches of recitative add to the impression of an operatic scena. Finally, and carrying this parallel further, there are six variations on a tender theme that seems a parent of Florestan's in the Act 2 Terzetto from *Fidelio*, also in A major. As in op. 12 no. 1 the interest is evenly spread, and after a Beethovenish digression at the end of the fifth variation he turned for the last to the six-eight time so much favoured by Mozart for codas and final variations, as in his own Violin Sonata in E flat K.481, for example.

The next in this group, op. 30 no. 2 in C minor, is undoubtedly a greater and more challenging work, and the rejection in the sketches of a third statement of the opening figure in favour of the downward scale already intensified the drama:

Ex. 12

Beethoven's C minor daemon soon produced a vigorous exchange of chords, more apposite in a duo than those in the op. 18 no. 4 Quartet in that key, and bringing an abrupt move to E flat for the second group, thus emphasising the contrast of keys and ingredients as in the Fifth Symphony. The martial dotted rhythm in the second subject, scored in economic two-part writing, and its sequel of rushing scales and agitated syncopations, led one imaginative writer to hear or see in it a charge of Prussian cavalry [!]. One may be better content to observe that the urgency of the music forbids, for the only time in the series, the usual exposition repeat. Instead, a new cantabile theme arrives, the violin's property, accompanied by the opening motif in the bass and effectively dovetailing exposition and development. The development becomes stormy and the coda more so, stretching the medium in Beethoven's fieriest C minor manner; and at the close the violin rides the storm with the first subject while the piano sides with the elements.

In the Adagio, sketched in G major but settling in A flat, a more veiled key for strings, the prevailing character is cantabile for piano and violin in turn. The suspensions in the theme may be felt compassionate, but the crotchets need measuring with care to take account of their later demisemiquaver accompaniments. Towards the end, as in other Beethoven slow movements, there are dramatic interruptions, ironically with rapid scales of C *major*; but the disturbances, while recalling the outer world of action, are short-lived. C major is however the key of the scherzo, a sharply pointed movement with a more melodic, and amusingly canonic, trio; but its high spirits are dashed by an explosive finale that carries C minor through to the end. Again Beethoven gives the utmost significance to the quaver figure that launches it in the bass: it has only to appear on the horizon for the listener to sense an imminent return of the rondo-subject.

The third of the op. 30 sonatas, no. 3 in G major, stands in even greater contrast to the C minor than the first of the set. In the first movement Beethoven presents a series of epigrams, some closely related, and all certain of their effect. The character here is bright and witty but does not exclude tenderness; nor is there any loss of logic or 'line' in the movement's prodigality. The development, where a composer's seams often show, is a natural continuation, taking the opening 'rocket' theme into dark keys and dark regions of the piano with answers from the violin four octaves above. The duality had been established from the outset: a unison theme breaking into repartee, with wilful and provocative dynamics. For the middle movement Beethoven wrote a minuet 'ma molto moderato e gra-zioso', and the sketches show the trouble it caused him; but having achieved its haunting songlike theme he allowed it to return again and again, unadorned except for changes of scoring. At the start, for example, the violin plays an inner part, a favourite device of Mozart's. In the finale however Haydn is clearly the influence: the general rusticity and perpetual motion are reminiscent of the popular 'Gipsy Rondo'. It deals moreover with the adventures of a single theme and, from the violin's entry, its contrapuntal companion. The drone-bass, traditionally bucolic, is no obstacle to modulation. It moves with the theme, sometimes surprisingly far, as on the last page.

In 1803 Beethoven composed the Sonata in A op. 47 for the visiting mulatto violinist George Bridgetower, though its subsequent dedication to Rodolphe Kreutzer gave it its name. The 'Kreutzer' was the only Beethoven violin sonata to begin with a slow introduction. In fact he offered the visitor a grand opening gesture – four bars of unaccompanied violin – and thereafter rose to the occasion by writing for both players in an unmatched virtuoso style. This was explained in the elaborate title of the first edition: 'Sonata for piano and violin obbligato, written in a decidedly concertante manner, as though a Concerto'. The word 'obbligato' must of course be construed as 'obligatory' and not in its later misuse as 'optional', but note that the piano takes precedence. After the violinist's opening challenge the piano hints that A minor, nor major, is to rule the first movement, and in the subsequent dialogue a simple rising semitone figure is dwelt upon before the violin takes it up resolutely to launch the main Presto. As a 'prime motif' it also plays a great part in the second group and the development, along with much standard passage-work, but the stirring emotional effect is out of all proportion to the means. (It even stirred one of Tolstoy's short-story characters to a *crime passionnel*.) The only serene theme in this demonic movement, mostly in semibreves, marks the arrival of the second subject, and even this is turned from major to minor when the piano takes it over. Yet the impact of the first movement, Tovey maintained, should not lead one to underrate the rest of the sonata, for the Andante and its variations are on a grand scale, and there are thematic links between the first movement and the finale (see Ex.13).

The scope of the variations derives from the breadth of the Andante theme itself. Vaughan Williams found the second variation, in which the violin performs a spectacular moto perpetuo, a trivial prelude to the tragic third one, but Beethoven often exulted in such

Ex. 13

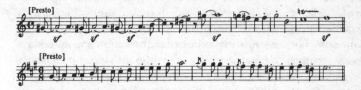

leaps from the mundane to the sublime and vice versa. Variation 4 is lavishly decorative in an ethereal high register, though still within the range of Mozart's keyboard, after which a long coda takes a reluctant farewell of various features of the theme. A peremptory A major chord then obliterates the slow movement's F major and announces the finale, which begins in a mock-fugal style incorporating, perhaps unknowingly, the first movement's rising semitone; but if the counterpoint is short-lived the six-eight rhythm and energy are certainly not. The sketches show that this full sonata-form Presto finale was intended for the earlier and milder A major Sonata op. 30 no. 1, but that was surely in its own initial stages. As it stands, it is only applicable and appropriate to the 'Kreutzer'.

Having composed nine violin sonatas within half-a-dozen years, nine years were to elapse before he returned to the form for his tenth and last, op. 96. In 1808, however, he produced the A major Cello Sonata op. 69 and the two piano trios op. 70. The Sonata, his only middle-period one for cello and piano, begins quietly on the cello alone, an effect as magical in its own way as the solo opening of the Fourth Piano Concerto. In fact the work inherits something of the concerto's warmth and ease, though in neither case do these qualities inhibit the well-placed moments of brilliance and drama. There is pathos, too, in the first movement's development, when a fragment of the opening subject yields an expressive dialogue in minor keys, with phrases prophetic of the 'Arioso dolente' in the Piano Sonata op. 110 and also curiously reminiscent of the gamba solo in 'Es ist vollbracht' from the *St John Passion*, another Bach work Beethoven can hardly have known. Yet he still seemed reluctant to exploit the cello's natural singing quality in an extended slow movement. There is a busy scherzo in A minor with tied-note syncopations and a through-composed trio in the major that comes round twice. Then follows an Adagio cantabile in E major with an exquisite theme for the piano, to which the cello provides a tender counterpoint before taking it over; but it soon reveals its introductory nature by moving to the home-key in preparation for the finale. This is both buoyant and brilliant, and its second subject begins with a brief but memorable exchange exploring the higher singing reaches of the cello; but the lyrical expansion of the first subject in the coda is largely confined to the piano, while the cello provides a bass below the pianist's left hand, partly contrapuntal, partly in harmonic support. Yet the cello's versatility, its rapid changes of register and function, had been a feature from the start.

When Beethoven came to this group of chamber works in 1808 he had behind him the experience of the three 'Rasumovsky' quartets op. 59. No. 1 in F had been notable for its royal treatment of the cello, and both the op. 70 piano trios begin by giving it pride of place. In op. 70 no. 1 in D it emerges from the unison opening on a sustained F natural, which has a far-reaching sequel like the ambiguous C sharp at the start of the *Eroica*: in the exposition it is quickly resolved, but in the recapitulation it leads, via D minor, to a new and mysterious modulatory episode. Otherwise the first movement is remarkably concise, with a splendid drive and continuity, well-ordered textures, and so much deriving from its unison subject. The work's most original feature is however the slow movement, a Largo in D minor that centres on a forlorn phrase Beethoven noted down among sketches for the Witches' scene in *Macbeth*, one of his many unfulfilled projects; and the general atmosphere of mystery, with a haze of tremolos and measured trills in the piano part, led to the familiar title, the 'Geister' (or 'Ghost') Trio. After this the D major finale may seem plain sailing, yet it is also prone to strange hesitations and twists of key. Two later digressions, first to B flat and to E flat on the reprise, are initiated by long improvisatory passages for the pianist's right hand alone, further examples of the imaginative textures in which these two trios abound.

If the E flat Trio op. 70 no. 2 is less immediately arresting than the 'Geister' it offers subtler rewards. It restored the four-movement scheme of the op. 1 trios, even prefacing the first with an introduction, which is not only recalled at the end of the movement but lends its opening theme to the transition in the Allegro itself. The contrapuntal opening, again led by the cello, establishes an intimate manner; and a feeling of civilised discourse with a minimum of rhetoric pervades the whole work. The development of the trill, at first merely a passing feature, is a prophetic example of Beethoven's new resource. There is an unusual key-sequence for the middle movements: C major and minor for the second and A flat for the third, a procedure curiously reversed in the E flat String Quartet op. 74 of 1809. The characters of the movements are quite different however, for in the Trio a double-variation set on the Haydn principle, alternating major and minor themes, is followed by a minuet-like Allegretto instead of the expected scherzo. Here the theme, mood and key look back to the variations of the op. 26 Piano Sonata and forward to the popular Schubert Impromptu D.935 no. 2. This gentle manner called for the contrast of a lively and extended finale, which thrives on its opening figures but is also rich in its variety of harmonic movement.

The virtues of the op. 70 trios were soon to be overshadowed, unfairly maybe but unavoidably, by Beethoven's next chamber work with piano, the Trio in B flat op. 97, regarded by many as the greatest work of its kind. It was one of several masterpieces dedicated to the Archduke Rudolph but the only one to adopt his title as a nickname. The 'Archduke' Trio was completed in 1811 and sketches for all four movements appear in a notebook of the previous year, though further research suggests that the noble Andante theme may have been a by-product of Beethoven's earlier work on the slow movement of the 'Emperor' Concerto. It was his only trio to begin with the piano alone. This quiet but sonorous opening establishes a grand manner within a few bars and, in Beethoven's hands, provides immense resource for later development, each phrase within the theme being so clearly defined. A quick crescendo soon introduces the cello and violin in turn, with rhetorical gestures to be further expanded in the recapitulation, before the theme is resumed in a threefold texture; but the promise of a grander counterstatement is deflected into a sequential transition to the second group. The orientation here, G major instead of the expected F major, again raises the question of the mystique of key-relations, for it was to be followed in the first movement of the 'Hammerklavier' Sonata, also B flat, and the first of the Trio's second-group themes has a strong likeness to the opening of the Fourth Piano Concerto, also G major (see Ex.14).

The development, as already hinted, derives almost entirely from the figures of the first subject, though the subject itself, being open-ended, does not find its real fulfilment until the closing bars of the movement.

Ex. 14

The second movement of the 'Archduke' is the scherzo, and its general lightness of texture – strings alone to start with – is offset by the sheer size and weight of the trio-section with its dark minor-key fugal wanderings and, in compensation, the vigorous waltz-theme that breaks out three times in different keys. In fact the score asks for a complete return of the scherzo and trio, apart from the normal 'da capo' of the scherzo, as with some other middle-period works like the Seventh Symphony. Whether this is followed or not, the darker music of the trio still makes a further appearance in the coda. The placing of the scherzo second brought the remaining slow movement and finale into direct juxtaposition: they follow one another without a break, another middle-period trait, and in the 'Archduke' the dramatic contrast is heightened by the choice of the distant key of D major for the Andante and its variations. The hymn-like D major theme is again propounded by the piano with the strings joining in on the repeats, though in the second half the repeat is confined to the last four bars, thus intensifying the emotional fervour of the closing phrase. This pattern is reproduced in four variations that proceed by the traditional subdivisions of the beat, triplet quavers yielding by stages to demisemiquavers, though such a matter-of-fact account cannot describe the subtly changing relations between the players or the unworldly serenity of the music. When the theme itself returns it is deflected into other keys, opening up an extensive coda incorporating an apotheosis, in the aftermath of which a tender cadence-phrase is passed between violin and cello, the music fades, and a quiet change of harmony leads to the abrupt arrival of the finale.

Yet a sudden leap from repose into the world of action was typical of Beethoven in all periods, and keen analysts may trace a kinship between the cadence-phrase just mentioned and the lively rustic dance of the finale. The form is a sonata-rondo, and on its third appearance the 'dance' exploits the higher reaches of the cello against tremolandos in the piano with spectacular effect. The har-monic ambivalence of the theme, which leans heavily on the sub-dominant key of E flat, had its precedents, as in the rondo of the Fourth Piano Concerto, and called for the stabilising influence of a lengthy coda. This however springs its own surprises, a change of time from two-four to six-eight and of key from B flat to A major; but after a page of *presto* the home-key is just as dramatically restored, and in it ever-new versions of the rondo's figures run their way with apparent leisure until a further increase of tempo ends the movement.

If the 'Archduke' Trio turned out to be Beethoven's gloriously rich and spacious farewell to the form as a whole, two isolated movements for the medium deserve a brief mention here. In the summer of 1812 he produced a simple unpretentious piece in B flat WoO 39, dedicated to the ten-year-old Maximiliane, daughter of Franz and Antonie Brentano, 'for the encouragement of her piano-playing.' This explains the importance, yet the undemanding nature, of the piano part, and how it could ever have been considered as a rejected or alternative finale for the 'Archduke' is a mystery. A certain mystery also surrounds the ten variations for piano trio on a popular song, 'Ich bin der Schneider Kakadu' from *Die Schwestern von Prag* by Wenzel Müller, about which Beethoven wrote to Härtel at Leipzig in July 1816 that 'these belong to my early works, but they are not poor stuff'. Maybe they date from his prolific period of variation-writing in the mid-1790s, but they have an unusually portentous and mock-serious introduction, and the extended com-pass of the piano-writing in the later variations suggests considerable revision.

The Kakadu's key of G major and variation-form take one back to the Violin Sonata op. 96 of 1812 which, more than the 'Archduke' Trio, has the feeling of a valedictory work. If Beethoven in fact rethought parts of the Sonata to suit Pierre Rode's restrained manner of playing, the result was beneficial. Nine years had elapsed since his last violin sonata, the 'Kreutzer', with its extrovert bravura style, and in most ways op. 96 is its diametrical opposite. It also opens with the solo violin but in the gentlest possible way, reminding one again that G major had been the key of the Fourth Piano Concerto. The brief four-note figure, adorned with a trill, is at once echoed in the tenor register of the piano before blossoming into an unusually tender and lyrical first subject, and the more rhythmic elements in the transition and second group are suitably restrained. This also affects the development, which flows in a gentle unbroken line with no place for dramatic gestures, unless one senses a miniature drama in the quiet exchange of trills that beckons back the first subject. Development of this subject is left for the coda, and it was typical of Beethoven to gather the threads together in an abrupt final cadence in order to clear the air for the profound meditation of the next movement.

The Adagio of op. 96 begins with one of those intimate but noble chorale-like themes that recur in Beethoven from the *Pathétique* Sonata to the Ninth Symphony and the late quartets. It is given to the piano, and the violin enters with a gentle dovetailing of its final cadence before offering a more openly-expressed melody, yet complementary rather than conflicting in mood. These roles are later reversed, and the piano's decorative version of the violin's original theme leads to some touching exchanges towards the end. Not that the movement really ends, for the violin imposes a quiet C sharp on the closing E flat harmony, and through the alchemy of an augmented-sixth chord the G minor scherzo follows without a break. This terse movement, surprisingly in the tonic minor, keeps doggedly to its pattern of stressed upbeats until the trio-section, back in the slow movement key of E flat, introduces a more aspiring theme and develops it as a widely spaced three-part round. After the 'da capo' a brief coda translates the scherzo-theme into G major, ending with an abrupt flourish and the only actual *forte* chord in the movement. This gesture also serves as an effective foil to the opening of the finale, a set of variations on a gentle-paced and childlike theme, no doubt influenced – as Beethoven told the Archduke Rudolph – by the violinist Rode's dislike of 'noisy passages'. There is, however, enough brilliance in the even-numbered variations to provide the necessary contrasts, but the penultimate, fifth variation, traditionally in much slower tempo, recaptures the deeply meditative mood of the Adagio and ends by gravitating again to its key of E flat; and even the lively coda is broken off for a mysteriously subdued contrapuntal episode and, in the last bars of all, for a moment of tender retrospect.

The importance of the key of E flat in all four movements of a sonata in G major is an example of Beethoven's growing fondness for 'mediant relations' – that is to say with keys a third above or below the home-key. Working in the reverse tonal direction, the innocent-sounding variation theme in op. 96 is at once distinguished and elevated by its passing modulation from G to B major. Was this an inheritance perhaps of a similar move in the slow movement of the Violin Concerto, which incorporates variations and is also in G major? But mediant relations, whether between subjects or movements, form a recurring topic as one approaches late Beethoven. The C major Cello Sonata op. 102 no. 1 plunges into A minor for its first Allegro, and the Piano Sonata op. 101 moves from A major to F major for its Alla Marcia. The two cello sonatas of op. 102 were moreover Beethoven's last important chamber music with piano and must concern us here.

The strange circumstances surrounding the op. 102 sonatas have been discussed in relation to the lull in Beethoven's creativity during the years 1813 and 1814. In retrospect it is easier to trace a direct line of descent from the restraint of the op. 96 Violin Sonata and the intellectual concentration of the Piano Sonata op. 90, even in its easeful rondo, to the concise forward-looking manner and spiritual profundity of the cello sonatas. The first in C major has superficial links with a more distant past: in the slow introduction, a movement in itself, that had been a feature of the op. 5 sonatas of 1796; and the quiet opening on the cello alone, like and yet so unlike the A major Sonata op. 69. In op. 102 no.1 the give-and-take is infinitely subtler, communing and confiding rather than conversing (see Ex.15).

This gives all the more point to the resolute unison opening of the A minor Allegro vivace, a tightly-woven sonata-form movement that scatters fragments of its dotted rhythm up to its equally resolute close. Then follows an Adagio, also of an introductory nature, that resumes the mood of communing in a more elaborate and tonally elusive manner until it actually recalls the opening of the work. The finale, light in texture and mood, arrives almost unawares, but the isolation of its initial figure shows its clear derivation by inversion and diminution from the original cello phrase: the subject is playful and in a popular vein, but yields some explosive disagreements later as well as much contrapuntal interest. For an outright fugue we have only to turn to the next sonata in D major op. 102 no. 2.

Although these two works evolved side by side, they offer reverse procedures, for at the opening of the D major the piano proposes (an all-important leaping figure) and the cello disposes (in a more singing manner). The more usual three-movement plan is

121

Ex. 15

restored, and for the first time Beethoven wrote a full-scale slow movement for the medium. It is the heart of the work, and its key of D minor may recall one of the profoundest of his early movements, the *largo e mesto* of the D major Piano Sonata op. 10 no. 3. The scoring of the opening chorale is dark, but it is followed by impassioned dialogue and, at the turn to the tonic major, mutual consolation. Towards the end the music drifts away in a mood of deep introspection typical of Beethoven's last-period works, until the cello tentatively offers a simple rising scale and, with the piano's assent, sets off the final fugue. The fugue may be criticised for its severity and its awkward treatment of the medium. Intellectual vigour is however one way of tempering or dispersing overwhelming emotion, and Beethoven's absorption in counterpoint was to feature increasingly in his still later works.

The op. 102 cello sonatas offer a paradox: the opening up of new worlds of expression in a genre to which Beethoven never returned. All his later sonatas were for piano solo, and when he returned to chamber music he confined himself to the ideal medium of the string quartet. The 'Kakadu' Variations for piano trio, published in 1824 as op. 121a and apparently reworked in 1816, scarcely count, since Beethoven conceded that they were basically a much earlier work. Transcriptions have only been mentioned in passing in this general survey, but it is noteworthy that his own had favoured the piano in the 1800s – the piano trio version of the Second Symphony, the arrangement of the Septet for piano, clarinet (or violin) and cello – whereas in 1817 he adapted the C minor Trio op. 1 no. 3 as a string quintet *without* piano. His ambivalent attitude to the piano increased with his deafness, and his works for strings alone, especially the quartets, are so significant that they call for a new heading. As a postscript, however, mention must be made of his handful of pieces for the unlikely combination of mandoline and piano, WoO 43 and 44, written on his tour to Prague and Berlin in 1796, though possibly intended for his Viennese friend Wenzel Krumpholz. There are also the alternative versions of the op. 25 Serenade for flute or violin and piano (op. 41), and of the op. 8 one as a 'Notturno' for viola and piano (op. 42), the latter especially welcomed by viola-players in view of the sparsity of such duos.

8

Chamber music without piano

Works for strings

By the time Beethoven arrived in Vienna to study with Haydn, the string quartet, like the symphony, must have been regarded with a certain awe by the serious composer. There were enough striking precedents from Mozart and Haydn alone, and Haydn was still busily active in both fields. It was natural that Beethoven should hesitate, though when he eventually took up the challenge of the quartet he did so at three crucial times in his career, making the terms 'early', 'middle' and 'late' more than usually appropriate. This is borne out by the opus-numbers: six quartets op. 18; three quartets op. 59, with which it is convenient to link the two isolated works op. 74 and op. 95; and the late series from op. 127 to op. 135. The op. 18 set is, however, better described as 'late early' since it dates from around 1800 and was completed after the First Symphony. He had already exercised himself in the even more exacting medium of the string trio, as well as adapting his Wind Octet in E flat as the String Quintet op. 4, with two violas. There was a Mozartian precedent for this too, in the arrangement of the C minor Wind Serenade K.388 as the String Quintet K.406.

The string trio for violin, viola and cello also produced a single but outstanding masterpiece by Mozart, the Divertimento in E flat K.563; and since it was published in 1792, the year of Beethoven's own E flat String Trio op. 3, it is tempting to suspect an influence, especially on op. 3's adoption of the six-movement divertimento form with its two minuets and two slow movements. This was the work so greatly admired by William Gardiner of Leicester, having been brought to England by the Abbé Dobbeler later that year. It already showed a real grasp of the sparer medium, with a judicious use of double-stopping and even some extended two-part writing, as in the second subject of the first movement which arrives as a duo for violin and cello. From the structural viewpoint, too, the opening syncopations provided a useful recurring motif, both as an accompanying figure and, in the development, a powerful subject in its own right:

Ex. 16

There are effective contrasts in the extra movements, the capricious elements in the Andante and the first minuet giving way to the more reflective lyricism of the Adagio and the sustained melodic line of the second minuet, while the humour of the finale's rondo-returns is worthy of Haydn. Among the inevitable transcriptions of op. 3 an authentic version for piano solo was published during Beethoven's 'lean' period (1814) though this hardly justified a recent claim that it was another and long-lost piano sonata.

Four more string trios were to follow, the first of them the Serenade op. 8, which also spread itself on the lines of a divertimento, opening and closing with a lively march and including a set of variations on a closely-related theme. Here the key was D major, but a D minor Adagio prepared the way for an F major Polacca that replaced the awaited second minuet. Its winning theme earned it an independent popularity, judging from the arrangements of the Polacca alone, even one for flute and guitar. The viola version of the whole Serenade (op. 42) has already been mentioned: if not

Beethoven's own work, it presumably had his approval.

With the three string trios op. 9, however, any disarming associations of serenades or divertimenti were thrown overboard: the four-movement plan at once aligned the medium with the quartet and symphony, as it had done with the ambitious op. 1 piano trios and op. 2 sonatas. In fact the first op. 9 trio, like op. 1 no. 2, adds a slow introduction that prepares the opening figure of the following Allegro. It is in the development, where this four-note motif accompanies other ideas, that one senses the influence of Beethoven's contrapuntal studies. For the slow movement, a tenderly expressive piece in three-four time but with continuous triplet motion, Beethoven moved to E major, an exotic mediant relation of the Trio's G major, imparting in its context a dreamlike quality to the music. The scherzo, light and amiable, has a more solidly scored trio in C that finds its way back to the varied 'da capo' through a trial of sequences. After publication Beethoven composed a second trio-section giving prominence to the cello, though it still has a fair share of interest in the work as it stands. Meanwhile the presto finale of op. 9 no. 1 is a brilliant moto perpetuo, or near-perpetuo, in sonata form. There are however three disruptions of its general opera buffa manner: a flat-key diversion in long notes in the second group and on its return, and a more contrapuntal episode in the development. The developments in all three trios show Beethoven's growing powers of concentration. The first movement of op. 9 no. 2 in D is another example, with ideas passed in smooth counterpoint between the players, leading to a skilfully disguised return of the first subject. Apart from the more simply scored minuet the cello has several moments of glory in its high 'Prussian' register: in the D minor slow movement, anticipating its eloquent treatment in the greater and more tragic one of the op. 18 no. 1 Quartet; and in the rondo-theme of the finale, where it plays above the viola at the start and continues to do so while adding an open-string drone-bass beneath. If these bucolic touches still suggest Haydn, the gentler part-writing in the episodes is Mozartian. Another possible influence may have been Boccherini, most of whose string trios were for two violins and cello, but whose first set of six with viola had been published as early as 1773.

With the third of the op. 9 string trios any thoughts of influences fade. As with the op. 1 piano trios it seems that the key of C minor unleashed a creative daemon just as it was to do later. If a model has to be sought, then Mozart again comes to mind, considering Beethoven's great admiration for the C minor Piano Concerto K.491. Many of Mozart's most dramatic C minor works had opened with unison themes or phrases, and in op. 9 no. 3 Beethoven's is confined to the descending half-scale C – B – A flat – G, a basic idea that was to dominate the late quartets in various permutations. In the finale of the C sharp minor Quartet op. 131 it appears in the same descending form, and its counterstatement in viola and cello is briefly but vividly forecast in the first-movement recapitulation of op. 9 no. 3:

Ex. 17

The workmanship is striking throughout, looking beyond the forthcoming C minor Quartet op. 18 no. 4 to the taut and dramatic first movement of the E minor 'Rasumovsky' op. 59 no. 2. In the slow movement Beethoven turned to C major for a noble serenity, filling out the opening into a quartet texture with double-stops. The six-eight scherzo, back in C minor, has no longer any trace of its minuet ancestry, while the urgency of the finale is underlined by its preference for minor keys, the second group beginning in E flat minor and returning via G minor to C minor. Although C major had played a part in the actual reprise, the quiet major-key ending, like that of the C minor Piano Trio, is a typical Beethoven surprise.

The finale of op. 9 no. 3 had opened with a swirling scalic figure that was to be reworked, in a more relaxed mood, in the last movement of the String Quartet in F op. 18 no. 1. Such cross-currents between works were not uncommon, and the sketches show that the op. 18 quartets were taking shape as the op. 9 trios were being completed. Having decided at long last to broach the quartet medium, Beethoven planned a set of six. In such cases the printed order does not necessarily reflect that of composition, and on stylistic grounds no. 4 in C minor was probably the earliest, while no. 1 in F was one of the last to achieve its final form. The version of op. 18 no. 1 that Beethoven gave to Amenda in 1799 was revised fastidiously, and the art of writing quartets 'properly' involved some drastic thinning-out of texture, as shown in these parallel passages from the finale:

Ex. 18

The Amenda version had already been through its own refining process. In the earlier sketches we see Beethoven working on the opening subject in common time, experimenting with rhythmic variants until a change to three-four gave wing to the first movement.

Yet the result seems completely spontaneous, with the opening figure dominating all, though Beethoven pruned some of its appearances in the 1801 version. The scherzo and finale share some of the first movement's good-humoured blend of caprice and intellectual strength, but the second movement, the Adagio, is the most memorable. Despite his reservations about programme music he admitted that this tragic D minor movement was inspired by the tomb-scene in *Romeo and Juliet*, and over a sketch for the closing bars he wrote the words 'les derniers soupirs'.

There is no place for such tragic overtones in the next quartet, op. 18. no. 2 in G. At the start a delicate flourish from the first violin establishes a mood of airy lightness and Mozartian grace, though its forceful recapitulation on the cello against the insistent crotchets of the transition motif is a thoroughly Beethovenish example of 'dramatic' counterpoint. The C major Adagio is more conventionally ornate, but its statuesque quality gives way to a quicker middle section that turns its stately cadence figure into a sprightly dance, and on the return the cello leads in the still more florid part-writing. The work continues with a busy but moderate-paced scherzo in which a semiquaver figure is bandied about – does it caricature the Adagio theme at the start? – and the trio-section's crotchets are kept firmly in check by counterpoints of triplet quavers. The finale, tersely witty in a Haydnish way, is entertaining for the surprise keys in which the opening subject reappears but it also has its contrapuntal interest.

The D major Quartet op. 18 no. 3 reminds one again that 'writing quartets properly' involved effects of the utmost economy. The opening on the first violin is an example: a long-breathed theme gently supported from the third bar by semibreves from the other players. Here the effect is warmly serene, but when the movement rouses itself rhythmically and dynamically Beethoven compensates by introducing unexpected key-changes at important structural points: the sudden move to C major, en route for A major, at the start of the second group; the magic return to D major for the recapitulation out of a cloud of C sharp major harmony, more strictly the dominant of F sharp minor; and the further recalling of the second subject in E flat in the coda. One does not need technical knowledge to respond to these modulations as changes of mood, or of tone of voice; or to sense the unusual key of the Andante (B flat) which opens in a deep sonority with the second violin playing above the first. The old adage about 'playing second fiddle' is also alien to the true art of quartet-writing. In the third movement, a cross between minuet and scherzo, Beethoven manifested the 'emotionalising' of the dance-form that Mozart had shown so eloquently in the G minor String Quintet and elsewhere. It is marked by strange pauses and unsettled tonality, and its turning to minor keys is more fully realised in the clear-cut sequences of the trio, leaving the finale to restore the high spirits of D major in a volatile six-eight beginning with an energetic duo for the two violins.

Op. 18 no. 4 in C minor has aroused most argument about its dating and its merits. It shows little sign of the refining art that had elevated the first of the series. The outer movements abound in rough-hewn textures and orchestral effects: antiphonal chords between the first violin and the rest of the quartet, much makeshift filling-in and, in the first movement, internal tremolos and other repeated-note patterns; and the sectional treatment of the rondo simply draws attention to the harmonic squareness of its theme. There may have been, as Robert Simpson has suggested, a sardonic humour at work, for there is promise enough in the 'Sturm und Drang' manner of the very opening, part of which is picked up by the second group in the major key. The contours of the first subject recall the *Sonata Pathétique* of 1799, also in C minor, and the sonata's finer development and integration of ideas, including those of its rondo, seem to confirm an earlier origin for the quartet. The lack of a true slow movement is also curious. In its place Beethoven wrote a light-footed 'scherzo' in fugal style, taking a backward glance at the fugues in Haydn's op. 20 quartets, but perhaps seeming dry because the Andante of the First Symphony was to treat a similar opening fugato in a far warmer and less stringent manner. The following minuet is more in keeping with the emotional world of the first movement, though the strangely scored A flat trio, with its busily fluttering first violin part, leaves the impression of a peculiar hybrid – like the C minor Quartet as a whole.

The fifth of the set, in A major, has a more definite link with Mozart. 'Now *that* I call a work' Beethoven said of Mozart's quartet in the same key, even making his own score from the printed set of parts. If K.464 was a conscious model for op. 18 no. 5 the parallels are not of theme or style but of form and texture. Coming to it after the C minor Quartet one is struck by the economy of the part-writing, as in this extract from the development of the first movement:

Ex. 19

Beethoven followed Mozart in placing the minuet second and writing a slow movement in variation form, but whereas Mozart's variation-theme had been strikingly beautiful in itself Beethoven chose a basic text, simplified from the sketches into a direct march down and up the D major scale. In the finale he paid more obvious debts to Mozart in the antiphony between the upper and lower pairs of instruments and the introduction of a subject in long note-values to contrast with the busier surroundings.

Whereas Mozart's example may have contributed to the unified impression of the A major Quartet, the last in the series, op. 18 no. 6 in B flat, has a strange overall effect. It opens with a bright epi-grammatic movement in which sonata form is carried through with the same regularity as in the Piano Sonata op. 22. The slow move-ment is ornate in a conventional way, but impersonal in the light of those in op. 18 no. 1 or no. 3. With the scherzo there is a radical change of scene and style, and an obsession with syncopations that mock at its three-four time-signature. After the more plain-sailing trio, with continuous athletics for the first violin, the return is heralded by a brief but violent outburst in B flat *minor*. The introduction to the finale, however, brings a disruption of a far more profound nature. Beethoven entitled this Adagio preamble 'La Malinconia' and within a few bars led the music through remote tonal, in fact átonal, regions:

Ex. 20

The 'Malinconia' theme returns during the otherwise cheerful finale and may be felt to throw a shadow over the last page, where the coda is preceded by four bars of hesitant 'poco adagio'. This juxtaposition of mystery and light, or of problems and solutions, takes one back beyond the 'chaos' in Haydn's *Creation* to the purely musical world of Mozart's 'Dissonance' Quartet. Perhaps Beethoven felt the need to deepen the emotions in the final stage of the last of his op. 18 quartets? The result is a dual-character movement that uncannily forecasts the 'Muss es sein?' finale of his last quartet of all, op. 135 in F major, of a quarter-of-a-century later.

Two other works call for comment as a postscript to discussion of the op. 18 quartets. In 1802 Beethoven made a quartet transcription of the Piano Sonata op. 14 no. 1, transposing it from E to F major, as already mentioned in connection with the original. Op. 14 no. 1 is perhaps too well known as a sonata to gain much acceptance in a medium Beethoven enriched so fully; but the String Quintet in C op. 29 is another matter. Discounting op. 4 and op. 104 as other interesting arrangements, and not forgetting some later isolated movements such as the Fugue in D op. 137, the two-viola Quintet op. 29 was Beethoven's only real successor to Mozart's masterpieces in this form. Since it dates from 1801 its relation to his work on the op. 18 quartets is clear, though the opening bars show a new interest in long-flowing lyricism that is also carried over into the decidedly Mozartian slow movement. The absorption with short rhythmic motifs, which had been such a feature of the quartets, returns in the scherzo; and the trio, having given melodic prominence to the first viola, builds up a massive and sonorous paragraph out of a one-bar fragment of the theme. The finale is however the greatest surprise, a six-eight Presto richly endowed but dominated by its first subject, with the mysterious but explosive tremolandos and semiquaver swirls that gave the work its nickname, 'The Storm'. A further surprise is the late appearance and recurrence of a minuet-like episode in a formal dotted rhythm. Here the marking 'scherzoso' suggests an element of parody, but the choice of keys, A major and C major, also recalls the unusual tonal scheme of the first movement, in which the second group substituted A major and minor for the orthodox dominant. The Quintet is original enough to annul any direct comparisons with Mozart's four mature masterpieces. It deserves attention as a further, and unique, example of 'late early' Beethoven, though as with other media his next chamber works for strings were to show an astonishing development of style.

For an explanation of the vast gulf between the op. 18 and op. 59 quartets one must in fact look to other forms: to the grand expansion of style in the *Eroica*, to *Leonore* and its overtures, and, in the piano music, the 'Waldstein' Sonata. Beethoven worked on the three 'Rasumovsky' quartets op. 59 from 1804 to 1806, and in deference to the Count who commissioned them he introduced Russian themes in the finale of the first quartet and the third movement of the second. He did not do so overtly in op. 59 no. 3, though it is possible to read a certain Russian melancholy into parts of its slow movement. To criticise Beethoven for flouting the original character of the themes is irrelevant: they were not being 'quoted' but adopted and integrated. The 'Rasumovsky' quartets are sufficiently contrasted to make a programme in themselves, though the first two were received with initial bewilderment and only the third, with its old-style minuet and mock-fugal finale, gained immediate acceptance.

The new scale of op. 59 no. 1 in F is apparent in the length and breadth of its opening subject, which is passed in mid-theme from the cello below to the first violin aloft and held together with a pulsating background of static harmony and suppressed energy. If the manner of this opening is without parallel in Beethoven's works, it is also typically economical, since the theme is the source of so much that follows: the transition material, the cadence theme of the exposition, the fugato in the development, and of course its own harmonised-out apotheosis in the coda of the first movement. Even the finale's Russian tune, beginning in the same cello register, seems to derive from it. Instead of the usual scherzo or minuet-and-trio Beethoven wrote a highly original through-composed scherzando movement, placed it second, and began with a one-note rhythmic idea on the cello that serves as a springboard for a host of miniature themes, lyrical, witty or pathetic, and often passed round in the sparest of textures. In stark contrast the Adagio indulges a mood of sad introspection, also enhanced in due course by the cello in its higher registers. It was here in the sketches that Beethoven made his strange note about the weeping willow over his brother's grave. Was this in fact an oblique reference to Caspar Carl's marriage, or to the child Franz Georg who had died in infancy in 1783; or did he still harbour thoughts about the 'other' Ludwig who died before he was born? In any case, the Adagio, like other middle-period slow movements, leads into the finale without a break, and if Beethoven knowingly misconstrued his Russian theme as cheerfully diatonic instead of soulfully modal, he made partial amends by taking a reflective farewell of it in slower tempo towards the end.

After the spacious opening of the first 'Rasumovsky' the second in E minor plunges at once into a world of high drama. The first two chords are more than introductory, playing a vital role in the first movement's development. They may even be felt as a latent accompaniment to the following subject, a tense but subdued idea that is immediately repeated a semitone higher on the Neapolitan harmony of F major, paralleling the 'Appassionata' Sonata and anticipating the more vehement harmonic moves at the start of the F minor Quartet op. 95. In fact the first movement of op. 59 no. 2 foreshadows the still tauter drama of op. 95 in its concentrated part-writing and abrupt changes of texture, ranging from strong unison passages to the suppressed but extended use of chords in cross-rhythm. At the end the movement falls away quietly as though aware of the advent of the serene slow movement in the tonic major. The chorale-like opening of the Molto Adagio is indeed serene in the noblest sense and Beethoven admitted that it was inspired by contemplating the starry heavens. Its one forceful statement towards the close is so ecstatically harmonised that it must be quoted with a bar or two of its calm aftermath:

Ex. 21

The 'scherzo' of the quartet is an Allegretto based almost entirely on the rhythmic figure of its first bar, and its restless minor-key character is twice interrupted by the E major Russian theme 'trio' with its fugal entries and humorously forced canons. As with some other scherzos of the middle period, the long extra repeat creates a momentary illusion of a perpetual motion; but the prevalence of E minor and major throughout the quartet threatened monotony in a four-movement work. This Beethoven avoided by devising a finale theme that opens as though in C major, creating a gravitational conflict that is only fully resolved in favour of E minor on the last page. The sketches show that this novel and dramatic tonal scheme occurred to the composer well in advance of the energetic dotted rhythm of the subject itself.

The third 'Rasumovsky' quartet, definitely in C major, began by exploiting a distant approach to the home-key in a slow introduction enshrouded in harmonic mystery. As with Mozart's 'Dissonance' Quartet, the arrival of the C major Allegro comes as a sudden release, or discovery, and the similarity of some of the semiquaver passages is striking. The most Beethovenish feature is the growth of new material from the simple upbeat quaver-and-rest to the Allegro. Among the sketches it is curious to find a repeated-note theme that later became the Allegretto of the Seventh Symphony. Perhaps it was considered for the slow movement of op. 59 no. 3, since its key of A minor remained when a more flowing idea in six-eight emerged, notable for the pathos of its opening phrases, the surprising grace of its secondary theme, and the prolonged use of cello pizzicato.

After this uniquely haunting movement – maybe with Russian overtones? – Beethoven wrote a Classically-shaped minuet instead of his customary scherzo, possibly because of the brilliant finale that was to follow; perhaps too because his written remark 'let your deafness no longer be a secret' had led to a new philosophy including a more relaxed acceptance of his past inheritance. Yet there is a purely musical link between the opening bars of the minuet and the fugue-subject of the finale, the one a free inversion of the other, and this Beethoven seemed to demonstrate by adding a linking coda to the former. The finale's fugue-subject, first given to the viola, is amusingly garrulous but the movement is only intermittently contrapuntal. It develops into a near moto perpetuo that is a tour de force for the players and, in its extrovert energy and high spirits, a further testimony of the composer's newly relaxed mastery. This manifested itself in a more intimate manner when Beethoven returned to the form in 1809 for the solitary Quartet in E flat op. 74, nicknamed the 'Harp' because of the prominent use of pizzicato arpeggios in the first movement.

Once again Beethoven began with a slow introduction. In op. 74, however, the mood is neither mysterious nor dramatic but tenderly lyrical, with a subdominant leaning in the opening phrase that exercises a calming effect on the first subject of the Allegro. Apart from its colourful pizzicato, the movement's surprise comes in the coda, where the 'harp' arpeggios support a prolonged display of concertante virtuosity from the first violin; but calmness is restored in the warm lyricism of the Adagio, in which the viola's pizzicato accompaniment towards the end may be felt as retrospective. The scherzo in C minor is however at once volatile and dramatic, taking its energy from a four-note rhythm that inevitably recalls the Fifth Symphony and, when it hammers in unison on the dominant of F minor, the 'Appassionata'. Yet Beethoven called for a certain restraint in the context of the quartet, *forte* but 'leggiermente' at the start, and *sempre pp* in the transition to the variation-finale. Schubert seemed to recall this last passage at the start of his own C minor Quartettsatz. Meanwhile the trio in C major is encouraged to enjoy its athletic counterpoint in the fullest sonority on both its appearances – a relic or parody maybe of the 'species' exercises Beethoven had once worked for Albrechtsberger? Op. 74 was the only one of the quartets to adopt variation form for its finale. The theme, a binary one in which eight bars are answered by twelve, has a family likeness to the opening of Haydn's E flat Quartet op. 76 no. 6 in its pattern of short phrases, and the variations proceed traditionally by introducing quicker note-values and highlighting different instruments, the viola in no. 2, the second violin and cello in no. 3. Another feature is the alternation of vigour and tenderness, and the quartet's abiding impression seems to be summed up in the two quiet chords that end the increasingly brilliant coda.

Despite the contrast to be expected between a composer's adjacent works the gap between op. 74 and the F minor Quartet op. 95 of the following year (1810) is astonishing. The breakthrough in op. 95, so different from that in the *Eroica* or the 'Rasumovsky' quartets, was not in terms of expansion but of compression. The F minor Quartet, which was announced as a 'quartetto serioso', is likely to be one of the shortest of all by the stop-watch, yet in density and concentration, though not the only criteria for musical worth, it marked a new departure, already hinted at in the Piano Sonata op. 78 and to be further fulfilled in the works of the next decade: the Cello Sonatas op. 102 and the Piano Sonatas op. 90 and op. 101. To set the opening bars of op. 95 alongside those of the 'Appassionata' Sonata, in the same key and with the same Neapolitan (G flat) move in its first subject, is to grasp the quartet's speed of action. Both are intensely dramatic, but the terse resolute subject of the Quartet establishes a new time-scale, a new dynamic force. As with the 'Appassionata' and the first 'Rasumovsky' Quartet there is no exposition repeat, though with op. 95 the reason is more obvious:

such an intensely compact movement, with its explosive mood-changes, abrupt silences, and brief consolatory ideas, could scarcely stand formal repetition.

The slow movement, in D major, is equally concise, reconciling lyrical expression with intellectual precision. One marvels at the later *upward* harmonisation of the cello's opening scale, at the subtle minor-key inflections that disturb but deepen the otherwise serene main theme, and the setting-off of a fugue by the viola on a new theme that is actually a latent counterpoint to the former one. Beethoven has neither the time nor the need to force the ideas together, but refines the music away to a bare octave and, as in the 'Appassionata', a quietly held diminished-seventh chord. On this chord the scherzo breaks in, though not so called and still bearing the marking 'ma serioso'. If its unrelenting energy and persistent dotted rhythm stretch the medium, the trio does so in other ways: in texture, with the second violin carrying the melodic line an octave and more above the first's accompanying figures; and in tonality, ranging from G flat major to B minor on its first appearance, and picking it up in D major on its return – all in the basic context of F minor. The finale, though on the same concise time-scale as the rest of op. 95, introduces its tenderly agitated sonata-rondo with a few bars of Larghetto. Tovey likened the most haunting phrase in the rondo itself to one in the coda of Mozart's C minor Piano Concerto, which Beethoven admired so much. The Quartet, however, has an altogether surprising coda. Is this swift sunlit ending in such stormy surroundings yet another forecast of the 'Muss es sein?' finale and its attendant philosophy in op. 135? Meanwhile op. 95 proved to be Beethoven's farewell to the quartet for almost a decade and a half.

The long interim period has been described: the creative lull and the new awakening. Yet the quartet remained in abeyance. Beethoven toyed with ideas for string quintet and in 1817 produced the brief D major Fugue that was later published as op. 137, and it is interesting to find that the scherzo theme of the Ninth Symphony was also conceived as a quintet-fugue. Quartet textures, however, continued to abound in other media, as in the late piano sonatas; and in the last solo section of the Ninth many singers have complained of being wafted to heaven in terms of florid string-quartet writing. By this time (1824) Beethoven was already at work on a new series of quartets commissioned by another music-loving Russian, Prince

Nicholas Galitzin, to whom three of these late works – op. 127, op. 130 and op. 132 – were dedicated.

Although Beethoven received Galitzin's request in 1822, the E flat Quartet op. 127 was not finished until 1825. By the end of 1826 however he had not only completed the other two Galitzin quartets, op. 132 and op. 130, but added op. 131 and op. 135, besides composing a new finale for op. 130 to replace the *Grosse Fuge*, which was subsequently published separately as op. 133 and dedicated to the Archduke Rudolph. As a series the late quartets were Beethoven's last testament and for many his greatest achievement, though for years they evoked bewilderment as well as admiration. For example Tchaikovsky, whose idol was Mozart, found in these last works 'glimmers and nothing more . . . . the rest is chaos'. Time however has proved that Beethoven's late masterpieces are imbued with intellectual and spiritual qualities that invalidate any normal comparisons or assessments. Joseph Kerman has described the E flat op. 127 as Beethoven's 'crowning monument to lyricism'. This could certainly apply to the first two movements and perhaps to the finale too, where the animated main theme is stretched out, rather than speeded up, in an unconventional coda that reveals its lyrical potential against a murmuring background of triplet semiquavers. The first movement, in a lilting three-four time but harmonised with the subtlest fluidity, is however introduced by a short majestic passage that returns at crucial points in the structure. This appears in the keys of E flat, G and C, whose tonics had been salient notes in the initial statement. The idea of a completely integrated introduction was to recur in op. 130: it had its forebears, but the merging of the two-four Maestoso into the three-four Allegro in op. 127 showed a closer than ever relation.

The slow movement was to explore the richness of variations in a continuum unimaginable in the neatly articulated sets in op. 18 no. 5 or the 'Harp'. Its Adagio theme, the result of many reworkings and character changes in the sketches, is warmly lyrical on the broadest scale, and the rapt manner of its introduction must have appealed to many Romantics who were otherwise unable to enter into Beethoven's spiritual world. If not Tchaikovsky, certainly Wagner, who wrote reams of ecstatic prose about the late quartets, and who seemed to recall this opening and its key of A flat in the tranquil section of the love-duet in Act 2 of *Tristan*, 'O sink hernieder'. The comparison is of course superficial, for the Adagio of op. 127 is not

concerned with earthly or even legendary passions but with profound contemplation. There is however a conversational element in
the sharing of the melodic line between the first violin and the cello,
and of a more playful nature in the two-violin dialogue of the second
variation, which leads through an inspired modulation to the intensely sustained third variation in which the cello is again elevated
in Mozart's 'Prussian' manner. The key here is E major and there is a
deep poignancy when the cello substitutes a G natural for the violin's
G sharp when it takes over the phrase in the same register:

Ex. 22

[Adagio molto espressivo]

Such richness of texture is typical of the whole movement, and on the
return to A flat one notes, as with the late piano sonatas, Beethoven's
increasing absorption with trills. This even leaves its mark on the
capricious subject and inversion in the scherzo, a highly inventive
movement with a fleet trio in E flat minor that settles from time to
time on the drone-bass of its own 'second subject', in which one may
discern recollections of the *Pastoral* Symphony of so many years
before. The finale, already mentioned for its unusual coda, shows
Beethoven's acute awareness of tone-colour even in his deafness, the
marking 'sul G' (G string only) for the first violin giving the main
subject a distinctive sonority, further enhanced by the prominent A
natural that adds a recurring modal flavour to its E flat surroundings. This Lydian tendency, in one sense archaic but integrated with
no suspicion of pastiche, was to play its most famous role in the slow

movement of the next quartet in order of composition, op. 132 in A minor.

While working on op. 127 Beethoven noted down a basic four-note motif in various canons and inversions. It was to appear in differing guises throughout the next three quartets, notably as the subject of the *Grosse Fuge*, and was first put to expressive purpose in the opening bars of the A minor Quartet op. 132, which reflect quietly on its possibilities before a sudden flurry of semiquavers from the first violin sets off a passionate Allegro. It is in the development that the unity of these ideas, the first subject of the Allegro and the opening motif is revealed by bringing them together in counterpoint. Otherwise the Allegro preserves the outlines of sonata form even though its through-composed nature produces the second subject (or group) in F major in the exposition and C major in the recapitulation, saving the only extended affirmation of the tonic for the coda.

The second movement of op. 132 retains the outward form of a minuet and trio more closely, momentarily recalling that in Mozart's much-admired A major Quartet K.464; but the time-scale of the 'minuet' is vast despite its entire derivation from the two opening figures, one a counterpoint to the other. In the equally spacious 'trio' Beethoven began and ended with the sounds of a celestial musette, creating a ravishing texture above and below the sustained open A string of the first violin. The heart of op. 132, however, lies in its extraordinary slow movement, explicitly entitled 'Hymn of Thanksgiving from a Convalescent to the Deity, in the Lydian Mode.' Knowing of Beethoven's own sufferings, it is impossible not to respond to the music's subjective overtones, though the expression, more than in the 'Arioso dolente' of the op. 110 Piano Sonata and the Cavatina of the op. 130 Quartet, seems sublimated into the universal. His studies of the early church styles are known from his work on the *Missa Solemnis*, and in the Lydian sections of the 'Heiliger Dankgesang' they yielded a chorale in slow minims, interwoven with imitative figures and elaborated in two variations. Two interludes move from the 'Lydian' F major to D major and a livelier three-eight tempo, and over the first Beethoven wrote 'neue Kraft fühlend' – 'feeling new strength'. Is it coincidental that this sudden joyfulness of spirit should turn to the key of the Joy theme in the finale of the Ninth Symphony?

These internal contrasts are carried a stage further in the lively self-contained march that Beethoven interposed between the Lydian

Hymn and the A minor finale, which is itself introduced by a passage of dramatic instrumental recitative. The fact that the opening of the finale, a passionate lyrical subject of great beauty, was derived from a rejected sketch for a purely orchestral finale to the Ninth, suggests a link of an amusingly esoteric kind. When Schiller's 'Ode to Joy' took over in the symphony its theme was also preceded with recitatives in the cellos and basses, which seem parodied in the first violin's mock-dramatic lead-in in the quartet. A more serious parallel with the Ninth may seem far-fetched and paradoxical since the means and media are so different: the ultimate triumph of the major over the minor key. If the ecstatic breaking-in of the major key at the end of op. 132 also depicted a triumph of the human spirit, it made superhuman demands on the players comparable with the strenuous vocal climaxes in the Ninth. The same was to be true, to an even greater degree, of the *Grosse Fuge*, the original finale of Beethoven's next quartet, op. 130 in B flat.

The number of movements in the late quartets continued to increase: op. 127 with the usual four, op. 132 with five, op. 130 with six; op. 131 was to have seven, though played without a break; until op. 135 returned to the four-movement plan. There were however Classical precedents for six-movement works, and op. 130 showed its remote allegiance to the Divertimento by including two dance-type movements and two slow (or slowish) ones, though in the most contrasted styles imaginable. Even more than with op. 127 the first movement is an astonishing amalgam of a slow introduction and a main allegro, the integration of the former continuing right into the coda. Two further points can only be summarised here: the harmonic enrichment of the exposition material in the recapitulation, enhanced by the distant keys of the second group (G flat, later D flat); and the simple violin and cello dialogue in the coda, as though the vigorously contrapuntal first subject had posed a question only to be answered in the last bars. This was a formal feature that Beethoven had pursued from earlier times: the first movement of the *Eroica* and the finale of the *Pastoral* symphonies are cases where the 'ideal' version of a theme is left until the end.

The second movement of op. 130 is a brief and rapid scherzo in B flat minor and *alla breve* time, and although it passes in a flash one just has time to admire the interplay of the middle parts. The trio, however, is the first violin's showpiece, and the explosive chromatics at the lead-back turn out to be humorously relevant. Humour of a more restrained nature is to be found in the first of the 'slow' movements, an Andante packed with scherzando elements and full but mercurial textures. One imagines the quick-witted Verdi of *Falstaff* admiring it, especially in such prophetic passages as the following:

Ex. 23

The key is D flat, a 'deflected' mediant prominent in the first movement and closely related to the B flat minor of the second; and the introductory phrases, stressing the notes B flat-B double-flat (alias A natural), seem to recall the opening of the whole work, consciously or not.

After the flat keys of the previous movements in op. 130 the arrival of the 'Alla Danza Tedesca' in G major is surprising enough, since we find its opening phrase in the sketches in A major – perhaps intended for op. 132? – and B flat. However the B flat-G major relationship had been explored in the 'Archduke' Trio and 'Hammerklavier' Sonata, and the G major Piano Sonata op. 78 had opened with an inversion of the same figure, also marked 'Alla Tedesca'. The subtly inflected sequel in op. 130 is however worlds apart, though the popular German dance element remained in its regular four-bar phrasing, as it was to do in parts of the E major scherzo in op. 131; but the handing round of the fragments of the theme towards the end, beginning with bars 5 to 8 in reverse order, is a purely intellectual pleasure:

Ex. 24

Coming to op. 130 after the intense emotions of op. 132, the listener may well find the earlier stages of the work more detached and more intellectually concentrated, but such impressions must change radically with the fifth movement, the Cavatina. Beethoven admitted his deep involvement with it, an even more personal, confiding and consoling document than the Lydian Hymn of op. 132, written to be played for the most part with a hushed expression, *sotto voce*, but offset by a strangely disquieting and fragmented middle section marked 'beklemmt' or 'afflicted'. The episode soon passes back however to the comforting diatonics of the Cavatina itself, with the final tonic chord of E flat notated in tied quavers to clarify the meticulous dynamic inflections.

The uppermost note of this chord, the mediant G, was to be taken up in powerful unison by the *Grosse Fuge*, the quartet's original finale, and in quiet playful octaves by the Allegro that replaced it. As a sequel to the Cavatina the 'Great Fugue', with its stupendous renewal of energy, was the most dramatic continuation possible. Its official title is really a misnomer, for the movement incorporates an introduction, a double-fugue, a slower and only mildly contrapuntal section brought about with an abrupt modulation from B flat to G flat, a scherzo that is soon overwhelmed by a resumption of the fiercest fugal developments, followed by a stream of afterthoughts and retrospects. Yet perhaps the label is, after all, a fitting one, for the 'work' (as it became in its independence as op. 133) amounts to an exhaustive survey of a single subject's rhythmic and fugal possibilities – in Beethoven's words 'tantôt libre, tantôt recherché'. The subject itself was clearly a further growth from the four-note figure that had opened op. 132, and related to the more compact fugue-subject that was to appear in op. 131; though there is no direct evidence that Beethoven planned the three works, to the exclusion of op. 127 and op. 135, as a triptych.

Ex. 25

The first players and listeners must have found it hard to accept the *Grosse Fuge* within a framework that contained the Alla Tedesca and the Cavatina; and Beethoven was to replace it with the lighter finale that reflects the sparer manner of his last quartet of all, op. 135. Before rediscovering the virtues of Classical precision and restraint he continued to expand the form. The first months of 1826 produced the vast single span of the C sharp minor Quartet op. 131, single in the sense that its seven movements are played without a break. It opens with a fugue in slow tempo on the subject quoted above. The noble pathos of the music, far removed from the fierce counterpoint of the *Grosse Fuge*, may owe something to Bach's fugue in the same key in Book 1 of 'The 48', which Beethoven had known since his youth. The heavily stressed A and D naturals in the subject and answer are, however, intensely personal, adding strength and poignancy to the closing section. There are long-term implications here, to be followed up in the swift six-eight second movement (D major) that appears in the shadow of the fugue as though from a vast distance but quickly generates surprising rhythmic energy; and in the elaborate A major variations that form the central core of the work. The stage for the variations is set by a brief third 'movement', a mock operatic interlude ending with a coloratura flourish from the first violin, as if to push memories of the *serioso* fugue still further away before introducing the simple A major aria. The variations are unique in their range of textures. The innocent-sounding theme, shared bar by bar between the two violins, invited melodic efflorescence but hardly the grotesque two-part counterpoint of the third variation or the harmonic concentration of the fifth. The apotheosis is, however, expectedly adorned with trills, though in the closing phases the tonality (A major) is undermined by digressions and the actual ending is strangely hesitant and disembodied. At this point the cello, which had proved a disruptive element in the otherwise serene sixth variation, throws out a fragment of theme that sets a new creative process in motion. The *alla breve* Presto that seizes on it as a starting-point is in effect a scherzo played as a continuum but incorporating a recurring trio with folklike themes in regular four-bar phrasing. Although the basic key carries forward the pattern of rising fifths – D major for the second movement, A major for the variations, and now E major – the gravitation to the quartet's home-key of C sharp minor is strong, and the vain hammering on its dominant, G sharp, is followed by a repeated drift to G sharp *minor*, which proves to be the key of the brief but profound Adagio that separates the scherzo from the finale. As for the finale, it is in the fullest minor-key sonata form, intensely rhythmic but with a wondrous lyricism and opening up of texture in the second group; and its manifest links with the opening fugue complete the circle of the quartet Beethoven considered his greatest.

The fact that the lighter textures of the last quartet of all, op. 135 in F, were conceived and sketched while Beethoven was completing op. 131 need no longer surprise us, since he had frequently composed widely different works side by side. To regard op. 135's reversion to a Mozartian time-scale as somehow retrograde is a serious misapprehension. After the grandeur of its predecessor it may seem closer to the world of comedy than tragedy, but it radiates a spiritual serenity and philosophy of acceptance that transcends both. The light interplay of the first movement, 'so very beautifully composed' as Joseph Kerman says, is followed by a scherzo in which a lively but bland off-beat theme and its bass change places in invertible counterpoint. Its diatonic F major is disturbed by an outburst of unison E flats in cross-rhythm, only 'righted' in the final bars. The middle section with its scales and turns is the real surprise, culminating in a lengthy ostinato passage in A major, with the first violin executing a vigorous dance high above the continuous drumming of the other players.

The slow movement is profoundly calm and in D flat, another mediant relationship, and here the subjective emotions experienced in the Cavatina of op. 130 are at last sublimated into a song of 'rest and peace', as Beethoven noted in the sketches. It is in fact a theme with four variations, but compared with the elaborate sets in op. 127 and op. 131 the textures are sparer and simpler, befitting the marking 'semplice'. References have already been made to the finale, which bears the title *Der schwer gefasste Entschluss*, roughly rendered as 'the hard-won decision'; and the words 'Muss es sein?' and 'Es muss sein!' – 'Must it be? It must be!' – are set to the slow introductory figure and the opening bars of the Allegro, the latter a free inversion of the former:

Ex. 26

There is a hint here of the dark questioning phrase that is humorously brushed aside at the opening of the first movement, and those in search of hidden unities may like to compare the finale's second subject with the contours of the slow movement theme.

Whatever view one takes of the implied programme – an ephemeral jest, or an eternal profundity ironically disguised – the impression remains that Beethoven in his last completed work summed up his life's struggles, his resignation and his ultimate philosophy and faith, in music of disarming lightness and simplicity. The lightness, distilled from a lifetime's experience, is deceptive, for the grave 'Muss es sein?' subject is to return in more weighty and menacing tones; and there are momentary shadows of doubt on the very last page, before the second subject is resumed in a still lighter pizzicato. Thus Beethoven ended his work in a medium that had meant so much to him – except for the new finale for op. 130, which occupied him during the last fateful months of 1826 and yet retained some of this new-found lightness of mood and texture. Did Schubert pay a conscious tribute to it when he ended his B flat Piano Sonata of 1828 with a two-four movement that also hovers between the dominants of C minor and B flat?

Works for wind and for wind and strings

Beethoven's music for wind and piano has already been discussed. Apart from the ever-popular Septet, his other chamber music with wind scarcely approaches the splendour of Mozart's 'Gran Partita' K.361 for thirteen players or his Serenade in C minor K.388 for wind octet. Nor did he have occasion to emulate Mozart in a quintet for clarinet and strings, a horn quintet or an oboe quartet. The word 'occasion' is important here, for much wind-music was written to order for entertainment purposes or to exploit the gifts of a particular player, as with the clarinettist Anton Stadler and Mozart. Beethoven may not have inherited Mozart's unique ability to 'rise to an occasion' especially when an unusual medium was involved, though he produced a useful and last-minute work for the horn virtuoso Punto in the Sonata in F op. 17. As a free-lance Beethoven could pick and choose, and it is noteworthy that most of his wind works were early. This does not take account of such later curiosities as his marches and other pieces for military band, WoO 18 to 22, which date from around 1810 at the height of the Napoleonic crisis and hardly count as chamber music; or the solemn *Equali* for four trombones WoO 30, written in Linz in 1812 and sung in a vocal arrangement at his own funeral; or the rarity of an Adagio for three horns, apparently dating from 1815.

There was however a traditional demand for wind music at the Bonn court, both for out-of-door performances during the summer months and as entertainment or *Tafelmusik* for the Elector's dinner-table. Duets for pairs of wind instruments would hardly have been effective for either purpose and were presumably written for the players' own enjoyment. Beethoven composed three such duos for clarinet and bassoon WoO 27, probably before leaving Bonn, and one in G major for two flutes WoO 26 with an amusingly precise dedication 'to his friend Degenhardt by L. van Beethoven, 23 August 1792, midnight'. Two more substantial wind works date from the same year and were scored in the Mozartian manner for an octet of oboes, clarinets, bassoons and horns. The Octet in E flat (op. 103!) was the source of the String Quintet op. 4, and in its busier but less polished original it would have provided excellent 'table music' for the noisiest of banquets, with its rumbustious tuttis and frequent *ff* markings that were scaled down in the string version. Yet there is delicacy, too, in the minuet and its lightly-scored trio, and plenty to show off the individual players, as with the oboe in the slow movement, the clarinet in the finale, and the fanfare of horns at the end. The other work, a leisurely Rondino, WoO 25, in the same key and with the same scoring, favours the horns from the start in a more melodious manner. It may have been an offshoot from the previous work though hardly, as Maynard Solomon suggests, an alternative finale. Perhaps the Octet aspired to be a Divertimento with extra movements and then changed its mind, leaving the Rondino to fend for itself.

Horn-players will find a different challenge, and some brilliant concertante writing, in the Sextet for two horns and strings, yet again in E flat and curiously known as op. 81b, having been published belatedly by Simrock in the same year as the Archduke Rudolph's 'Lebewohl' Sonata, henceforth known as op. 81a. The Sextet may have been carried over from Bonn but is usually ascribed to Beethoven's early years in Vienna (1794 or 1795). All three movements explore the conversational possibilities of the medium, amounting to witty repartee in the finale's rondo-theme, with the second horn in the lead. In the slow movement, however, they play the main theme in three-part harmony with the cello, but with material less beguiling than in the earlier Rondino. The misleading opus-numbers continue with the Trio for two oboes and cor anglais, also composed in 1795 but published as op. 87. Here the unusual medium was presumably dictated by the brothers Johann, Franz and Philipp Teimer, who gave the first performance, and for whom Beethoven probably composed his Variations on Mozart's 'Là ci darem' for the same instruments. The novelty of the cor anglais, which was never part of Beethoven's orchestra, did not deter him from writing lavishly for it in the Trio, which is a substantial four-movement work.

The Serenade in D op. 25 for flute, violin and viola offered

another rare genre with a tendency to top-heavy monotony that
Beethoven avoided by creating a wide range of imaginative textures.
The adoption of a six-movement divertimento form magnified the
challenge and the incentive, for though some of the movements are
short, others spread themselves generously, like the first minuet with
its two trios and the Andante with variations. The Serenade begins
with an 'Entrada', in reality a simple binary movement with an
added trio-section and 'da capo'. Marion Scott described the actual
opening on the solo flute as 'a fanfare that might come from a fairy
turned gamin'. To others it may suggest the bird-song of the *Pastoral*
Symphony of the next decade. Beethoven rests the flute from time to
time and indulges the sparer medium of a string duo, sometimes
taking the viola high above the violin, or emulating a quartet texture
with double-stops as in the Andante theme. The finale with its
'Scotch snaps' is however splendidly virtuosic for each player in turn,
giving extra point to the brilliant unison coda.

In 1796, the year of the Serenade, Beethoven had returned to the
pure wind ensemble for the Sextet in E flat op. 71, a medium of
clarinets, horns and bassoons that yielded a solitary March in B flat
WoO 29 two years later. The op. 71 Sextet, after an impressive
unison introduction, sets off its first Allegro with the clarinet, pays
attention to the first bassoon in the Adagio, opens the minuet with
the pair of horns, and gathers all the forces together for the quiet
martial theme of the rondo. It may be a coincidence that the minuet
begins by quoting the opening of Mozart's String Quintet in E flat
K.614 but it is hardly accidental that Beethoven should be drawn
back again to this favourite key, though more suited to the clarinet
and horn than to strings, for his most famous work in this category of
chamber music, the Septet op. 20 of 1800 for clarinet, horn, bassoon,
string trio and double-bass. Its immediate popularity, far surpassing
that of his more profound works, annoyed the composer; but its easy
mastery of a hybrid medium made it the prototype of many multiple
chamber works by Moscheles, Hummel, Spohr and others, with
Schubert's Octet as its most famous successor.

The Septet is a six-movement divertimento in form, with an
introduction that at once proclaims the importance of the first violin.
Beethoven probably had Schuppanzigh in mind when he wrote the
work, for there is some spectacular virtuoso writing in the second
variation of the fourth movement and in the scherzo, and the finale
even introduces a substantial cadenza before the reprise. Having

experimented with the delicate problems of balance in the light-weight Serenade op. 25, he gave the larger forces in the Septet a firm footing by sacrificing a second violin and adding a double-bass, which lends an orchestral character to the tuttis but is used with discretion elsewhere. In the variations, for example, the first one is confined to the string trio, and the opening theme of the finale appears as a duo for violin and cello, even on its reprise. The wind have a triple role to play, supporting the strings, ranging themselves antiphonally as a group or in pairs, or disporting as soloists. The second movement, an Adagio cantabile, favours the clarinet but the bassoon and horn have later shares in the melodic line. For the third movement Beethoven re-used the minuet theme from the Piano Sonata op. 49 no. 2, double-dotting the quavers and adding a new continuation and a trio showing off the horn and clarinet. The fourth is the variation movement expected of a divertimento, and specula-tion that its theme was a Rhenish folk-song at least testified to its simple and winning nature. In the following scherzo the most winning feature is the cellist's moment of glory in the trio, though the prevalence of the home-key called for a brief introduction to the finale in the tonic minor, its quiet martial manner resembling the interlude in the Horn Sonata of the same year. The popularity of the Septet is easy to understand: it abounds in good themes with little trace of the 'learned' style, even in the first movement's development, and the finale crowned them all before rounding off the work with an applause-seeking display of violin virtuosity.

Beethoven wrote no wind chamber music of importance after the Septet, though one or two isolated pieces have been mentioned, to which may be added the 'Mödlinger' Dances WoO 17 of 1819, for clarinets, horns, two violins and bass. The *Equali* for trombones really occupy a category of their own. In 1800, the year of the Septet, Beethoven produced his First Symphony and his wind-writing there-after was largely directed to the orchestra, while in chamber music the string quartet and works for strings and piano became his preoccupation. The great significance of the symphonies and con-certos must be our next concern here.

9

Symphonies

Beethoven did not leap fearlessly into the world of the symphony like the child Mozart on his visit to London, or slip into it as an extension of the quartet or divertimento as Haydn had done. By the 1790s the symphony, like the quartet, was a force to be reckoned with, and he did not enter either field until the turn of the century. He had naturally contemplated the form before this. There is a very early sketch in C minor labelled 'sinfonia', and there are extensive ones for the C major symphony dating from his mid-twenties. His eventual First Symphony (1800) owed its key and the scalic opening of the finale to this unfulfilled work. As public music it displayed none of the profound emotions expressed, for example, in the slow movements of the piano sonatas op. 7 and op. 10 no. 3; nor did it emulate the storm and stress, and indeed the smouldering orchestral effects, of the more recent *Pathétique*. It has its surprises – the misleading opening 'out of the key', the precipitous minuet that is really a scherzo, and the playful introduction to the finale – but its moods are neutral, even conventional, as though Beethoven had decided to test his powers on safe ground before venturing into uncharted territory. The introductory moves, though harmonically simple, were arresting enough in their approach to C major by way of full closes in F and G major:

Ex. 27

The prominence of the wind-players was noted by the first

critics, and a few bars later Beethoven alternates full wind-and-drum chords with strings to establish C major beyond doubt. This antiphonal treatment of strings and wind is carried into the Allegro, which is dominated by the three-note motif and rising staccato crotchets of the first subject, the crotchet arpeggio also accompanying the conversational phrases in the second group. The first subject had embraced a sequence in the supertonic, like the String Quintet in C op. 29, and its triumph on stable tonic harmony in the coda set a pattern for many later movements. The symphony's 'slow' movement is in sonata form but lightweight, almost the minuet that the third movement is not, beginning with a fugato and adding a running counterpoint on its return. Here the most original passage is the cadence-theme, with violin triplets set against cross-rhythm chords and a quietly insistent rhythm on the drum.

In the third movement 'Menuetto' is at once countered by the marking 'Allegro molto e vivace'. Did Beethoven, as in the 'Spring' Sonata op. 24 and the *Eroica* Symphony, first plan a more normal minuet and then speed it up? There are, however, lively minuets in Haydn – the 'Surprise' Symphony's is 'Allegro molto' – and Beethoven adds the excitement of lively modulation, moving rapidly to D flat in the second section, after which the trio's amusingly square wind-band, with asides from the strings, remains firmly in or near home. The lead-in to the finale is the famous joke in which the scale-figure is unfolded slowly in violin recitative; and if the movement's humour is again Haydnish, there are plenty of Beethovenish passages too, as with the new march-theme in the coda, around which the original scales play. One turns to the earlier C major Piano Concerto for a comparably witty ending, noting that the concerto's rondo is grander and richer in secondary material, and the symphony's sonata form more modest and compact.

The Second Symphony (1802) establishes a grander manner in the size and scope of its slow introduction, though it begins with a direct call-to-arms and affirms its key of D major in a theme given to wind and strings in turn. Before long, however, a series of abrupt modulations presages Beethoven's dramatic middle-period style, and a powerful unison climax in D *minor* is often cited as a prophecy of the first movement of the Ninth Symphony. The main Allegro again shows his resource in dealing with a cliché, the semiquaver figure in the first subject, which becomes a motif on its own before the exposition is over. The second subject, on the other hand, has an unusually martial character, perhaps a Revolutionary influence, and plays an important part in the development. Once more the coda fulfils the aspirations of the first subject, having reached a resplendent climax through a rising progression of chromatic chords. Yet the symphony still casts backward glances at the eighteenth century, especially in the lyrical outpouring of the Larghetto, where many turns of phrase suggest Haydn or Mozart, and Haydn certainly in the bucolic cadence-theme with its notoriously high asides from the horns. The scherzo is wholly Beethovenish, throwing its three-note figure around the orchestra in humorous fashion, and two features of the trio may be noted: a further forecast of the parallel place in the Ninth, especially when the bassoon counterpoint arrives; and the strong assertion of F sharp, dominant of B minor, in the strings. This D major – B minor relationship links up with the pauses in the coda of the finale and was also a characteristic of the 'Pastoral' Sonata op. 28.

Lengthy sketches for the finale of the Second Symphony were examined by Nottebohm in his first published commentary on a complete Beethoven sketchbook of 1801. They show that the cantabile transition theme was a later thought, since it does not appear in the first two drafts, and they also reveal an apparent plan, eventually compressed, for an outsize rondo with four episodes. Much of the finale's vitality derives from the explosive opening gesture and the two-note figure that sets it off, and the lead-backs through multiple reiterations of this figure were formal expansions that Beethoven incorporated in other works, such as the finale of the E minor 'Rasumovsky' Quartet op. 59 no. 2. In the symphony the 'gesture' is poised on dominant-seventh harmony until its brilliant resolution on the chord of D major at the end of the coda:

Fig. 28

The immense expansion of form and content in Beethoven's Third Symphony, the *Eroica*, (1803) has inevitably been discussed in the post-Heiligenstadt part of the biography. The incentives, whether Bonaparte, or heroism in general, or simply an inner artistic compulsion, are understandable, though the actual achievement remains staggering. Some time presumably elapsed between the primitive 'Wielhorsky' sketches and the progressive work in 'Landsberg 6', the so-called 'Eroica' sketchbook. Here one idea was firmly fixed from the start, the opening subject with its E flat arpeggio turning dramatically to the alien and ambiguous C sharp:

Ex. 29

The sketches suggest that Beethoven planned a 'shock' beginning with a pair of irregularly spaced dominant-seventh chords, though perhaps as the sequel to another slow introduction. These were filled in to clarify the rhythm but eventually replaced by the two simple but arresting E flat ones, providing the firmest possible launching-pad for the tonal adventures to come. In the end it is striking how subsidiary or transitional ideas were seized upon to produce paragraphs of colossal cumulative power. One such idea, phrased in pairs of crotchets across the three-four time and heard early on, was to generate the most shattering climax in the development. Much has been made of the 'new' theme that follows this climax in the remote key of E minor, and which analysts have tried to derive from the rising triad of the first subject, though Beethoven provided a more obvious unifying factor in the accompanying syncopations.

It became clear that sonata form on such an epic scale demanded a coda of unusual proportions, with room enough to recall the 'new' theme before carrying the first subject home as a triumphant round in its most fundamental form. Such a peroration to a first movement had no symphonic precedent, though the ending of Mozart's 'Jupiter' Symphony had pointed the way to Beethoven's climactic codas. The marking 'con brio' is a key to the first movement's character, and it should go without saying that the comfortable 'moderato' or 'non troppo' sometimes heard can only remove or undermine its elemental drive. The Funeral March, on the other hand, benefits from the broadest tempo compatible with sustained intensity of line. Some naive observers queried Beethoven's placing of the march second, as though to kill off his hero early in the proceedings; but a symphony is not a biography, and to borrow his later remarks on the *Pastoral* Symphony, he was expressing feelings rather than depicting events. Viewed objectively the march is a very slow movement on a large scale and in rondo form, but the scoring of the theme for low-lying strings, with rumbling basses suggesting muffled drums, sets a tragic mood from the start, enhanced by a counterstatement in the most plaintive register of a solo oboe. The theme's afterthoughts are spacious, thus delaying the first episode, which brings the tender consolation of C major but produces triumphant cadences of a military nature. The second episode, however, provides the emotional climax, a double fugue that breaks in soon after the return of the march; and the disintegration of the latter in the coda is a stroke of genius foreshadowing the return of the Arioso in the op. 110 Sonata and the 'beklemmt' passage in the Cavatina of the op. 130 Quartet. Structurally and emotionally the *Eroica* stands ahead of its time as a landmark in musical expression.

It was also imaginative to follow the grief-laden ending of the Funeral March with a rapid scherzo that runs half its course in a subdued pianissimo and to pick out its salient melodic feature with oboe or flute in keys other than the tonic, B flat or F major, saving the home-key statement (E flat) for the sudden and long-delayed *ff*. The addition of a third horn enabled the trio to live up to its name for once, and the E flat fanfares inevitably recall the triadic theme of the first movement, even more so in the sketches. For the finale Beethoven took as his text the *Prometheus* theme and its bass that had already produced the piano Variations and Fugue op. 35. The *Eroica* inherited some of its procedures and added others, and it is far too facile to describe the finale's unique form as an amalgam of variations and fugue. Its sequence of events may be summed up as (a) a downward rush of strings obliterating the E flat key of the scherzo in order to emphasise it afresh, and beginning as though in G minor: (b) variations on the bass of the theme eventually yielding the theme itself; (c) a fugato on the bass; (d) a return of the theme in D major with varied repeats and leading to (e) a central episode in which a march in dotted rhythm is superimposed on part of the original bass and in G minor. From this point the events are freely reversed, creating a kind of arch-form which can be clarified by continuing with the letters in retrograde order: (d) the first part of the theme returns in C major; (c) a second fugato on the inverted bass; (b) variations are resumed but in slow tempo; and finally (a) the music drifts yet again to G minor, to be interrupted by a quick rush of strings parallel to the opening and veering rapidly to the home-key of E flat for a brilliant coda. The importance of G minor at the three crucial points is easily overlooked, though it serves as a foil to E flat and reinforces the symmetrical aspect of the whole.

The strength of the *Eroica* finale lies in its wide variety of textures and treatments, most of which are offshoots from the simple binary theme and its bass. Its most sublime moment surely comes after the climax of the second fugal section when the wind offer the *Prometheus* theme 'poco andante' and in a new and richer harmonisation; and this elevated manner, far removed from its origins in the ballet and as a contredanse, epitomises the grander and deeper emotions of the symphony as a whole. When the poet Christoph Kuffner asked Beethoven to name his favourite among the symphonies he replied 'The Eroica', though the year was 1817 and the Ninth had yet to come.

Apart from the First, the odd-numbered symphonies are the weightiest in the series, though it would be wrong to regard the more relaxed even ones as less typical or important. When Schumann described the Fourth Symphony as 'a slender Greek maiden between two Norse giants' he overlooked the masculine vigour of the outer movements, thinking more perhaps of the lyrical aspects of the slow movement and the charm of the trio in the scherzo. The Fourth Symphony (1806) opens moreover with a slow introduction of minor-key darkness and mysteriously measured tread, which invoked the scorn of Weber through its sparseness of notes. Yet its sense of space is immense. The opening moves, having established the key of B flat minor, are then diverted by a semitonal rise into remote regions, giving the unexpected outburst of dominant-seventh harmony preceding the Allegro the alarmingly dramatic effect of a sudden sunrise at midnight. The dominant seventh provides the springboard, and the detached quavers of the first subject may be felt as an outcome of the much slower ones in the introduction. In fact the energy of the Allegro vivace owes much, as Tovey said, to 'the variety, the contrasts, and the order of themes and sequences, varying in length from odd fractions of bars . . . . to the 32-bar and even longer processes in the development.' The exposition pursues its varied course with confidence and humour, incorporating a clarinet-and-bassoon canon in the second group and rounding off the whole section with a brilliant syncopated theme deriving from an earlier transition idea.

Though the development is based entirely on the figures of the first subject, two features deserve mention: the melodious counterpoint that blossoms in sequences and in smooth contrast to the detached quavers; and the enharmonic use of the timpani's B flat as A sharp when the music, as in the introduction, has wandered into distant keys. It may be argued that the drumrolls on the third of a remote chord, a dominant seventh on F sharp, are of necessity always B flats as if reminding the orchestra of the movement's proper key. In any case the alchemy works, the harmony resolves poetically in that direction, and the drumroll is heard in its new and true context. The exciting crescendo leading to the recapitulation resembles a parallel one in the 'Waldstein' Sonata, though being based entirely on tonic harmony the effect in the symphony is more original, simpler and stronger.

In the slow movement, doubtless admired by Schumann, the lyric grace of the first theme is introduced by a rhythmic figure that hints at the latent strength underlying the outward tenderness. It flares up from time to time, but is also heard in the forlorn high register of a bassoon and appears quietly on the timpani at the end. The most dramatic contrast in this sonata-rondo comes in the middle episode where a forceful minor-key version of the subject yields to a delicate interweaving of arabesques in first and second violins in the exotic region of G flat major. The scherzo is the first in the symphonies to bring round its trio-section a second time, and the third statement of the scherzo itself is accordingly abridged. It makes great play with cross-rhythms, alternating with unison phrases and minor-key inflections, and these elements are expanded with a wider modulating scheme in the second part. The trio however is carried through mostly on a tonic pedal, and its 'poco meno mosso' allows more room for its lyrical but playful exchanges between wind and strings. As for the finale, it is an extrovert affair with many glimpses at the past, as in the Mozartian 'Alberti bass' treatment of the clarinet in the second group. Its main topic is the opening semiquaver subject and its tendency to build up sequences in perpetual motion: it taxes the bassoon in the recapitulation and the basses in the coda, and is eventually handed round at half-speed before being whisked away in a surprise ending. The brusque treatment of dynamics should temper any lingering notions of Schumann's 'Greek maiden' or of the slightness of the 'even numbers'.

The Fifth Symphony (1808) took longer to complete, and sketches already appear in the 'Landsberg 6' sketchbook of 1803–4. Its immense popularity is no doubt bound up with the 'fate' associations of the first movement and the stirring triumph of the C major finale. Extra instruments – three trombones, piccolo and contrabassoon – are reserved for the finale, and the colossal strength of the first movement is achieved with normal Classical forces, though Weingartner remarked of its coda: 'Are they giants whom we hear scraping and blowing?' Even the famous opening is given to strings and clarinets alone, saving the full force of the tutti for the recapitulation and coda. Although familiarity makes it hard to hear those initial five bars out of context, they are in fact tonally ambiguous. It is only in the continuation that the key of C minor is confirmed, and if the exposition is repeated as it should be, the opening is heard decidedly in the relative major of E flat. If one aspect of the movement's compression is the growth of whole areas from the four-note opening 'motto', there is also a remarkable treatment of the related horn-call that heralds the second subject. The theme that follows can be proved to be a variation upon it; and more striking still is the derivation of the latter part of the development from the minims of the horn-call. Unlike Mozart's practice of recapitulating the second subject in the tonic minor in minor-key works, Beethoven, after admitting some minor-key inflections, allows C major to triumph for awhile, only to deny it with overwhelming force in the coda. The brief oboe cadenza that follows the return of the first subject is incidentally the outcome of a melodic thread woven into the reprise some bars previously.

In the sketches the slow movement theme appears as a 'tempo di menuetto' with trite sequences. Its eventual form as a subject for variations incorporates a sequel that moves dramatically to C major for a martial counterstatement, but after one complete variation a second in quicker note-values breaks off on a dominant-seventh pause. At this point a more improvisatory manner sets in, involving a wide range of thoughts about the subject. The form of the movement is thus unusual in its move from literal variation-writing to free, though the Adagio of the Ninth Symphony was to close with a similar though more homogeneous coda of afterthoughts.

The third movement fulfils the purpose of the scherzo or minuet in its three-four time and overall ABA form, but is a wholly original conception with little remaining of the dance origin. The opening theme, looming up in unison from cellos and basses, is followed by questioning phrases and half-closes. Beethoven noted that the first idea shared the contours, though not the character of the finale theme in Mozart's great G minor Symphony; and we may also note that the half-answers look forward to the major-key opening of the op. 101 Piano Sonata. In the symphony the real 'answer' is the resolute subject in the horns that harks back for many to the 'fate' motif of the first movement. These contrasting ideas are developed in a through-composed way that precludes the possibility of the usual internal repeats. The trio, with its bustling fugato in the cellos and basses, is however clearly in binary form, though the repeat of its second part is more lightly scored and extended to prepare for the return. Here the question arises about Beethoven's original and maybe his ultimate intentions for the movement. The first set of parts and indeed the autograph score, despite its verbal additions and illegibilities, indicate a doubly alternating scherzo and trio such as we find in the Fourth, Sixth and Seventh symphonies.

It is understandable that the long repeat should have been abandoned at the marathon concert in December 1808, and in a letter to Breitkopf and Härtel of 21 August 1810 Beethoven seemed to have settled on the shorter version. In spite of his instructions two redundant bars were retained in the printed score at the return of the opening theme, evidently a relic of the 'first time bars' leading to a complete 'da capo'. The 1810 letter does not dispose of the matter, for in April 1820 Franz Oliva reported in a conversation book that he had just heard the Fifth played by the Dilettanten in Vienna, adding that 'they left out half the third movement [the scherzo]; the fugal movement [the trio] was only played once, then they came to where the violins play pizzicato and went straight into the finale'. Although Beethoven's reaction was not recorded, it seems clear that Oliva, who was close with the composer at the time, expected the long repeat. As it stands it seems strange that so powerful a work as the Fifth Symphony should dispense with even *one* full return of the scherzo, and though the evidence is confused there are aesthetic grounds for reviving Beethoven's original plan, especially in view of Oliva's remarks.

The usual procedure is for the one playing of the trio to lead to a ghostly and abbreviated reprise of the scherzo, which then subsides into an even more mysterious transition in which long-held notes in the strings are barely kept alive by a rhythmic figure on the drum. After this suspense the violins outline the opening theme of the movement, developing it in rising sequences and breaking into C major but withholding a crescendo until the last moment: thus the brilliant daylight of the finale bursts forth, with the trombones making their first important appearance in a symphony. As Robert Simpson has pointed out, the exposition repeat in the finale is rarely observed, but with the restitution of the full 'da capo' of the scherzo it is really needed to balance the extra weight of the previous movement, thereby delaying the retrospect of the scherzo that precedes the recapitulation and justifying, in fact demanding, the prolonged affirmation of C major in the coda. A brief quotation from the second subject is given for the sake of its unobtrusive bass, which acquires such immense importance in the development and coda:

Ex. 30

The 'Eroica' sketchbook also contained at least two harbingers of the Sixth Symphony, the *Pastoral* (1808): a sketch for the two-four rustic dance in the 'Peasants' Merrymaking', and another in twelve-eight quavers labelled 'the murmuring of the brook' and noted in two keys, C and F, with the comment 'the larger the stream, the deeper the note'. It was not until 1808 however that Beethoven began to work on the *Pastoral* in earnest, and a sketchbook of that year is largely devoted to it, the remainder concentrating on the two piano trios op. 70. On the very first page he made memoranda about 'programme music': 'the listener should be able to discover the situations for himself' and 'every kind of painting loses by being carried too far in instrumental music' and so forth. In spite of these reservations he preserved the title and its subheading 'Recollections of country life' and gave descriptive subtitles to the five movements too, but added the proviso 'more the expression of feeling than tone-painting'. The very first phrase, coming to a pause in the fourth bar, is a marvellous example of Beethoven's ever-growing resources, since most of the first movement can be derived from some fragment of it:

Ex. 31

Meanwhile violas and cellos sustain a bare fifth through the first three bars, a drone-bass redolent of rustic music-making and the first of several in the symphony.

A feeling of natural growth is reinforced by the many self-repetitive figures, as in the development, which remains poised for a dozen bars or more on a single harmony until some sudden change – B flat to D major, G major to E major – opens up new vistas and reveals the leisurely tonal scheme of the music. This relaxed mood is manifest in the second group too, beginning with a three-part round on simple tonic and dominant harmony and closing with a drone-bass cadence-theme. Yet the movement leaves an impression of prodigality, leading the sympathetic listener to agree with Sir George Grove that 'when the sameness of fields, woods and streams can become distasteful, then will the Pastoral Symphony weary its hearers'. Thus Beethoven, according to the title, expressed his 'joyful feelings on arriving in the country'.

The Andante has the more specific label 'Scene by the brook' and opens by transforming the earlier twelve-eight sketches into a flowing melodic pattern in the lower strings. Once again the movement is largely diatonic and the richly lyrical outpouring remains for a long time in the home-key of B flat until a gentle drift in the opening theme moves to the dominant, bringing wider melodic sweeps in its train. An exploration of more distant keys is left for the development, during which the opening material moves by stages from G major and E flat to G flat and C flat; yet the flow is unbroken as the music drifts back for the more richly scored recapitulation. The coda introduces its celebrated bird-calls, identified in the score as the nightingale, quail and cuckoo, yet these two brief cadenzas are thematically relevant rather than realistically avian: compare the nightingale's appoggiaturas with the second violins' cross-phrasing in the first bar, and note that the cuckoo reproduces the tessitura of the first violins' initial motif.

Though the *Pastoral* is unique among the symphonies in having five movements, the last three are played without a break and have a continuous programme: the peasants' merrymaking, the storm and the thanksgiving after the storm. Antony Hopkins proposed a fanciful but plausible timetable for the symphony: morning and afternoon for the first two movements, evening for the peasants' revelry, interrupted by a nocturnal storm and followed by the glowing serenity of a Sunday morning. One may accept or reject such realism, bearing in mind the composer's own guardedness, and listen to the *Pastoral* as a satisfying piece of absolute music. Yet there is no denying the element of parody in the merrymaking, though its opening alternation of F major and D major is deeply poetic, having as a prototype the childlike Bagatelle op. 33 no. 3. The third statement of the opening is cut short, pictorially speaking, by a distant roll of thunder and a staccato figure in the strings suggesting raindrops. One may note that the fury of the storm is unleashed in the 'Appassionata' key of F minor and with a theme resembling its first subject; that the rumbling cellos and basses had been foreseen in a sketch of tremolos marked 'thunder – basses'; and that the 'raindrop' quavers are augmented into hymnlike minims as the storm abates and gives way to the warm-hearted thanksgiving of the finale.

For the storm Beethoven added a piccolo and a pair of trombones to the orchestra, retaining the latter to enrich the sonority of the finale. The dynamic climax of this leisurely sonata-rondo comes in the coda, but the emotional climax really lies in the hushed transformation of the rondo-theme that follows. This intimate mood is resumed as a muted horn recalls the yodelling figure that opened the movement, and it was typical of Beethoven to cut it short with two abrupt final chords.

The Seventh Symphony (1812) was described by Wagner as 'the

apotheosis of the dance', but its cosmic energy was ridiculed when a later age actually danced a ballet to it. All four movements depend on the reiteration of basic rhythms. Even the 'slow' movement is neither andante nor adagio but 'allegretto'. The first is however preceded by an introduction on a grand scale, and the rather imprecise marking 'poco sostenuto' has led to a wide divergence of interpretations: suffice it to say that the strength of the semiquaver scales that later accompany the minims of the opening should be borne in mind from the start. Beethoven's long-range treatment of tonality (or key) was never better exemplified than in this symphony. For instance the introduction soon side-slips from its home-key of A major through distant chords of C and F major before climbing up to its first scale-accompanied tutti; and these happen to be the keys destined for its own 'second subject', a lilting theme on woodwind complemented by sustained notes and melodic fragments in the violins. The link with the Vivace, in which the exchanges of a solitary octave E between wind and strings are slowed down to a state of immobility, is a good example of what Basil Lam has called Beethoven's art of composing-in the 'spaces' in his music. Eventually the bare exchanges are, as it were, fertilised by a short upbeat, thus giving birth to the six-eight dotted rhythm of the Vivace. The persistence of this rhythm is a test of stamina for performers; and the importance of C major and F major in the development is a unifying factor from the introduction that recurs in all four movements. It may have been the grinding bass ostinato in the coda that led Weber to declare Beethoven 'ripe for the madhouse', but it provides a splendid building-up of tension before the final climax. For once the dotted rhythm is suppressed, only to break out with renewed vigour, and the ostinato itself, though seeming new, can be related back to the opening bars of the first subject:

Ex. 32

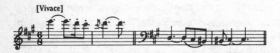

The Allegretto, marvellously framed between two wind chords, derived from a sketch of six years before and has been mentioned in relation to the C major 'Rasumovsky' Quartet. Its march-like theme is a haunting creation, and the A major-minor harmony in its twelfth bar gives it a melancholic effect, to be inherited by a flowing counterpoint in cellos and violas. Variations play a large part in the movement, but the variants are confined to accompanying figures and the theme is always present in them with its counterpoint a regular companion. The basic rhythm ♩ ♫ |♩ ♩, which appeared to influence Schubert so much, continues in part as a pizzicato bass when minor turns to major for two episodes featuring the clarinet. There is also a quiet fugal development that produces an abrupt climax, and a coda that scatters the original subject between different instruments and registers. The success of the movement was immediate: it was encored at its first performance and has been a popular favourite ever since.

In view of the Allegretto's key of A minor, Beethoven decided on F major for the scherzo, the only one in the symphonies not in the tonic. Although F major plays its own strong role in the Seventh, the opening section of the scherzo makes an impulsive move to A major, as though wanting to be in the home-key; and in due course the insistence on the note A effects a modulation to D major for the trio. Whereas the scherzo derives immense energy from units of one, two or four bars, the trio spreads itself with a theme in the wind supposedly akin to an Austrian Pilgrims' Hymn, giving rise to a tradition of lethargic performance quite at variance with Beethoven's more modest retarding of tempo from 'presto' to 'assai meno presto'. The fact that the trio comes round twice in full and even returns briefly in the coda is hardly compatible with a slow tempo, which also makes the dynamic marks implausible, as with the long-held notes in the violins, written without nuances in contrast to those in the theme itself. Yet very few conductors have taken Toscanini's literal and logical view of the relation between scherzo and trio.

The finale's sustained energy matches that of the first movement's Vivace. Its first subject, a brusque binary theme with a pattern of semiquaver swirls in the strings and strong cross-accents in the wind, begins by sitting heavily on a dominant pedal, the bass-note E; but the music settles firmly in the tonic for the transition material before moving to unexpected regions for the second group. This fulfilled a memo in the sketches: 'goes first to F sharp minor, then C sharp minor.' The development, like the first movement's, moves in triumph to C major, hence F major, and there is an inspired lightly-scored 'false reprise' in B flat before the real recapitulation. Even those unfamiliar with the language of keys will note the new harmonic twists in the return of the second group. Then the coda: a new lease of life and energy, moving through new areas before settling on a long dominant pedal, while the first and second violins vie with each other over the figures of the first subject. This is one of countless examples in the Classical and Romantic repertory that benefit from the separation of first and second violins to the left and right of the conductor, a practice largely ignored in modern perform-ances. Incidentally the final phase produces two vociferous climaxes on the note G natural, alien to A major, though the actual ending is precisely punctual and relevant.

Beethoven temporarily ignored his note about a further sym-phony 'in D minor' and produced the Eighth in F major (also 1812). Coming after the Seventh, its far more compact scale disappointed its first audiences – 'because it is so much better' said the composer – but within this scale it has proved no less masterly, no less 'new'. It opens with a self-contained theme and an initial motif that plays no further part in the exposition but provides the mainstay of the development and coda and is humorously thrown away at the close. It is in the broad transition theme and the oblique approach to the second group that Beethoven displays a new manner, with a wide range of textures concisely juxtaposed and enlivened by cross-rhythms. The vitality of the music again depends on a literal obser-vation of the extreme tempo-mark, not merely Allegro but 'vivace e con brio'.

The two middle movements are without precedent in the sym-phonies, though the Piano Sonata in E flat op. 31 no. 3 had offered something similar: in place of a slow movement an Allegretto scherzando in two-four time, and instead of a scherzo a true moderate-paced minuet. The second movement of the Eighth derives its humour from the mechanical chording of the wind, apparently caricaturing Maelzel's metronome; and in fact the main subject was adapted as a vocal canon on the inventor's name. In the minuet, two heavily stressed bars emphasise the three-in-a-bar character before the arrival of the theme, while the scoring of the trio is notable for its horns and busy cello accompaniment, an effect greatly admired by Stravinsky. The finale carries far more weight than its lightly-scored opening would suggest, though the suddenly loud and out-of-key C sharp that disrupts the proceedings promises a later and drastic harmonic adventure. The semitonal shift from C to C sharp is, however, paralleled when the second subject arrives in A flat before subsiding on to G and, in Tovey's words, 'relaxing with a slow smile' into the orthodox dominant key of C major. The scale of the latter part of the finale is remarkable. Robert Simpson debunked the theory that half the movement is coda, suggesting instead an outsize sonata-rondo with two developments and two recapitulations. It is on its third appearance that the strange C sharp succeeds in forcing the first theme into F sharp minor, to which the brass and timpani respond by pulling it back again into F major, a classic case of instrumental limitations producing a masterstroke of sublime humour. For the finale Beethoven tuned the drums in octave Fs, as he was to do in the scherzo of the Ninth; and in the Eighth this led to original effects of colour in unison with the bassoon. As for the prolonged affirmation of F major in the closing bars, this was in keeping with the scale of the movement, despite the common reference to the Eighth as 'little'.

Although Beethoven had written to Breitkopf in 1812 about 'three new symphonies', i.e. beginning with no. 7, the third 'in D minor' turned out to be a long-term project indeed. Just as many years separate the Eighth from the Ninth as from the First, though the intention to set Schiller's 'Ode to Joy' dated back to 1793 or earlier, and a setting of the words 'Muss ein lieber Vater wohnen' appears in a sketchbook of 1798 and 1799. There was no suggestion of a symphonic context, which would have been most unlikely at that time, and even in the last stages the incorporation of voices in the Ninth was not undertaken lightly, as the sketches show. They also indicate that a different type of choral symphony on a religious text was projected, though this was set aside after the decision had been taken to make Schiller's 'Ode' the climax of the Ninth itself.

Yet for all its revolutionary aspect and impact the Ninth Symphony (1824) still owes much of its strength to Classical tradition. Its spirit has inevitably been linked with outside events, the aftermath of the French Revolution, the Napoleonic wars, the dignity of the individual, the sufferings and hopes of mankind, including Beethoven's own; and yet in simple musical terms it may be held as the greatest example of the triumph of the major over the minor key. Where the Fifth had pointed the way, the Ninth intensifies, deepens and makes explicit. There are places maybe where the medium quakes and quivers under the weight of thought and emotion; where

Beethoven seemed to fight against or reach out beyond instrumental and vocal limitations, though this had long been a characteristic tendency. His deafness used to be blamed for miscalculations, yet few conductors nowadays adopt the re-scorings suggested by Wagner or Weingartner. These so easily become the thin edge of a large wedge: moreover the limitations often contain the strength or become the mother of invention. In the scherzo, for example, the restriction of the octave-tuned drums to the minor third of the key influenced the tonal course of the movement.

Once we accept the choral finale, the first movement, arguably Beethoven's greatest achievement in sonata form, would appear to set forth the problems that he sought to resolve with Schiller's aid: the word 'despairs' appears in the sketches. Despite its influence on the Romantics, especially Bruckner, the mysterious opening is unique: a quiet bare-fifth tremolo on the dominant of the key, with a two-note fragment quickly gathering momentum and breaking into the powerful unison of the first subject – how many later works have found inspiration here, and how few, if any, have approached its drama and economy? Yet Beethoven soon repeats this whole process, veering from D minor to B flat major, the eventual second-group key, which is forthwith denied vehemently until the music yields to it again for a complete change of scene. And what 'second group' can compare with this for richness and continuity, for its alternation of consolation and doubt, or for the resolute way it gathers strength for its final fanfare on the chord of B flat? But the dotted rhythm of the fanfare contains that of the opening two-note figure: all that is needed is the downward step of a semitone from B flat to A to recall it. For the only time in the symphonies there is no exposition repeat, though as in other cases – the F major 'Rasumovsky' Quartet, the first movement of Brahms's Fourth Symphony – the music makes *as if* to repeat before opening up new vistas. The new moves in the Ninth include a brief touch of D major, which leads by way of G minor to a development of unsurpassable drive, drama and pathos. The ironic use of the tonic major recurs, with full force at the moment of recapitulation and in gentler guises in the reprise of the second group and in the coda. All these D major events are sooner or later deflected into D minor, and the movement ends with an expanded statement of the first subject and a shattering sense of finality (see Ex.33).

Yet in this same D minor the scherzo follows, with its octave-

Ex. 33

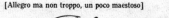

tuned drums settling the tonality. The opening bars, surely the most electrifying start to any scherzo, were probably a late thought, whereas the succeeding fugato was sketched and resketched for almost a decade. The fugal treatment is also, in another sense, introductory, for once the whole orchestra is involved, harmonic emphasis takes over. It goes without saying that no symphonic scherzo can compete with the size, energy and economy of the Ninth's for, setting aside the D major trio as a haven apart, the scherzo itself is a large-scale sonata movement with each part repeated. Three features must be mentioned in addition to the dramatic use of the timpani: the complete domination of the opening rhythm, the unique harmonic flavour caused by the orientation of the second subject (C major), and the change from four to three-bar phrasing in the development. At the end the trio makes as if to return but Beethoven cuts it short, for the energy of the whole, physical and mental, could have propelled it into eternity.

There were good reasons for placing the Adagio of the Ninth *after* the scherzo and before the opening clamour of the finale, though the sketches reveal changes of mind here too. Even in the movement itself the themes appeared to Beethoven in reverse order, the second one (note again its eventual key, D major) being sketched as a 'beginning', the actual B flat opening at a later stage. Both were preserved, and the principle of variations and episodes established, with the B flat theme the subject of increasing elaboration. To describe these ideas as ineffably tender and serene would still be an understatement; yet late in the movement two arresting fanfares disturb the tranquillity, the second probing deep unexplored regions before resolving back into further variants. Tenderness in Beethoven's case does not imply a lack of strength or awareness, even of inexplicable mysteries. This Adagio also contains the celebrated passage for the fourth horn, in the interlude preceding the second B flat variation, suggesting that Beethoven knew his player owned one of the newly-invented valve instruments.

Having settled on the 'Ode to Joy' and rejected ideas for an instrumental finale, Beethoven faced the problem of justifying the intrusion of the human voice in a symphony. His plan to revive and reject themes from the previous movements in vocal recitative was also modified: first, instruments must be tried and found wanting. The cellos and basses come near to words and their eventual acclamation of the 'joy' motif cannot be doubted. Yet perhaps it might? Who but Beethoven, one wonders, would have dared to allow the finale to develop so far as a purely instrumental movement, and then to intervene, return to the start, and to sum up the meaning of the cello-and-bass recitatives with the baritone's brief words 'O Friends, no more these sounds!'? The flash-back has been criticized as a miscalculation, but the drama of spontaneously reversing a decision is not alien to an art that spreads itself across time. It could be argued that it brings art still closer to life, for we seem to share Beethoven's problems and triumphs as we listen to him. One of his triumphs was the creation of a theme, through countless rewritings, of a fundamental simplicity and appeal. It had already grown from a hushed unison to a jubilant acclaim from the orchestra alone, and now, aligned with Schiller's words, it reaches an overwhelming climax at 'und der Cherub steht vor Gott.'

The choral finale of the Ninth is, to borrow from Schiller, 'all-embracing', for the great unexpected chord on the word 'Gott' opens the door to the most secular version of the theme imaginable – 'Froh, wie seine Sonnen', with tenor solo – though it inspires the orchestra to a vigorous double-fugue and, in due course, the chorus to a resumption of the original. When the tempo broadens to encompass a new theme (G major, with trombones) that literally 'embraces the millions', a profound feeling of awe descends at the mention of the Creator beyond the stars: 'Ihr stürzt nieder, Millionen'. The great chorus that brings the 'Joy' and the 'Millionen' themes together in counterpoint has its clear message for mankind, and this alternation of awe and jubilation is carried through to the closing pages of the final Bacchanale. Awe must also strike the listener today at the manifestation of mind and spirit revealed in the Ninth Symphony. Its influence on Wagner in particular was profound and lifelong, and the alliance of symphonic thought and explicit emotions must have struck him as an obvious precursor of music-drama, though Beethoven can hardly have viewed the Ninth in such a light. How his Tenth Symphony would have turned out we can hardly conjecture, though Schindler identified a 24-bar fragment in the sketches as an idea for the scherzo, beginning in this surprisingly familiar vein:

Ex. 34

10

Concertos

Despite the importance of Beethoven's concertos the list is short by Mozartian standards. It comprises the five for piano, one for violin, the Triple Concerto, and some shorter but related pieces: the two violin Romances and perhaps, on account of its dominating solo part, the curious but prophetic Fantasy op. 80 for piano, orchestra and chorus. There are sketches for other works in the genre: a fragment of a violin concerto in C (WoO 5) dating from his last years in Bonn, but breaking off in the development of the first movement; an abandoned concertante for piano, violin and cello (1802) which has some bearing on the subsequent Triple Concerto; and a projected piano concerto in D (1814 or 1815), which could have been an interesting venture indeed, coming on the threshold of the third period. One very early work outside the usual canon was actually completed when the composer was fourteen, though he saw no reason to revive or publish it and the score was lost: a Piano Concerto in E flat (WoO 4). A copy of the solo part survived however, in which Beethoven had noted details of the tuttis and scoring, and a reconstruction by Willi Hess was performed by Edwin Fischer at Potsdam in 1943. Its musical value is slight, though the orchestra of two flutes, two horns and strings is unusual, and the florid but discursive keyboard writing testifies to the skill of the young virtuoso. If this was precipitated by some special occasion in Bonn, the Beethoven of eleven years later had more pressing reasons to display himself with orchestra to the Viennese public.

Beethoven's first 'mature' piano concerto was the B flat (1795), known as 'no. 2' because of its delayed publication. Although he described it as 'not one of his best' its freshness of spirit and invention have kept it firmly in the repertory. If the main subjects have Mozartian traits, their treatment is less poised but more robust, wilful and explosive, in fact more Beethovenish. Even the first tutti, having established its tonic and dominant, makes an abrupt move to a distant key, D flat, by appropriation rather than logical modulation, accompanied by an equally sudden drop from *ff* to *pp*. One might expect the soloist to adopt this kind of gesture, but it is left, here and later, to the orchestra:

Ex. 35

The various ways of introducing the solo had been well explored by Mozart, and Beethoven was to offer new solutions in his later concertos. In the first two he brought in the piano with new but fairly neutral material, but the entry in the B flat was at least adventurous in its gradual descent from the highest to the lowest notes of the available keyboard. It was in the rounding-up of the solo exposition that he showed his more forceful personality, turning the traditional passage-work into rugged chromatic sequences, adding some brisk repartee between tutti and solo, and steep dynamic gradients to prepare for the final trill. On the other hand the development, incorporating the orchestra's semitonal shift, settles down to light-weight exchanges with elementary arpeggio figures from the piano, but the return is dramatically prepared and a fully-scored sketch for it appears in the 'Kafka' miscellany. The only original cadenza for the first movement is in a later style but, like the longest of those for the C major Concerto, too good to miss. Its recurring fugato reminds one that B flat was to become Beethoven's fugal key (op. 106, op. 133) and the fact that it dwarfs the orchestra's modest cadence-theme might be justified as a ripe example of Beethovenish humour.

The slow movement, with its noble melodic line and its purposeful decorations in the solo part, is of a higher order; and the climax here is the coda, with its recitative, its long pedal-marks, and the dying echoes of the theme. The finale, with its syncopated rondo-theme, much mulled over in the sketches, replaced an earlier movement with an Andante middle section (WoO 6) and has greatly helped the work's popularity. The coda springs a Haydnish surprise when the piano offers the subject in the wrong key (G major) and the wrong rhythm (unsyncopated), only to be firmly corrected by the orchestra.

Nevertheless no. 1 in C major (1795, final version 1800) is a far grander work, with clarinets, trumpets and drums added to the orchestra. The opening tutti, having offered its martial first subject in both *p* and *f*, makes an original departure in presenting the second subject's initial phrase in a sequence of foreign keys to be duly completed and extended in the usual dominant after the solo's entry. There is also a march-like cadence-theme that forms an important sequel, but the very opening with its octave leap provides the most dominating figure. Much of the solo writing is based on elementary patterns with a touch of caricature, owing more to Clementi than to Mozart, but there are already foreshadowings of the 'Emperor' in the energetic left-hand triplets and the veiled right-hand chromatics. The largest of the two completed cadenzas is in a post-Waldstein style, like that for the B flat; and though it storms away for five minutes and tails off into a 'joke' ending, it offers a splendid example of Beethoven's improvising manner and the concerto is robust enough to take it.

The slow movement, though hardly more expressive than the B flat's, is far more extended, and the long coda resolves into an eloquent dialogue between the piano and the first clarinet. This larger scale also applies to the finale, which bristles with wit and vitality: in the length and capricious phrasing of the rondo-theme, the cross-accents and modulating sequel in the first episode, and the irresistible abandon of the second, all typifying the composer-pianist's growing confidence. The short-slur articulation in the rondo, ♪♪♩, is a feature more readily executed by the orchestra than the piano. Czerny reported that Beethoven played the first note as an acciaccatura, and Schnabel treated it roughly as such in his recording, making a disparity with the tutti and removing the contrast with the episodic variant ♪ ♪♪♩. Yet the different versions, as in the rondo of the B flat Concerto, are a source of humour in the coda, which also has a surprising moment of quiet reflection from oboes and horns after the piano has finished.

With the Third Concerto (1800) we approach the middle period manner, and in its final form (1803) Beethoven utilised the new keyboard extension, adding brilliance to some of the passage-work and length to the downward swooping scales. The key of C minor already had its Beethovenish associations and a minor-key concerto offered its own dramatic possibilities, with Mozart's D minor and C minor as admired precedents. Beethoven's move to E flat in the opening tutti has however been criticised for forestalling the solo's prerogative, but the backtracking into C minor via C *major* is a typical manoeuvre with a touch of intellectual humour about it. After the solo entry, with its simple but arresting C minor scales, the course of the movement is firm with clearly posted landmarks. Beethoven made no attempt to emulate Mozart's changing order of events in the recapitulation of the C minor K. 491, but he followed Mozart in carrying the solo part into the coda and achieved a magic effect in the quiet duet for piano and timpani after the cadenza.

The slow movement is in E major, beginning with a rapt contemplative theme on the piano to which the orchestra adds a more openly expressive version, but the mood of quiet communing continues in the middle section, where a dialogue between bassoon and flute is accompanied by undulating arpeggios in the solo. On the return the opening subject is distributed conversationally, eventually generating a climax and cadenza. The solo version of the theme had been marked by a sudden disruptive C natural in the bass of the penultimate bar, dissolving into a half-close; and at the end of the movement, after many dying falls, the orchestra produces an abrupt *ff* chord of E major, a gesture too often underplayed in performance. Despite the still muted strings, it is surely an awakening, forward-looking rather than retrospective, as the predominant third of the chord, G sharp, shows in its immediate translation into the A flat of the rondo-theme. The importance of the minor ninth, A flat, had been noted in early sketches for the rondo, but despite the minor key this finale radiates wit and well-being and especially in its major-key episodes. Its unity is assured by the simple semiquaver turn in the second bar, which is common to most of the themes including the lyrical clarinet subject that opens the middle episode. The lead-back from this is however highly adventurous, beginning with a scholarly fugato in the strings and leading to a humorously non-fugal entry by the piano in A flat octaves. This process that launched the finale is reversed: the A flats become G sharps, and an ethereal version of the rondo-theme appears in the slow movement key of E major. The coda, like the final variation in the Mozart C minor, is in six-eight time; but whereas Mozart pursued his tragic mood to the end, Beethoven's is a wholly brilliant affair in the major.

In 1804 Beethoven completed his Triple Concerto in C for piano, violin and cello, which comes at the halfway mark in his seven mature concertos and is in many ways a work of transition and experiment. It was his only finished example of the hybrid 'sinfonia concertante' for two or more soloists that had had such a vogue in Paris and led to several important works by Mozart. In Beethoven's case there was inevitably some sacrifice of formal tautness in the need to distribute the interest between the three players, who are treated both as a trio and as individuals. The spreading is in fact far from even, since the cello takes the lead in all three movements and mostly in a high register. The first movement in particular may be felt too spacious for its content. If some of the material seems run-of-the-mill – the arpeggios in the development, the scales in the coda – it may be argued that some other middle-period works, like the 'Waldstein' Sonata, thrived on such things. Their less successful integration in the concerto is hardly to be wondered at in view of the unfamiliar formal problems. There are however masterstrokes, such as the quiet opening on cellos and basses, and the re-entries of the orchestra on an interrupted cadence were to be inherited by the Violin Concerto.

In the Largo the time-expansion problem was solved by extreme compression.Once again the cello leads with an eloquent and high-ranging theme, which is then restated by the trio with the piano in an accompanying role. The link with the finale is managed with drastic simplicity, a sketch rather than a genuine transition, in which a quickening repeated-note on the cello eventually breaks into the rondo-theme of the Polacca, another high-altitude challenge for the player. There is an unexpected turn to E major for the violin entry that effectively counterbalances the slow movement's A flat and later serves as a springboard for the A minor middle episode. In this a more extrovert aspiring theme is shared out between the players against a regular polonaise rhythm. Although it has a more lyrical sequel there are sufficient elements of display in the Triple Concerto for it to dispense with cadenzas as such, though an embryonic one may be detected towards the end of the quick two-four section of the coda in the Polacca, aptly placed between a brief six-four chord and the trills leading back to the original tempo.

To turn from the Triple Concerto to the Fourth Piano Concerto in G major (1806) is to exchange an interesting and unjustly neglected work by a master for an undisputed masterpiece of the highest order. To allow the soloist the first word in a Classical concerto would have been a rarity, though Mozart approached it in his early E flat Piano Concerto K. 271; but the masterstroke in the G major is the gentle manner of the opening, with its half-close that surprises the orchestra into its still quieter reply in the distant key of B major. Yet such moves, in Beethoven as in Mozart, may have delayed but did not undermine the Classical principle of orchestral exposition. The tutti in the Fourth Concerto, having found its way back by gentle stages to the tonic, is notable for its lyrical warmth, though it rises to two resplendent climaxes, the second of which falls away to a cadence-theme which is one of many variants of the piano's opening phrase. The pervading rhythm of three upbeat quavers bears a superficial likeness to the 'fate' motif of the Fifth Symphony and the two works were sketched simultaneously, but the characters of their first movements could hardly be further removed. The concerto breathes warmth of heart and serenity, even in its rapid passage-work, much of it in triplet semiquavers. The re-entry of the solo is, however, dramatic, breaking in on the cadence-theme with an improvisatory passage before resuming its dialogue with the orchestra. Mozart had indulged in surprise entries of this sort, but in his first three concertos Beethoven traditionally rounded off the tutti before the solo entry. Beethoven left two cadenzas for the first movement, the one beginning in six-eight time being most often played, in which the piano takes over the richest of the second-subject themes for the first time; but the work's popularity led to a spate of alternatives from generations of pianist-composers including Clara Schumann, Brahms and Busoni. In all cases the cadenza closes into a ravishingly poetic coda in which the solo dominates to the end.

The Andante of the G major is a unique drama carried out with the simplest of means. Only the orchestral strings are used, playing in octaves until the closing bars. They begin in an aggressive *forte*, to which the piano responds in quiet but fully harmonised phrases, starting on the very chord of B major that had marked the orchestra's entry in the previous movement. The piano's restraint eventually subdues the strings and only then does it show its latent strength by flaring up in a brief cadenza. Concord is at last established in the closing bars, after which the orchestra exchanges E minor harmony for C major and the rondo begins with hushed animation. The Romantics understandably read extra-musical meanings into the Andante, whether Orpheus taming the forces of nature, or more simply 'the quiet answer that turneth away wrath'; but though we describe it as unique, once more we can find a foreshadowing of its process in the last variation and coda in the slow movement of Mozart's later E flat Concerto K. 482.

Although the finale begins with four bars of C major harmony, the theme soon arrives at a firm cadence in G, incorporating a falling fifth A-D that is much used in the coda, but the opening subdominant bias gives an unusual orientation to the rondo-returns, each prefaced with a short cadenza. If the movement reconciles lightness of texture with passages of brilliant repartee, it also finds a lyrical haven in its second main theme, where the widely-spaced two-part writing over a deep bass-note shows Beethoven's growing dependence on the pedal for special effects of colour, as in the finale of the 'Waldstein' Sonata. The rondo-theme has its warmer transformations too, richly sustained on divided violas and a solo cello in B flat, and eventually settling *on* as well as *in* G major after the cadenza. One curious side-issue is that a rejected sketch for its opening bars became, in slower tempo and the key of B flat, the semiquaver motif that accompanies the Prisoners' Chorus in *Fidelio*.

The G major may be considered the most perfect of the piano concertos from many viewpoints, and in his Fifth and last Beethoven was to seek a more overtly triumphant mood with stronger contrasts and a more magisterial grandeur. Before moving on to the so-called 'Emperor', two intervening works must be discussed, the Violin Concerto op. 61 and the Fantasy op. 80. The glorious solo writing in the concerto obviously inherited the experience of the nine of Beethoven's ten violin sonatas that preceded it and especially the 'Kreutzer' op. 47, which he described as concerto-like in manner. There were other more direct though modest forebears in the two Romances for violin and orchestra op. 40 and op. 50. The former in G major, with its chordal and chorale style opening for the solo, is less immediately attractive or grateful than the F major with its high tessitura and finely-drawn melodic line. Both were thought to date from around 1802, but the F major may have been earlier (*c*.1798); and another theory, bearing in mind their style, scoring and isolation, conjectures that both may have been potential slow movements for the much earlier unfinished concerto (WoO 5). A more decisive influence on op. 61 was probably the Triple Concerto already mentioned.

The indifference shown to Beethoven's only Violin Concerto (1806) during his lifetime seems hard to grasp in view of its sublime qualities, such as the wonderfully poised balance between tender lyricism and virtuoso display and its general warmth and serenity. It took the young Joseph Joachim's historic performance with Mendelssohn in London in 1844 to reveal the work as a *ne plus ultra* for the aspiring soloist. Its premiere with Clement in 1806 was a last-minute affair and hardly propitious, and Czerny's account of its 'great effect' conflicts with contemporary complaints of its lack of continuity and long-windedness, no doubt levelled at the time-scale of the first movement. Tovey described its many strokes of genius as 'mysterious in radiantly happy surroundings', yet these mysteries – like the opening drum-taps and the strange D sharps at the entry of the first violins – may have struck those early listeners as simply bizarre or humorous. The four (or five) repeated notes once again provided a basic but telling motif adaptable to any context. Thus they introduce and punctuate the two main subjects of the first movement, and form a quiet but constant background to the G minor cantilena in the development. Another subtle masterstroke is their momentary melodic elevation, in which the previously unsupported D sharps are harmonised out:

Ex. 36

Otherwise the material is almost wholly diatonic, culminating in a noble and important cadence-theme that falls away on dominant-seventh harmony to make way for the entry of the solo. This dovetailing of tutti and solo, well known to Mozart, made for continuity and was adopted in differing ways in Beethoven's last two piano concertos.

Two tonal moves in the D major exposition became recurring features: the restatement of the second subject in the tonic minor, and the earlier intervention of a more martial tutti in B flat, providing dramatic contrast and serving both as transition and ritornello. It invariably arrives through an interrupted cadence, a structural device noted in the Triple Concerto, and though untouched by the soloist, it was used, unidiomatically, in Joachim's cadenza, Beethoven having left none. An original cadenza does however exist for the piano version of the work incorporating a timpani part. Attempts to transcribe this back for violin have been unconvincing, partly because the piano-and-drum duet was a special feature that Beethoven also adopted in the Third and Fifth piano concertos and hardly adaptable. The piano version of the concerto itself, though occasionally performed, is little more than a pragmatic curiosity. The sublime moment after the cadenza, for example, when the violin plays the second subject quietly on the lower strings with a simple pizzicato accompaniment, becomes a commonplace in the makeshift keyboard arrangement.

The Larghetto of the Violin Concerto is also remarkable for its sustained calm, only slightly disturbed by the chromatic sequences in the theme. It continues with variations in which the violin weaves celestial arabesques aloft, but after a fuller statement of the theme by the orchestra alone a freer manner takes over. Two further ideas emerge, even more profoundly serene, alternating with a further variation and closing into a brief memory of the first solo entry. Yet astonishingly the movement has remained in its key of G major throughout, making the orchestra's abrupt move to the dominant in preparation for the finale an electrifying event. It was here presumably that Clement turned the request for a cadenza to his own ulterior purpose! The Rondo, as with the other later concertos, including the Triple, then follows without a break. Its recurring six-eight subject is too familiar for comment, except to note that it was a stroke of genius to lift it two octaves from the G to the E string for its immediate counterstatement and to leave it with a questioning phrase. This is the cue for an extended orchestral tutti; though the ultimate answer may be found in the coda, where an engaging oboe and violin duet brings the theme home after a mysterious drift as far afield as A flat. The episodes of this sonata-rondo are more clear-cut than in any of the concerto finales apart from the earliest in B flat: the first and third introduce the only bouts of double-stopping in the work, while the second shares a touch of G minor pathos with the first bassoon, recalling the inspired and more expansive move in the development of the first movement.

It seems more logical to turn to the 'Choral' Fantasy (1808) at this point, than to leave it for discussion with Beethoven's other vocal music. Though scored for piano, orchestra and chorus, by far the greater portion concerns instruments alone, and the vocal contribution – to a text by Kuffner in praise of nature and art – is confined to the last stages. Despite its much smaller scale, the work's relationship to the Ninth Symphony is clear, as Beethoven later pointed out, and this is manifest when the voices enter with a theme previously given out by the piano as a subject for concerto-like variations and interludes. The theme also anticipates the 'Ode to Joy' in its stepwise simplicity, and derived from a much earlier setting of Bürger's 'Gegenliebe'. The instrumental variations range widely in key and tempo and are bound together by freely modulating episodes, but the whole work is prefaced by a lengthy exordium from the piano, improvisatory in manner and having no apparent thematic connection with what follows. The orchestra's tentative entry, leading to some hesitant exchanges with the piano before the arrival of the main theme, is recalled dramatically at the start of the choral finale; and the application of the word 'finale' to the original orchestral entry suggests that Beethoven actually improvised, and probably at far greater length, when the work was first performed in December 1808. The idea of a grand solo opening has however a direct bearing on his Fifth Piano Concerto (1809), sketches for which followed closely on those for the Fantasy.

The Fifth Concerto in E flat was the last Beethoven completed, a fact usually related to his gradual withdrawal from public performance, and Cramer's nickname has survived too long for us to quibble about its political implications. The title 'Emperor' at least befits the majesty of the work from its opening bars, which establish the pianist in the grandest manner before settling down to an equally grand orchestral exposition. Unlike the quiet beginning of the Fourth Concerto, this initial display of strength, with basic arpeggios and scales used in a wholly arresting way, is heralded and punctuated by orchestral chords. The succeeding exposition, stirred on by the unprecedented challenge, remains more firmly than ever in the home-key apart from a move to the tonic minor at the start of the second group; but this stability, vitally and traditionally Classical, makes the soloist's first quiet move to other regions a dramatic event. Meanwhile the orchestra has derived immense energy from the simple figures of the first subject, just as the solo is to do towards the end of its own exposition. One might write in technical terms of the first movement's long-term key-scheme, of Neapolitan relations and enharmonic modulations, and of the orchestra's peremptory returns to the dominant or tonic; but the great popularity of the 'Emperor' testifies to the drama, colour and emotion that these moves convey. Two obvious features are the chromatic scales with which the pianist re-enters and departs from the scene, and the exchange of stormy octaves between solo and orchestra in mid-movement. One important innovation was the abolition of the optional cadenza in favour of a brief written-in flourish. If this removed a time-honoured prerogative, no virtuoso could complain in view of the brilliant opening and its reprise, and the continuing domination of the piano to the end of the coda.

Beethoven sketched a slow movement theme in C major before settling on B major for the Adagio. The soloist's quiet reflections on an orchestral subject of great beauty and serenity set a pattern for many concertos of the Romantic period, whether the nationalist Grieg or the Classically-minded Brahms, and the celeste-like treatment of the piano towards the close was praised by Berlioz. The choice of B major not only offered links with first-movement events but afforded a dramatic return, through B flat to E flat, for the breaking-in of the finale. Here the rondo-theme is hinted at gently before being taken up vigorously, and any old-fashioned complaints about Beethoven's over-reliance on tonic and dominant harmony are rebutted by the athletic energy of its cross-rhythms and the range of keys and treatments in the long middle episode. The greatest surprise of the coda is the piano-and-drum duet that subsides into a moment of calm reflection before the final run-up. How could such brilliant contrasts have failed to impress that first Viennese audience in 1812?

11

Music for the stage

It seems appropriate to include Beethoven's overtures and incidental music in this chapter as well as ballet, opera and operatic projects. All his overtures, except for the 'occasional' and seldom-heard *Namensfeier*, were written for the theatre, even though most of them outstripped their original purpose and found a lasting place in the concert hall. The chances of hearing Goethe's *Egmont* or Collin's *Coriolan* with Beethoven's music are rare, but the dramatic force of the two overtures, heard out of context as absolute music, is staggeringly self-sufficient. This was one of Beethoven's eternal problems in his approach to opera: the harnessing of such musical power to the requirements of a libretto, an aria or ensemble. The history of the three *Leonore* overtures proves the point, for in tightening up the spacious drama of 'no. 2' into the more formally perfect 'no. 3' he reduced the impact of the opera itself. This he acknowledged by composing the shorter and less dramatic *Fidelio* overture for the final version. Yet to suggest that Beethoven, one of the most dramatic of all composers, added little or nothing to the development of opera is an ironic half-truth. Few nowadays will deny that *Fidelio* is a profoundly moving masterwork, though it could be argued that it achieved greatness in spite of its tacit acceptance of the conventional trappings of the German Singspiel, with its artificial mixture of musical numbers and spoken dialogue.

Yet it happened that Beethoven's favourite Mozart opera, *Die Zauberflöte*, was also a Singspiel that transcended the medium's limitations through the genius and spiritual quality of the music; and by a curious coincidence it was Schikaneder, Mozart's librettist and first Papageno, who offered Beethoven his first operatic contract. Although the Schikaneder project, *Vestas Feuer*, was abandoned, it provided a step towards *Fidelio*, even if an oblique one. The influence of Beethoven on the future of opera was also oblique, but subtle and far-reaching. His greatest heir was Wagner, even though Wagner's debt was primarily to Beethoven's symphonies and quartets.

Would the overture to *The Flying Dutchman* have taken its present form if Wagner had not been obsessed with the D minor first movement of the Ninth Symphony and its haunting 'empty fifths'? Or the chorus of anvils in *Rheingold* have adopted its incessant dotted rhythm if he had not come to it fresh from conducting the Seventh? It was also symbolic that when Wagner consecrated the founding of Bayreuth to the sounds of Beethoven's music he chose, not *Fidelio*, but the Ninth Symphony.

Beethoven's problems with *Fidelio*, and his inability or reluctance to carry through his many other projected operas, cannot be ascribed entirely to inexperience. As a viola-player at Bonn he was exposed to a fair cross-section of the operatic repertory between 1789 and 1792, though unlike the young Mozart his aspirations in that direction were to remain latent for many years. His only 'stage' work at that time was a curiosity, though it did call forth his first purely orchestral music, discounting the orchestra's contribution to his early keyboard concerto and to the two cantatas of 1790. The occasion was the *Ritterballet* (WoO 1) which was produced by Count Waldstein with members of the local aristocracy on 6 March 1791. The following year's *Theaterkalendar* described the event, in which the participants donned historic national dress to depict their German forebears' prowess in war, hunting, love – and drinking. Accordingly the eight musical numbers comprised a Kriegslied, Jagdlied, Minnelied, a German song and dance, an opening March and a final Coda. Since Waldstein was to be credited with the music, Beethoven kept to the simplest tonic-and-dominant manner to avert suspicion. All the items were in D major except for the plaintive but lilting Romanze (Minnelied) in B minor; the Jagdlied opened with a pair of horns redolent of the hunt; and the Coda rounded up the whole affair neatly by recalling the German song (no. 2) with its foretaste, already, of the finale of the 'Alla Tedesca' Sonata op. 79.

His only other incursion into ballet was a far more important one, coming at the time of the First Symphony and the op. 18 quartets (1800–1). Thayer suggested that the choice of subject, *Die Geschöpfe des Prometheus*, literally the creatures or 'creations' of Prometheus, may have been influenced by the recent success of Haydn's *Creation*, giving more point to Beethoven's play on words in the anecdote mentioned earlier (pp. 29–30). Although he was patronising about the ballet-master Vigano, he must certainly have been attracted by the legendary figure of Prometheus, the bringer of fire, who was also represented as hero and benefactor, and with whom Beethoven may have identified himself as a musician. In fact, as Marion Scott remarked, the hero on this occasion seemed to have acquired the combined gifts of Orpheus and Pygmalion, bringing statues to life though the power of harmony and, with the aid of Apollo in Parnassus, teaching them the blessings of culture.

With the disappearance of the original ballet most of the music fell into neglect, apart from the overture, which quickly became a favourite concert piece. Its dramatic opening chords epitomised the unusual harmonic moves at the start of the First Symphony, also in C major, and the lively string writing in the Allegro looked forward to the finale of the Fourth. Several of the ballet numbers are colourfully scored, including no. 5 with its cello solo and exotic use of the harp, and no. 14 with its basset horn. There is an engaging freshness about the Pastorale, no. 10, and an amusingly brisk forecast of Wagner's Pogner in no. 3. The opening Storm is also impressive, a forerunner of the more elemental one in the *Pastoral* Symphony, and owing something perhaps to Haydn's 'Representation of Chaos' in *The Creation*. The finale, however, has an interest for us beyond its musical value as a summing-up. It adopted two of Beethoven's recent set of Twelve Contredanses (WoO 14), no. 7 in E flat and no. 11 in G, the former destined for independent fame as the subject of the op. 35 Variations for piano and the finale of the *Eroica* Symphony.

The success of *Prometheus* must have kindled Beethoven's desire to write an opera at last, and may have influenced Schikaneder's invitation for him to do so. This desire, so often expressed in his letters, had been dormant during his first decade in Vienna, when the focal point of his creativity had been the piano. Yet his problems with vocal declamation, over which he continued to seek Salieri's advice, had not prevented him from composing a fair number of songs. In 1796 he even contributed two arias to a Singspiel by Ignaz Umlauf, *Die Schöne Schusterin*, and also wrote his impressive scena and aria 'Ah perfido!'. Here one already senses the musical character of Leonore taking shape: substitute 'Abscheulicher!' for 'Ah perfido!' and, in the aria, 'Komm, Hoffnung' for 'per pietà' and the prophecy becomes clear.

The path to *Fidelio* or *Leonore*, Beethoven's own preferred title, was however far from clear when he took up his lodgings in the Theater an der Wien early in 1803. First he was saddled with Schikaneder's libretto, *Vestas Feuer*, on which he worked without enthusiasm, abandoning it after a couple of scenes. On the other hand the attraction of Bouilly's 'Léonore' was obvious, and the notion of a rescue opera embodying a loyal, ideal heroine aroused his sympathy as, it seemed, no other topic was able to do. Bouilly's original text had already been set as a two-act opera by Pierre Gaveaux and performed in Paris in 1798, and two Italian versions by Ferdinando Paer and Simone Mayr were to appear respectively in Dresden in 1804 and Padua in early 1805, Mayr's librettist having reduced the plot to a single act and transferred the scene to Poland. Beethoven may have known Gaveaux's score, but the suggestion that Paer's opera influenced him and his librettist Sonnleithner by the year 1805 is hard to substantiate. He is known however to have heard the Paër *Leonore* in Vienna in 1809, sung in German, five years before his own final version; and it was out of deference to Paër that the Viennese authorities insisted from the start on the alternative title of *Fidelio* for Beethoven's opera.

Beethoven's three versions of *Fidelio* date from 1805, 1806 and 1814, though the earlier ones are normally referred to as 'Leonore' to avoid confusion, and this title is of course preserved in the rejected overtures, 'no. 2' being played at the first production and 'no. 3' for its revised version the following year. No. 3 is in fact an astonishingly comprehensive revision of no. 2: the changes involved greater clarity and conciseness, countless refinements in scoring and dynamics, the sacrificing of a rich but over-long development in favour of a normal recapitulation, and the reshaping of the coda to provide a more satisfying climax to the whole. Meanwhile the history of 'Leonore no. 1' has been much debated. Since its material has nothing in common with the others apart from the use of Florestan's aria, in place of a development and in the 'wrong' key of E flat, one might assume that it was written first and discarded as too light-weight. The Kinsky-Halm catalogue's date of 1805 has however been challenged in the light of the sketchbooks and replaced by 1806–7, in which case no. 1 must be regarded as a deliberate reaction to the others, perhaps intended for a projected production in Prague. Its posthumous publication as 'op. 138' was hardly helpful. One curiosity is the likeness of a woodwind figure in the coda to Florestan's phrase 'ein Engel, Leonoren' which does not appear in the earlier version of his aria. This would seem to support a later date in spite of no. 1's generally simpler style.

The failure of the 1805 version was not only due to the French occupation of Vienna: Sonnleithner's libretto and Beethoven's acceptance of it at least contributed. With the intention of providing greater musical scope the librettist made three acts out of Bouilly's two by enlarging the subplot of Marzelline's infatuation with the 'male' Fidelio and postponing the main action until Pizarro's entry in the new second act. Neither the drama nor the extra musical numbers could have been expected to sustain interest after the high-powered 'Leonore no. 2' overture; and the form of the Singspiel was a further hindrance, with the curtain rising on Marzelline's spoken self-communings. The story of the post-mortem, and of the cuts and changes Beethoven made with the help of Stephan von Breuning, has been touched upon earlier. Even in its revised two-act version the 1806 revival was ill-fated: *Fidelio* was put to rest for eight years until the Congress of Vienna in 1814, when a new librettist, Treitschke, was engaged to make further revisions.

Treitschke started off well by reversing the order of the first two numbers and leading straight into music with the Jaquino-Marzelline duet, its A major following naturally in the wake of the new E major overture. If the domestic scene with its knockings on the door reminds one of Figaro and Susanna and presents Beethoven at his most Mozartian, the dramatic situation is very different. Jaquino has lost Marzelline to Fidelio, at least for the time being, and her own C minor-major aria is also more effectively placed *after* the duet has clarified the triangular predicament. In 1805 the scene had been prolonged by a trio in which the jailor Rocco, Marzelline's father, had expounded on the topic of 'marry in haste, repent at leisure', thereby delaying the entry of Leonore herself and the moving quartet-canon 'Mir ist so wunderbar', in which the music at once plumbs a new depth of feeling. The canon has been criticised for not differentiating between the characters, but Ernest Newman made the human observation that Beethoven, having brought Leonore on to the stage, could now only see the ironic situation through her eyes, whether the plight of the half-jilted Jaquino or the mundane attitude of Rocco. Rocco's down-to-earth aria about money, apparently omitted in 1806 but restored in 1814, is, however, important since it has a backlash when Pizarro offers to bribe him into connivance at the murder of Florestan. The following trio, no. 5 in the final version is memorable for Leonore's resolute display of courage, 'Ich habe Mut!', and for the subtle but powerful contrast between her contribution and Marzelline's.

This ended the original first act, but the 1806 and 1814 versions moved on into the march that accompanies the arrival of the governor Pizarro and the guards. The news of the impending visit by the Minister to inspect the prison is the cue for Pizarro's vengeance aria 'Ha! Welch ein Augenblick!', a stormy D minor movement that was pruned here and there and greatly improved in its treatment of the guards' asides, which had been a barely audible background in the 1805 version. Their subdued comments were to be clarified by a six-bar rest from Pizarro and a dramatic modulation from D to B flat, the eventual key of the liberating trumpet-call in the second act and well known in its final form from the third *Leonore* overture. The duet in which Pizarro tells Rocco of his plan to dispose of Florestan is splendidly through-composed, ranging from sinister unison passages to the abrupt wind-chords at the fatal words 'Ein Stoss! – und er verstummt!' An important stroke in the final revision was the removal of the charming but embarrassingly redundant duet for Marzelline and Leonore, with its symbolic concertante parts for violin and cello. This originally separated Leonore's own aria from the Pizarro-Rocco duet, with a drastic loss of tension and continuity. In 1806, perhaps at Breuning's suggestion, there had been a move in the right direction by interchanging the numbers so that Leonore's scena preceded the Marzelline episode; but in the Treitschke version she enters far more dramatically with a new recitative, 'Abscheulicher! Wo eilst du hin?', suggesting that she has not only observed Pizarro and Rocco but overheard or half-overheard the plot to kill her husband. This change may have been influenced by Paer's *Leonore*, which had meanwhile reached Vienna. In her aria, too, the elaborate fioritura was simplified and made more purposeful, doubtless to the satisfaction of the first Leonore, Anna Milder, who took part in all three productions (see Ex.37).

The traditional scena, with its recitative, aria and cabaletta, was flexible enough to convey the emotions, reflections and aspirations of a character while effectively displaying a singer's versatility. It had served well for Mozart's Countess in *Figaro*, and it enabled Beethoven to fulfil his character studies of Leonore and, in due course, of Florestan. If the success of an opera also depends on the appropriate use of a chorus, Leonore's request (originally Marzelline's) that the prisoners should be allowed a brief airing in the grounds of the prison was a stroke of genius that produced one of the most moving moments in all opera. (Did she hope to see Florestan among them?)

Ex. 37

(1805) [Adagio]

die Lie — — — be wird's er - rei — — — — chen.

(1814) [Adagio]

die Lie — — be, die Lie-be wird's er- rei — — — chen.

The introduction to the Prisoners' Chorus is marvellously wrought, with its tentative string harmonies so evocative of a groping from darkness to light, and the bassoon and clarinet figure that so surprisingly derived from sketches for the finale of the Fourth Piano Concerto. In the extended finale of Act 1 the greatest achievement of the 1814 version was the removal of Pizarro's second aria, with its chorus of guards, in favour of an ensemble that projected the varied emotions and schemings against the background of a second chorus from the prisoners as they return to their cells. There is nothing here for superficial applause: instead of the commonplace sabre-rattlings of 1805 the act ends with the gentlest postlude in the orchestra.

The second act of the 1814 *Fidelio*, despite some important changes of detail, followed the general plan of the Act 3 of 1805 up to the halfway mark: Pizarro's frustration by Leonore's dramatic disclosure ('First kill his wife!') and the timely intervention of the trumpet-calls announcing the Minister's arrival. Thereafter it differed radically. In the early versions there was no scene-change, the denouement being enacted in the dungeon instead of the bright daylight of the parade-ground. Yet there was loss as well as gain in 1814, especially in the severe compression of the reunion duet for Leonore and Florestan, from which some beautiful music was excised. In fact the rejected version had much in its favour, with the couple left alone in the dungeon and still uncertain of their safety; and the 'O namenlose Freude' duet forming the climax of an extended scene instead of bursting forth spontaneously. This was the one legacy from Beethoven's work on *Vestas Feuer*, which may account for the uncomfortable word-setting in the new context; and here the revision in 1814 lessened the vocal strain, threw the emphasis more aptly on the word 'Freude' but lost the united abandon of the original:

Ex. 38

In fact the final scene in the *Fidelio* we know is a foregone conclusion, whereas in 1805 the drama continued. All three versions, however, quoted and developed the theme from the 1790 'Joseph' Cantata as Leonore was given the privilege of unlocking her husband's fetters.

Several points in the first part of the act justify the occasional revival of the earlier *Leonore*. The refashioning of Florestan's recitative was beneficial, and the new cabaletta, in which his vision of the 'angel' Leonore is marvellously depicted by a solo oboe, was an inspiration; but the rejected F minor close, more tragic and resigned, was also revealing of his true character. The melodrama, with the whisperings of Rocco and Leonore offset by orchestral fragments, may have belonged to 1805, though surely not its reference to Florestan's oboe theme? Most of the other changes were prunings, as with the long introduction to the grave-digging duet; but the addition of the contrabassoon, and of the swirling semiquavers at the rolling back of the stone, were other inspired strokes. The new change of scene in mid-act, however, created a hiatus and an embarrassingly long wait in most productions, though this could have been prevented by having a smaller and quickly removable set for the dungeon scene. Hence there arose the tradition of playing the 'Leonore no. 3' at this point. Although followed by Mahler, Toscanini and other famous conductors, the idea is now generally frowned upon. The pros and cons may be debated: it is wholly relevant to the opera, can cover up an awkward break, and invariably brings down the house: but it has the disastrous result of reducing the musical effect of the final scene. Strictly speaking, one may have *Fidelio* or 'Leonora no. 3' but not both at once – which is why Beethoven removed it after the 1806 production.

The key-scheme of *Fidelio* makes an absorbing study. All three 'Leonore' overtures are in C major, the opera's final key of liberation, whereas that to *Fidelio* is in E major, the key of hope and heroism in Leonore's aria. The music of the prison favours flat keys: Rocco's aria, the march, the prisoners' choruses, the trumpet-calls are in B flat; Florestan's recitative and aria are in F minor and A flat, turning to F major at his vision of Leonore and again at his actual moment of freedom. C major would seem to be the tonal centre of gravity, though apart from the final scene it is confined, except in passing, to Marzelline's Act 1 aria, actually in C minor and major, but originally planned in C major from the start. This was in any case a neutral situation in relation to the main plot, and it is more rewarding to note that in the second and third 'Leonore' overtures Florestan's aria appears in A flat in the introduction but is elevated to Leonore's E major when it is transformed into the second subject of the Allegro, eventually reaching the mean of C major on its final statement.

In spite of his problems with *Fidelio* Beethoven continued in his search for operatic subjects, and there is no place here to list the many librettists he approached, or who approached him. Several have been mentioned in the biographical chapters. After the further revival of *Fidelio* in 1822 Beethoven took Grillparzer's proposal of *Melusine* seriously, and the poet's suggestion that a recurring theme could be associated with the title-role throughout might have produced a pre-Wagnerian Leitmotif if Beethoven had not shelved the project. He had, however, maintained some contact with the stage through incidental music, and mention must first be made of his music for *Egmont*, composed in 1809 and 1810 partly out of his admiration for Goethe but also inspired by the subject of heroism and self-sacrifice. His devotion to the liberating hero of the Netherlands must also have stirred up thoughts of his own Flemish ancestry.

The music comprised the well-known overture, four interludes, two songs for Egmont's beloved Clara or Klärchen, and a touching orchestral piece depicting her own tragic end; a melodrama accompanying Egmont's thoughts on the eve of his execution; and finally, after the fall of the curtain, the Symphony of Victory so familiar to concertgoers as the F major blaze of glory from the end of the overture. Again one questions the effect of the finality of the overture on the more leisurely pace of the drama, since within so few minutes it symbolises the dominating force of the Spanish oppressor, the Duke of Alba, and in the Allegro the rebellious fervour of Count Egmont, with the coda clearly depicting his execution, the uprising of his people and the posthumous triumph of his spirit.

The overture *Coriolan*, dating from 1807 and written not for Shakespeare but for a play by Heinrich von Collin, was first heard in a concert performance and is another example of the power of music transcending the spoken word. As with *Egmont*, though in a somewhat freer manner, it adapts the principles of sonata form to the expression of human emotions and conflicts. Once again we witness, in the aural sense, the tragic destruction of the hero but with no aftermath of triumph: even the consoling E flat second subject turns to the minor key before the final collapse and disintegration of the C minor Coriolan 'motif'. Such pathos, with music as the servant of dramatic truth, had been marvellously expressed in the Funeral March of the *Eroica*; but in the two overtures the compression and economy of material are astounding, giving them a hold over music-lovers who know little or nothing of their backgrounds.

Beethoven's spirit could not respond so earnestly in the overtures and incidental music for Kotzebue's *Ruins of Athens* and *King Stephen*, written in 1811 for the opening of the new Imperial Theatre in Pest the following year. They are ostensibly imbued with national fervour and pay implicit homage to the Austro-Hungarian throne. In the former play, patriotism was carried to extremes as Minerva, daughter of Zeus, awoke from her long sleep to find Athens in ruins, Greek civilisation extinct, but Pest somehow thriving under benevolent rulers. *King Stephen*, described as Hungary's first benefactor, expressed similar sentiments, and Beethoven's music for both amounted to a medley of marches and choruses, with occasional recitatives, arias and melodramas. Little of it is heard today, except perhaps for the Dervishes' Chorus and the Turkish March from *The Ruins of Athens*, the latter having already served as the theme for the piano variations op. 76. Even the loosely constructed overtures have barely survived, and it is easy to understand the London Philharmonic Society's cool reception of them if they were expecting another *Egmont*. Beethoven also wrote incidental music for plays by Kuffner and Treitschke, but a further word is called for about *Leonore Prohaske*, a play by Dunckner involving the heroism of a female warrior. Shades of another Leonore must have crossed his mind here. Although banned from performance for political reasons, Beethoven's contributions (1815) had included a vocal romance with harp, a melodrama with harmonica, and – at Dunckner's request – an orchestral version of the Funeral March from the op. 26 Piano Sonata.

The opening of the Josephstadt theatre in Vienna in 1822 called forth an important work, the overture *Die Weihe des Hauses*, as well as adaptations of some of the music for *The Ruins of Athens* and a new chorus with soprano and solo violin to words by Carl Meisl. In the overture Beethoven paid deference to his admired Handel, both in the grandeur of the introduction and in the neo-Baroque fugal style of the Allegro con brio. The introduction is in fact grand enough to embrace four distinct phases or stages: after the opening chords, a broad ceremonial theme given first to the wind and then taken up by the full orchestra; some trumpet fanfares in quicker tempo with an excited bassoon counterpoint in scales; a still more contrapuntal episode on a staccato subject with (dare one say?) a touch of Rossini about it; and a passage of warm lyrical repose preceding the lead into, or up to, the fugal Allegro. Here the contrapuntal texture is pursued with immense vigour and monothematicism as in other late Beethoven works, and in a 'con brio' performance the energetic cross-accents should dispel any feeling of pastiche or pedantry.

Beethoven's music for the theatre was varied, sporadic and uneven. In opera it seemed that after *Fidelio* no subject was capable of holding him, though his treatment of words in the finale of the Ninth Symphony and even of the text in the *Missa Solemnis* continued to show his colossal dramatic potential. Even when absorbed in the late quartets he planned to compose a tenth symphony. If he had survived his last illness, opera might still have drawn him back.

12

Choral music

By comparison with Haydn, Mozart, Schubert or Cherubini, Beethoven's output of choral music, like his music for the stage, was small and of widely varying importance. Only the *Missa Solemnis* and the finale of the Ninth Symphony can claim almost universal acceptance as towering masterworks. One may occasionally hear his earlier Mass in C or, more rarely, his only oratorio, *The Mount of Olives*; but it seems to require a centenary, or a special act of homage or curiosity, to rescue and reassess a cantata like *Der glorreiche Augenblick* or even the more modest *Meeresstille*. Since the Fantasy op. 80 is primarily a work for piano and orchestra with a surprise vocal ending it has been discussed with the concertos, while the Ninth obviously takes its place with the other symphonies.

Yet the most impressive works of Beethoven's early years had been the 'Joseph' and 'Leopold' cantatas commissioned in 1790 by the Lese-Gesellschaft at Bonn. One may regret but understand the 'various reasons' that prevented them being heard at the time – delayed completion, unforeseen difficulty and lack of rehearsal – and that frustrated a plan to perform one of them at Mergentheim the following year, but their subsequent neglect is surprising. Did Beethoven, who wrote nothing comparable for chorus for over a dozen years, forget them so soon; and surely his friends Simrock and Waldstein, must have been aware of their importance, or for that matter Haydn, who is said to have accepted Beethoven as a pupil after seeing the score of one of them? Political implications probably played a part here: they were 'occasional' music and the occasions had passed. The history of the autographs is a strange one. In 1813 they were in the catalogue of the Baron de Beine's music library. They were then acquired by Hummel, who made no attempt to perform or publish them, leaving them for his heirs to dispose of, eventually, in an auction at Leipzig in 1884, after which their next owner, the Viennese writer Armin Friedmann, showed them to the critic Eduard Hanslick. As a result the 'Joseph' Cantata received its first performance in Vienna that year, and in 1888 they were both published as a supplement to the Breitkopf collected edition of Beethoven's works.

It was of the 'Joseph' Cantata that Brahms wrote to Hanslick: 'Even if there were no name on the title-page none other could be conjectured– it is Beethoven through and through.' The texts for both cantatas were by Severin Anton Averdonk, whose sister Johanna, a singing pupil of Beethoven's father, had shared in the composer's first concert as a prodigy at Cologne in 1778. Of the two works the 'Joseph' Cantata is the more striking for its depth of feeling and its prophecies, the sentiments of grief and gratitude being more potent than those formally welcoming a successor, who was in fact not destined to live up to the ideals and reforms of Joseph II. Averdonk's German text depicted Joseph as a benevolent ruler who had defeated the monster of Fanaticism and led his people from darkness into light. The opening and closing choruses, expatiating on the subject of death, were set by Beethoven in a stark C minor with impressive unisons and chords alleviated by delicate woodwind figures, though there is great variety of texture in the choral treatment, and melodic warmth at the move to E flat major, in which the first chorus ends. A bass and a soprano enlarge in turn on the deceased's good deeds, and it is in the soprano's first aria that we have the pre-glimpse of *Fidelio* at the words, equally appropriate to Leonore and Florestan, 'Da stiegen die Menschen ans Licht'. The parallel is strengthened by the choral background to the aria, and in the Cantata, which Beethoven did not ask of his Leonore at this point, the wide compass of the vocal line symbolises the ascent from darkness into light.

If the 'Leopold' Cantata gave less opportunity for such heartfelt expression, its welcoming character calling for conventional jubilation with trumpets and drums, the text afforded some retrospective glances. The opening soprano recitative, 'Er schlummert', seems a direct reference to the fourth section of the previous cantata, though there is nothing as arresting as the C minor choruses. The final paean in D major was however Beethoven's first attempt to express universal rejoicing, and must arouse distant thoughts of the Ninth Symphony as Averdonk appropriates, or chances on, the words from Schiller's Ode, 'Stürzet nieder, Millionen'.

Discounting one or two unison settings, including Metastasio's 'O care selve' in 1794 and the ephemeral 'Kriegslied' of 1797,

Beethoven's next significant work with chorus was *Christus am Oelberge* or *The Mount of Olives*. He admitted that it was written in great haste for the performance at the Theater an der Wien in April 1803, and it was twice revised before its publication in 1811 as op. 85. The text, prepared with the help of Franz Xaver Huber, was concerned with Christ's arrest and agony before the crucifixion, and may have been associated in his mind at that time with the more general theme of heroism and self-sacrifice that was soon to draw him to the subject of *Leonore* and later to Goethe's *Egmont*. Yet his one oratorio, which had several revivals during his life and some vogue in the Romantic period, has long dropped from the normal repertory. Although it is not hard to find reasons, such as inconsistency of style and uneven invention, *Christus* was an important work in his development. It gave him his first real experience of working with a chorus; and its markedly operatic style, with the alternation of recitatives, arias and ensembles, was a further step towards the first version of *Fidelio*.

The slow orchestral prelude, beginning in the fairly remote region of E flat minor but drifting to the dominant of C minor for the first of Christ's recitatives, sets a suitably anguished mood with muted strings. Its occasional consoling modulations are offset by outbursts of diminished-seventh harmony, the stock-in-trade for effects of drama and pathos but still of service to the judicious composer. The introduction is itself prefaced with a solemn unison arpeggio on horns, bassoons and trombones. One almost expects it to recur as a motif, knowing how resourcefully Beethoven had treated a similar figure in his D minor Piano Sonata of the previous year, but here it is purely introductory. According to Schindler, Beethoven later had misgivings over his setting of Christ's words in a declamatory operatic manner. He had, incidentally, no knowledge of Bach's *St Matthew* and *St John* Passions, which were still unpublished and virtually unknown at that time. His studies in recitative had come mostly from Salieri and, indirectly, from the works of Carl Heinrich Graun. In *Christus* the recitatives seem conventional and unimaginative for a subject which above all demands a reverential treatment. There is greater conviction in Christ's first aria, in which the principles of sonata form are effectively adapted to the emotions of anguish, trust and despair, reflected in the moves from C minor to E flat major, and from C major back to C minor. The problems of vocal contrast were solved by the appearance of a Seraph as observer and intermediary, though the soprano roulades and cadenzas seem oddly out of place alongside Gabriel's meaningful coloratura in Haydn's *Creation*.

There is however more to admire in the varied treatment of the chorus, from the accompanying of the Seraph's first aria to its cumulative effect as the soldiers come to pursue and bind the Saviour. Even here the clichés of opera are not far away, though the appearance of Peter produced a more fitting operatic trio. On the whole there is a shortage of the genuine contrapuntal writing that could have strengthened the impact of the ensembles and choruses: the fugal coda of the Seraph's aria is short-lived, and the final chorus also abandons its promising fugatos for more unanimous, though musically mundane, shouts of praise and joy.

Whereas Beethoven's only oratorio preceded his work, in fact his labour of love, on the first two versions of *Fidelio*, his next choral work, the Mass in C, came in the aftermath of that experience. It was, however, his first mass-setting, and despite its lukewarm reception at Eisenstadt by Prince Nikolaus Esterhazy ('What is this you have done again, Beethoven?') his letters suggest that he was proud of his achievement. It is bound to be partially eclipsed for us by the overwhelmingly greater *Missa Solemnis*, but nor is it fair to compare it with Haydn's last six masses, as Prince Nikolaus was bound to do. Haydn came to them with almost half-a-century of choral experience behind him; Beethoven, with a supreme mastery of instrumental forms, was faced with his eternal problem of word-setting and, in the case of the Mass, the additional requirements of the liturgy.

The intimacy of the setting is established in the first bar where, without orchestral preamble, the choral basses quietly usher in the opening Kyrie. Any risk of blandness in the largely diatonic phrases that follow is avoided by gentle modulations, even within the first sentence, where a touch of E major harmony foretells a more decisive move in the 'Christe eleison' section. There is distinction, too, in the informal interplay between solo voices and chorus that provides constantly varying textures throughout the whole Mass, placing it above its Viennese rivals of the time, *pace* Esterházy and always excepting Haydn. Mozart's C minor Mass and his Requiem were by now beyond direct comparison as high points of an altogether earlier Classicism. In the Gloria, Beethoven's more homophonic style called for the dramatic changes of pitch, key and dynamics that were to characterise the *Missa Solemnis*, as in the sudden hush and modal effect at the words 'adoramus te':

Ex. 39

Notice also the independence of the orchestral bass, which develops a motif heard earlier from the chorus. For the 'Qui tollis' Beethoven moved to F minor, Florestan's key of despair, once more showing the power of association: here the alto leads, with effective choral asides, and thereafter the other soloists enter contrapuntally, but the unison climax at 'ad dexteram patris' is another forward-looking gesture. The 'Quoniam' is also a splendid construction, with the grand chordal opening giving way to vigorous fugal treatment at 'cum sancto spiritu'. Both this fugue and the later one at 'et vitam venturi' are carried through with no trace of pedantry to their homophonic climaxes of Amens, showing a marked advance on the more self-conscious fugal writing in the oratorio of four years before. The 'cum sancto spiritu' fugue has a curious affinity with the Allegro theme of the second and third *Leonore* overtures, which seems more fully and consciously manifest in the accompaniment to the closing bars of the Gloria.

The Credo, though it has none of the blazing intensity of that in the *Missa Solemnis*, is also a highly original conception, beginning with hushed reiterations of the word before a dramatic crescendo completes the phrase 'in unum Deum', but the reiteration 'credo, credo' was a typical feature of the *Missa* as well. There is a parallel too in the hushed treatment of the Sanctus, throwing into relief the jubilant outbursts of 'Pleni sunt coeli' and the brief concluding 'Hosanna'. This last is traditionally recalled after the Benedictus, in which a tenderly intimate mood is set at once by the four soloists unaccompanied. The sparing use of the orchestra, which called for the luxury of double woodwind but excluded the expected trombones, is a feature of the closing sections; and at the end Beethoven prolonged the 'Dona nobis pacem' by recalling the music of the opening Kyrie, perhaps too briefly to make its point. Such subtleties were evidently lost on its early critics, but Beethoven knew that he had treated the text in a rare manner and seemed confident of its eventual success. When Breitkopf and Härtel turned it down he offered it to them as a free gift rather than allowing it to remain unpublished, adding that it was especially close to his heart. In spite of this it did not appear in print until 1812, in which year he wrote his incidental music for *King Stephen* and *The Ruins of Athens*. These, and the Fantasy op. 80 with its choral finale, have been dealt with elsewhere; but two subsequent cantatas must be mentioned here.

Der glorreiche Augenblick or 'The Glorious Moment', an elaborate and grandiose setting of a text by Weissenbach, was composed in 1814 to celebrate the Congress of Vienna. The approaching end of the Napoleonic wars and the dissolution of the Habsburg or 'Holy Roman' Empire called forth a triumphant paean of praise and optimism, scattered with such topical slogans as 'Europa steht!', 'Heil Vienna dir und Glück!' (the subject of an extended fugue), and significantly 'Stolze Roma trete zurück!' The expedient patriotic sentiments led to a work more interesting for its handling of large forces and its textural experiments than its musical inspiration. There are for example important concertante parts for solo cello and especially for solo violin, the latter weaving arabesques while the spirit of Vienna, personified in a soprano solo, echoes the exhortations of Schiller's 'Ode to Joy': 'Alle die Völker freundlich küssen'. Both the Benedictus of the *Missa* and parts of the finale of the Ninth could be found in embryo here; and the last chorus, beginning with a simple song for women's and children's voices, has a cumulative effect that also looks forward to the Ninth Symphony, reinforced by the cries of 'Welt, Welt' in the countersubject of the succeeding fugue. It was perhaps an ironic error of judgment that caused Beethoven to represent unity by setting three different lines of the text simultaneously in the passage preceding the fugue, thus making the words inaudible, since such a solecism was unavoidable in the fugue itself; but the Cantata ends with unanimous acclamation of the world's 'great moment' to the unbridled sounds of triangle, bass drum and cymbals.

The success of *Der glorreiche Augenblick*, like that of the 'Battle' Symphony, was short-lived, being geared to a passing event without transcending it. Meanwhile Beethoven's heart was more deeply involved in the final version of *Fidelio*. He also wrote two short patriotic choruses, 'Germania' and 'Ihr weisen Gründer glücklichen Staaten', the latter again addressed to the heads of state attending the Congress; but 1815 produced the more worthwhile (and decidedly non-political) setting of Goethe's *Meeresstille und glückliche Fahrt* ('Calm Sea and Prosperous Voyage') op. 112. This brief but attractive cantata, for four-part chorus and orchestra but without soloists, falls naturally into two musical halves: a serene opening Sostenuto depicting the stillness of the waters with dramatic vocal leaps to convey the immensity of the ocean; and a lively six-eight movement representing the voyage and its safe conclusion.

Although the two cello sonatas of 1815 have been cited repeatedly for their intrinsic importance and as harbingers of the late-period masterpieces, the repercussion on Beethoven's vocal writing was long delayed. There were, as before, occasional choral items of little weight, such as the setting of Schiller's *Gesang der Mönche*' (1817) for unaccompanied ensemble, or Stein's 'Hochzeitlied' (1819) with piano accompaniment. The more significant songcycle *An die ferne Geliebte* (1816) must await discussion with Beethoven's other songs, and it may be argued that a piano sonata, the 'Hammerklavier' op. 106, had a more direct bearing on his two greatest works involving a chorus, both of which inherited its colossal time-scale: the Ninth Symphony and the *Missa Solemnis*.

The latter, like the earlier C major Mass, was prompted by an occasion, though one of greater personal importance to Beethoven than the Esterházy commission: the enthronement of his friend and pupil the Archduke Rudolph as Archbishop of Olmütz in March 1820. Such an event suggested a setting of unprecedented grandeur, and in fact the *Missa Solemnis*, or Mass in D, was not completed until 1823, over three years too late for its original purpose.

Beethoven's attitude to religion may have been unorthodox, but his belief in a personal Deity can hardly be in doubt on the strength of his last works alone. Moreover, as his *Tagebuch* shows, his work on the great Mass was preceded and accompanied by a diligent study of ecclesiastical styles. Yet the arbitrary border-line between sacred and secular music had long been breached. Was it profane of J.S. Bach to incorporate concerto movements in church cantatas, or of Haydn when he praised the Lord with a cheerful voice and in the language of his quartets and symphonies? Conversely the *Missa Solemnis* must have seemed too vast, and in parts too dramatic and therefore too secular, for liturgical use, though this was apparently Beethoven's original intention for his Archduke-Archbishop. The *Missa Solemnis*, like Bach's B minor Mass, normally receives a concert performance even when performed in a cathedral festival. Its scale has long been taken for granted, and with it Beethoven's hard-earned skill in through-composing its great sections and sub-sections. Besides the strong characterisation of its clauses it unfolds with an overwhelming sense of unity and, one must admit, a symphonic inevitability. The five movements still correspond with the conventions or 'ordinary' of the Mass: Kyrie, Gloria, Credo, Sanctus and Agnus Dei; but their musical expression is unique in reconciling respect for tradition with the most intense personal fervour only possible in an 'enlightened' society.

The opening Kyrie impresses at once with its stability of key, compared with which the rapid inflections of the Mass in C are bound to pale. An orchestral prologue sets forth the harmonic structure of the choral entry, with clarinet, oboe and flute deputising in advance for the solo voices that are to flow so intimately from the choir's reiterations of 'Kyrie'. There is however a gravitation from D major to its near-relation B minor that at last produces the middle section of this ternary movement, the 'Christe eleison', with dramatic implications underlined by a change from alla breve to 3/2 and a more urgent tempo. Here the resolute minims for 'Christe' and the flowing crotchets for 'eleison' seem a sublime legacy and apotheosis of the second-species exercises in counterpoint that Beethoven had worked years before for Albrechtsberger. As this section closes in F sharp minor the return of the 'Kyrie' is managed by the simple manoeuvre of superimposing the original D major chords on the fading minor third of F sharp-A natural.

Beethoven's choice of D major for the *Missa Solemnis* was significant, reflecting his love of Handel and the Baroque associations with resonant open strings, trumpets and drums. In fact one could hardly imagine the Hallelujah Chorus, or the Gloria and Sanctus of Bach's B minor Mass in any other key. The D major of Beethoven's Kyrie had, however, been warmly expressive, with new departures in its closing section: a move to the subdominant for the choral entry, and a coda to restore the balance and crown the movement. In the Gloria the initial outburst of energy is carried through with the utmost brilliance. Here the word-painting called for abrupt mood-changes but with no change of tempo: the sudden *p* at 'et in terra pax' and the *pp* at 'adoramus te', in sharp contrast to the vigorous fugal treatment of 'glorificamus te'. There is however a broadening of tempo and a move to B flat – a recurring mediant relationship in the Mass as a whole – for the more tenderly flowing counterpoint of the 'Gratias agimus tibi' in which the tenor solo leads. Such changes in expression, from the gentlest human warmth to the most awe-inspiring grandeur, irradiate the first part of the Gloria, with the rising opening motif serving as an orchestral ritornello, until the mood alters radically at 'Qui tollis peccata mundi'. At this point the wind, led by the first clarinet, usher in a Larghetto in F major, moving back to D major for the choral restatement and with a dramatic diminished-seventh emphasis on the word 'peccata'. The climax at 'qui sedem ad dexteram patris' is one of several places where the choral sopranos are hard put to it to enunciate the words on a high B flat. With the 'miserere nobis' the range of keys widens, though it begins in D flat and closes on a pedal C sharp, its enharmonic. A subdued drumroll then heralds the 'Quoniam', which moves with grand orchestral gestures from A major via C major to the home-key of D major. It is important to note these keys, for the effect of C major in close context gives a modal flavour to the harmony that is further exploited at the end of the Gloria, which meanwhile launches into its final and grandest phase, a colossal fugal setting of 'in gloria Dei patris':

Ex. 40

The Handelian grandeur of the subject and the melismatic treatment of the word 'gloria' are counterbalanced by the Beethovenish sforzati and an unrelenting *ff* that is maintained for over sixty bars, with the countersubjects and subsidiary parts providing a continuous flood of Amens. When the whole texture suddenly fades, the solo voices begin a stretto on the same subject, lightly supported by wind-instruments; but this is soon deflected through a cycle of gentle but rapid modulations on to a deep dominant pedal for a resumption by the chorus, building up a further climax with its own strettos and augmentations. Eventually the Gloria breaks into quicker time for a lively antiphony of Amens with the fugue-subject an equally lively counterpoint; there are the outbursts of C major already mentioned; all of which is a stepping-stone to the final Presto, in which the original 'Gloria' three-four subject is carried to the most vociferous conclusion imaginable.

The Credo is a comparable conception, vast in its scale and its contrasts. The key is B flat, already noted for its mediant relation to D major, and the opening gesture, though personal enough in its emphatic reiteration of the word 'credo', has a grandeur fit to embrace the millions. There is the expected sudden hush at 'et invisibilium', and the dramatic repetition of 'et' is a continuing feature of the setting. Beethoven's counterpoint, it has been said, is more Handelian than Bachian, and the robust fugato at 'consubstantialem Patri' is an example; but the mystery of 'et incarnatus est' looks back to Palestrina in its Dorian spareness. There has been some debate as to whether this phrase should be sung by a solo tenor, as printed in the first edition, or the choral tenors, which makes for greater contrast with the solo quartet's development of it. In any case the scoring of the quartet section is wonderfully delicate and in fact picturesque, with a high flute suggesting the sounds of a symbolic dove, before it breaks into the warm D major harmony of 'et homo factus est'. This is surely one of the Mass's most inspired moments, coming as it does before the agonised D minor of the 'Crucifixus', in which the word 'passus' is handed between the solo voices against a poignant orchestral figure that anticipates the pathos in the first movement of the A minor Quartet op. 132. As in Bach's B minor Mass the music fades away to the phrase 'et sepultus est', but unlike Bach's peaceful resolution Beethoven pauses on a mysteriously unresolved interval of a fourth, adding to the drama of the 'resur-rexit'. It is here that Beethoven breaks in with six bars of unaccom-panied writing, the more astonishing for being declaimed vigorously in Mixolydian harmony with the bracing effect of a B flat triad in the context of B naturals to add to its archaism. The next fully-scored choral section begins with preluding upward scales to depict, more traditionally, the 'et ascendit'.

One might have supposed that the return of the original 'credo' subject, with its new bassoon counterpoints (hard to get across in performance), and its unifying effect in rounding up the remaining clauses of the rubric, would have provided a symmetrical rounding-up of the Credo itself. The final clause 'et vitam venturi saeculi, amen' is however the starting-point of a new double-fugue, first in a leisurely tempo and then, after an abrupt turn from the prevailing B flat to a cadence in D major, in quicker tempo with new countersub-jects. The next choral climax, however, returns to a broader manner altogether. Meanwhile the soloists have been silent, but they now enter as a quartet with a series of long-breathed Amens with chorus and orchestra in a passive role. Their flowing scales are eventually taken over by strings and woodwind; there are two tremendous shouts of Amen from the chorus on root-position B flat chords; after which the Credo ends quietly with a hint of the last fugue-subject in trombones, organ and orchestral basses.

The opening of the Sanctus, far removed from the outgoing splendour of Bach's or the lively jubilation of Verdi's in his *Requiem*, is hushed and inward as in Beethoven's earlier Mass; and the scoring without violins and with violas richly divided is typical of the composer in his moods of wonderment and introspection. One thinks again of the 'sturzt nieder, Millionen' in the Ninth Symphony, and the quiet harping on minor-ninth harmony before the D major outburst of the 'Pleni sunt coeli' strengthens the parallel. The first part of the Sanctus had been confined to the intimacy of solo voices, and many scores indicate this in the short but brilliant sections that follow, 'Pleni sunt coeli' and the first 'Osanna in excelsis', though here the strong orchestral background suggests a mistake and both are usually given to the chorus. In this case the contrast of the succeeding Praeludium, again with its divided lower strings, makes a still greater effect, representing the traditional organ interlude before the 'Benedictus' with its aura of sublime inspiration; though it is actually one of the few places where the organ is tacet until the closing bars. At its close the low-lying harmonies are replaced by an ethereal trio from aloft in the form of a solo violin and two flutes, which hover before descending in gentle sequences, thus initiating the Benedictus with an impression of real physical descent, whether the presence of Christ at the altar or the descent of the Holy Dove. The serene beauty of the Benedictus, in which the solo violin weaves its way as in a concerto while the vocal quartet and then the chorus discourse in a leisurely twelve-eight time, has been adversely criticised: by Sir Michael Costa, who a century ago struck out the solemn brass accompaniment because he thought its rhythm dance-like and therefore profane; and more recently by Martin Cooper, who found the violin solo and its character out of place: 'Indeed', he wrote, 'it would hardly be more unsuitable to introduce a ballerina into the sanctuary.' This is surely taking a backward glance by way of Tchaikovsky. Bach in his own way introduced a florid violin obbligato to the Benedictus in his B minor Mass, and there must be many who sense religious overtones in the slow movement of Beethoven's Violin Concerto. In the Benedictus, incidentally, the violin is silent when the chorus declaim their second 'Osanna', here integrated into the movement, rejoining them in the closing section in which the solo quartet plays no part.

The Agnus Dei is a two-part structure, opening with a grave Adagio in B minor, a rare key for Beethoven, that had only been hinted at in the Sanctus. Here the solo singers dominate in turn, beginning with the bass, and against their eloquent plaints the chorus provides a quiet backcloth to the words 'peccata mundi, miserere', now treated with far more restraint and resignation than in the Gloria. The pathos is intensified when a quaver counterpoint in the violins unfolds above the repeated crotchets of the 'miserere', including a hushed and wondrous move to the Neapolitan harmony of C major. At the end a tenderly expressive transition restores the key of D major and the lilting six-eight rhythm of the 'Dona nobis pacem' introduces the final stage of the work. It was over this that Beethoven added the words 'a prayer for inner and outward peace'. The warmth of heart in this music is epitomised in a memorable phrase first sung by the chorus unaccompanied:

Ex. 41

It returns later on the solo quartet and dominates the very last pages of the Mass. Meanwhile the falling sixth on the word 'dona' invites a fugal treatment with maybe a conscious tribute to Handel's 'and he shall reign for ever and ever' from *Messiah*. Beethoven's setting is the most overtly dramatic in the whole work. There are two orchestral interludes, the first veering to the 'other' main key of B flat for the ominous, and obviously military, sounds of trumpets and drums, answered by anguished cries of 'Agnus Dei' from the alto, tenor and soprano in turn; the second a Presto in animated counterpoint, developed symphonically but turning yet again to B flat for a more menacing fanfare, this time supported by the full orchestra except for the trombone and the organ, which are traditionally left to support the choral response. When these two nightmarish visions are past, the 'Dona' continues with its heartfelt plea for peace until the phrase quoted above returns to spread its benevolent wings amid wonderfully translucent orchestral colouring. In the otherwise silent bars, quiet drum-beats of a military nature and tuned to the now alien note of B flat are heard fading into the distance. For the first time the memorable phrase is given out 'ben marcato' and by the chorus in full voice, with the subtle and touching change from 'Dona nobis pacem' to 'Dona pacem, pacem'. It is then left for the orchestra to round off the work with six bars of formality, Beethoven's typical way of indicating that all has been said. His letters of the time refer to a second and even a third mass, including one in the unlikely key of C sharp minor; but after the *Missa Solemnis* his only choral music to materialise was to be the finale of the Ninth Symphony.

13

Songs

When Beethoven looked through some of Schubert's songs in his later years and commented on the 'divine spark' in them he probably reflected that his own activity in that field had been comparatively unimportant. Yet he left about eighty songs himself, not including ensembles or the copious folksong arrangements he made for George Thomson of Edinburgh. His solo songs made an oddly varied collection, ranging from early examples of the German Lied to the expansive Italianate manner of *Adelaide*, and from the simple strophic form of the first five Gellert hymns of 1802 to the through-composed song-cycle *An die ferne Geliebte* of 1816. Beethoven's problems with the human voice, much discussed and often exaggerated, were dwarfed in the colossal overall conceptions of the *Missa Solemnis* and the Ninth Symphony; and in this respect it should not be forgotten that Bach could also be accused of writing instrumentally for voices. In any case Beethoven's struggles with vocal declamation have been noted, in his mature studies with Salieri and in the successive versions of *Fidelio*.

As a composer of solo songs with keyboard, however, Beethoven had begun early with two miniature settings in 1783 or 1784, both published in a musical weekly called *Blumenlese: Schilderung eines Mädchens* and *An einen Säugling*, the latter to words by Döhring. The Lied, as a true duet for voice and piano, was still in its infancy, and although Mozart's exquisite *Das Veilchen* was written in 1785, Schubert's earlier Lieder owed much to lesser names like Reichardt and Zumsteeg. In the days of Beethoven's youth the North German school, turning from the widespread influence of Italian opera, had favoured a simple folklike style with the sparest keyboard support. Such songs by Schulz, Hiller and others were presumably well known in Bonn and far closer in spirit to the Singspiel aria than to the Italian models. Like Hiller, Beethoven's teacher Neefe was a prolific composer of Singspiele, though some of his songs, including his settings of Klopstock's love poems, struck a deeper vein of impassioned expression. He undoubtedly kept an eye on his young pupil's vocal as well as instrumental efforts, and there is in fact a touching F minor pathos in Beethoven's next known song, *Elegie auf den Tod eines Pudels*, WoO 110, of 1787.

In 1790, the year of the two cantatas, Beethoven's interest in the solo voice increased. There are the bass arias with orchestra, WoO 89 and 90, written for Joseph Lux, a buffo singer at the Bonn court. The second of these, *Mit Mädeln sich vertragen*, was his first Goethe setting, and its attractive abandon could have come from the simple-hearted Rocco in the first scene of *Fidelio*. Two songs with piano, *An Laura* and *Klage*, WoO 112 and 113, returned with subtler refinement to the folklike manner of the earliest ones. A more substantial offering was a set of eight songs to words by various poets including Goethe and Bürger. Although attributed to Beethoven's last years in Bonn (1790–2) some, like nos 3 and 4, may have been completed and were certainly adapted or re-used after his arrival in Vienna; and the group as a whole was destined to appear as op. 52 in 1805.

Most of the op. 52 songs are strophic and of the simplest construction, with the piano part largely content to double the vocal line, a tendency so contrary to the real flowering of the Lied, yet to be followed in many of the later songs, more appropriately maybe in the Gellert hymns. In fact op. 52 no. 1, a setting of Claudius's *Urians Reise um die Welt*, written to be sung 'with humour', has all the feel of a student's song, with its fourteen verses and recurring four-bar chorus. The others are obviously solo songs, some very brief like the last four, and all with Romantic overtones and picturesque piano codettas. Nos 3 and 4, Bürger's *Das Liedchen von der Ruhe* and Goethe's *Maigesang*, are more extended, with finely drawn melodic lines and shapely cadence-phrases that already look forward to Schubert. There are sketches for other songs dating from Beethoven's early Vienna years: for Rousseau's *Que le temps me dure*, with alternative settings, and for Goethe's *Erlkönig*, which was eventually published in 1897 in a completed version by Reinhold Becker, though inevitably overshadowed by Schubert's.

More significant is the setting of Bürger's *Seufzer eines Ungeliebten*, which Beethoven linked with its sequel, *Gegenliebe*, in a bipartite operatic manner – tripartite if one considers the opening recitative – and as a miniature 'scena' it seems to call for the orchestra that he employed in *Ah perfido!* a year or so later. The theme of the *Gegenlied* 'cabaletta', in which despondent love is at last requited, was to be adopted in the 'Choral' Fantasy op. 80. Meanwhile two Matthisson settings date from 1794 and 1795: *Opferlied* WoO 126 and *Adelaide* op. 46. *Adelaide*, a long through-composed song in two sections, slow and fast, may be criticised for subjugating the text to the principles of sonata development and the arbitrary use of harmonic clichés, but the attractive sweep of the music assured its popularity and the gratitude of singers. The complaint over its endless repetitions of word-phrases can hardly be levelled at the touchingly varied settings of the title-name. Its quiet reiteration at the very end is a gentle masterstroke that the Schubert of *Gretchen* must surely have admired. The *Opferlied* is quite another matter, hymnlike in the manner of the Gellert songs to come. Beethoven revised it in 1802, and more extensively in two much later choral versions. A comparison between the original opening and the 1824 version for soprano, chorus and orchestra op. 121b is revealing: the downward arpeggio remains though its position changes, and austerity has given way to tender compassion:

Ex. 42

With the exception of one or two short and isolated settings in the later 1790s — Herrosee's *Zärtliche Liebe* and Metastasio's *La partenza* — Beethoven's absorption in instrumental music, especially in the newly-conquered fields of the symphony and quartet, led him away from song composition. However in 1802, in the aftermath of the Heiligenstadt crisis, he turned to the simple pious sentiments of the Gellert Odes, which had already been set by C.P.E. Bach forty-five years before. The dedication of Beethoven's six settings op. 48 to

Count von Browne, whose wife died suddenly in May 1803, was a touchingly appropriate gesture. The first five of the hymns are composed in the simplest liturgical manner, unchanged through their many stanzas, but with the most basic keyboard support marked by occasional poignant harmonies, as at the start of *Vom Tode* (no. 3), or brief postludes, surprisingly decorative in *Die Liebe des Nächsten* (no. 2). The grandeur of *Die Ehre Gottes* (no. 4) is proclaimed in bold unison minims that seem a logical growth from the *Opferlied* of 1794. In such diatonic surroundings the emphatic augmented sixth on the word 'Namen' is a solecism that scarcely fits the other verses, but it may be felt to herald the distant modulations of the middle section. The last of the Gellert songs, *Busslied* (no. 6), has a completely different character, a Lied in style, with genuine piano-writing breaking into running counterpoints and routine arpeggios in the quicker major-key section, and only strophic in the freest sense of the term.

From his deeply personal attitude to religion Beethoven moved most readily to themes of friendship, love and nature. In *Das Glück der Freundschaft* op. 88 (1803), a strophic song with a varied and climactic coda, he unfolded a tender melodic line with a flowing accompaniment one could call Schubertian were it not also a forerunner of movements like the terzetto in Act 2 of *Fidelio* or the songlike rondo in the Piano Sonata op. 90. The setting of Sauter's *Der Wachtelschlag* WoO 129, of the same year, is remarkable for its complete emancipation of the piano-part which dominates a miniature drama, beginning with a quiet forecast of the *Pastoral* Symphony's quail and developing its dotted-rhythm motif in climaxes of menacing power. It is easy enough to point to places in the songs of the middle period where the desire for musical unity disrupts the natural word-setting. Beethoven did not always approach Schubert's ability to reconcile the two. His first setting of Tiedge's *An die Hoffnung* op. 32 (1805) illustrates the problem. The recurring triplets in the piano bind the song together and there are many bars where poetic justice is done to all three stanzas, despite the strophic form; but as Leslie Orrey remarked in *The Beethoven Companion*, the stretching out of the phrase 'ein Engel seine Thränen zählt' over a conventional six-four cadence, throwing the weight on to the word 'seine', is less felicitous. Beethoven had good reason to be drawn back to the sentiments of the poem in the depressed and unproductive year of 1813 and, having meanwhile met the poet in Teplitz, he produced a far more elaborate version with introductory recitative and great attention to word-imagery, op. 94.

The experiments with word-setting, obvious enough in the sketchbooks, were advertised more openly in the four very different versions he produced of Goethe's *Nur wer die Sehnsucht kennt*, WoO 134, of 1807 and 1808. The love-theme continues to run through the titles of Beethoven's middle-period songs: *Als die Geliebte sich trennen wollte* WoO 132, with words by Stephan von Breuning; and Reissig's *Lied aus der Ferne* and *Der Liebende*, WoO 137 and 139, of 1809. One former favourite that has worn rather thin with time is Carpani's *In questa tomba oscura* WoO 133, dating from 1807, a simple ternary song in which faithless love is chastised with conventional solemnity and, in the middle section, conventional tremolando effects. In 1809 Beethoven turned again to Goethe for the first three texts of the Six Songs op. 75, beginning with Mignon's song *Kennst du das Land*, which was to receive a later and more Romantically eloquent setting from Liszt. Mignon's longing to return to the childhood scene of the Mediterranean, with its citrus fruit, warm breezes, statues and mountains, was expressed by Beethoven in a simple strophic form with the piano-part yet again doubling the vocal line. The line itself is, however, beguilingly shaped, and each of the three verses has a dual character, turning from a questioning two-four time to a livelier six-eight at the prospect of Mignon's return, 'Dahin! dahin möcht' ich mit dir . . .' In the following year, 1810, Beethoven set three more Goethe poems, and here the first, *Wonne der Wehmut*, comes closest to the Schubertian ideal of the Lied. In fact the 'tears of love', so tenderly reflected in the piano's answering scales, seem to have inspired a miniature masterpiece from the first bar. Within its brief span it includes some deeply poetic modulations and inflections, appropriately at 'wie todt die Welt ihm erscheint' and 'unglücklicher Liebe'. The other two of this op. 83 group, *Sehnsucht* and *Mit einem gemalten Band* neither called for nor received such distinction.

In 1811 Beethoven again produced alternative versions of a song, Stoll's *An die Geliebte* WoO 140, though the variants largely concerned the texture of the accompaniment; and the lean year of 1813 yielded, apart from the new version of *An die Hoffnung*, a brief setting of Herder's *Der Gesang der Nachtigall* WoO 141, in which the piano opens with a full share of bird-calls. The spirit of the Congress of Vienna brought forth *Der Kriegers Abschied* WoO 143 with words by Reissig, and the bare fourteen bars and six verses of Rupprecht's *Merkenstein*, extolling the castle near Baden. Although this seems no more than a hastily-composed anthem or community song its setting as a vocal duet appeared impressively as op. 100, and Beethoven even produced an alternative setting for solo voice and piano WoO 144. Reissig's *Sehnsucht* WoO 146 of 1815–16, another poem of longing with an opening stanza evoking the stillness of the night, was a far more serious matter, and the sketches show the pains Beethoven took to achieve the serenity of the first line. The key of E major and the increasingly elaborate accompaniment for the second and third verses suggest it as a prototype for the variation theme of the op. 109 Piano Sonata of 1820. The simple but subtle diatonic harmony is already typical of Beethoven's third-period manner.

The year 1816 also produced Beethoven's most original contribution to the Lied in the song-cycle or 'Liederkreis' *An die ferne Geliebte* op. 98, a genre to be taken up by Schubert and Schumann and countless successors. Schumann seemed to acknowledge his indebtedness by quoting from the sixth of the songs at the end of the first movement of his Fantasy for piano op. 17. The poems by Jeitteles were unpublished when Beethoven set them and are thought to have been shown to him by a mutual friend, the playwright Ignaz Castelli. Once again the subject of longing and separation, a favourite topic in later song-cycles, exercised its attraction along with the many references to nature and the countryside, eternal sources of inspiration to Beethoven himself. His setting of the six poems, though mostly strophic within themselves, is even more closely woven than in most later cycles, since the whole is through-composed and the songs follow each other without a break. It was Schumannesque rather than Schubertian to recall the music of the first song at the end of the last, and Joseph Kerman has suggested that the closing stanza of no. 1 may have been added by Beethoven to prepare for this return. Such back-references were rare enough in Beethoven's earlier works – the Piano Sonata op. 27 no. 1, the Fifth Symphony – but the recent C major Cello Sonata op. 102 no. 1 (1815) and the A major Piano Sonata op. 101, written shortly after the song-cycle, both indulge in retrospects of their opening bars. With the songs a still closer unity is achieved through the piano's linking progressions, except between nos 3 and 4 (both in A flat) where the voice provides its own link with an expansion of the phrase 'meine Tränen ohne Zahl!'. There is also a symmetry about the poems, their metre, numbers of lines and stanzas (disregarding Beethoven's supposed addition to no. 1) that is matched in the key-scheme of the cycle: E flat, G major, A flat; A flat, C major, E flat. This is unified further by a gradual increase of tempo throughout the first five songs, culminating in the lively 'Es kehret der Maien' with its enthusiastic welcoming of springtime and all its symbolism, set to music of the simplest folklike nature. The sudden change to a more subjective mood, 'Nur ich kann nicht ziehen von hinnen', is one of the cycle's most touching moments, preparing the way for the resigned farewell of no. 6, though it, too, develops an excitedly fervent coda after the return of the theme of the first song.

By comparison with such recent settings as *An die Hoffnung* and *Sehnsucht*, the song-cycle, though charming and effective in its word-painting, marked a return to simplicity in its themes, harmony and textures. Yet such a rediscovery was a compensating trait in Beethoven's late works that seemed to balance the intense intellectualism of movements like the fugue of the 'Hammerklavier' Sonata, so soon to follow. Even the last quartets contained occasional folklike elements alongside their mental strivings and architectural triumphs. The question remains unanswered as to the identity of the 'distant beloved' of the song-cycle, since its formal dedication to Prince Lobkowitz is hardly helpful here. Was it still the Immortal Beloved of 1812 and hence presumably Antonie Brentano? Or in a more general sense did it epitomise Beethoven's lifelong failure to achieve a lasting love relationship?

Beethoven composed few songs in his later years, though two may be singled out for their more intimate revelations. *Resignation* WoO 149, with words by Haugwitz and dating from 1817, is a brief and touching through-composed song, its fragmented melodic line all the more affecting because of its subjective implications. Goeble's *Abendlied* WoO 150, in which a contemplation of the starry heavens turns to thoughts of religion and redemption, is set in E major, a favourite key for such reflections, if we recall Beethoven's remark about the night sky and the slow movement of the second 'Rasumovsky' Quartet so many years before.

Not every one of Beethoven's songs can be mentioned, let alone discussed, in a general survey such as this. It would, however, be unbalanced without a further reminder of the many unaccompanied Italian duets, trios and quartets, mostly on texts by Metastasio, WoO 99, that Beethoven wrote during his first decade in Vienna, partly as a result of his studies with Salieri. Then there are the numerous canons and quips, samples of which will be known to anyone browsing through Beethoven's letters. His folksong arrangements for Thomson do, however, call for a further paragraph.

In all, Beethoven made over 130 arrangements for George Thomson between 1809 and 1816, but their voluminous correspondence dates back much earlier to 1803, when Beethoven seemed to welcome the idea of composing some sonatas incorporating Scottish airs. The sonatas were never written, but the request to arrange Scottish, Irish, Welsh and other folksongs and popular airs was later taken up. The financial attraction during Beethoven's years of crisis must have been an incentive, and the addition of parts for violin and cello to the basic piano accompaniments, a common practice at the time, opened up the market and made for more favourable terms. Beethoven, who wrote to Thomson in French, haggled over money matters as usual and took offence when asked to rewrite some of the 'ritornelli', the preludes and postludes with which he framed the settings. Perhaps they were thought too difficult or unidiomatic, or both. When Beethoven adopted or adapted folksongs he could only make them his own, as he certainly did with the Russian themes in the 'Rasumovsky' quartets. The harmonisation of genuine folksongs, some of them with modal implications, is a debatable practice in any case, but many of Beethoven's versions have great charm and distinction, and there is endless variety in the introductory material. Some of the preludes are surprisingly free and could have set off independent sonata-movements; others derive from the songs, like that to 'Oh sweet were the hours' op. 108 no. 2, with its gracefully undulating triplets; while some, whether at Thomson's instigation or not, were in fact replaced and simplified, such as the drily contrapuntal start to 'The Massacre of Glencoe' WoO 152 no. 5. Beethoven's interest in his task and its possibilities led him to look further afield, or nearer home, for the twenty-three settings of continental folksongs incorporated in WoO 158, which were published not by Thomson but by Breitkopf – and not until 1941! It certainly seems likely that Beethoven's absorption in folk-music and other popular songs had a bearing on certain aspects of his later style, as noted with *An die ferne Geliebte* and even the 'scherzo' of the op. 131 Quartet.

14

Beethoven and posterity

During the Romantic period, which tended to underestimate Mozart and was still rediscovering Bach, Beethoven's influence was arguably more widespread than that of any other individual composer. Even such opposing geniuses as Brahms and Wagner admitted their debts to Beethoven first of all, despite Brahms's growing allegiance to Bach. He has even been blamed for the excesses of the Romantics – 'where the rot set in' was Britten's unfortunate phrase – as though the strong personal element in his music had distorted the fair face of Classicism and encouraged the extremes of self-indulgence. Yet it could be argued that Beethoven's architectural strength and endless concern with form and logic invariably elevated the subjective into the universal, even when the music seems as intensely personal as in the 'Heiliger Dankgesang' of the op. 132 Quartet or the ariosos and fugues of the op. 110 Piano Sonata. But Beethoven's greatest works, born of severe mental conflict and eternal self-criticism, could be viewed from many angles. When Wagner celebrated the founding of Bayreuth to the sounds of the Ninth Symphony he implied that the choral finale had at last broken the bonds of absolute music and paved the way for the fusion of symphonic thought and opera in music-drama. Brahms would have regarded the finale as an exception that proved the rule and pointed to the Classical strength of the previous movements.

Beethoven's universal appeal must be conceded even by the small minority of serious listeners who are unsympathetic to his work as a whole. The eventual realisation of the scope and stature of Bach and Mozart, as well as the increasing revivals of neglected music of all periods, in no way undermined Beethoven's popularity. His symphonies, sonatas and quartets are still mainstays of the repertory, touchstones for the interpreter, and apparently immune from changes of taste or the ravages of time. The most modest music-lover may keep to such well-tried favourites as the 'Moonlight' Sonata or the Fifth Symphony; the more intellectual listener will find an eternal challenge in the complex profundities of the 'Hammerklavier' or the 'Grosse Fuge'; while even those who know their Beethoven well may be continually surprised at the richness and originality of the earlier sonatas and chamber works.

The tacit acceptance of such an inheritance and the sheer weight of its influence have inevitably been questioned from time to time. Some critics have gone to extremes in attempting to denigrate Beethoven, especially when pleading other causes: like Norman Suckling, in his book on Fauré, who ridiculed the long stretches of tonic-and-dominant harmony in the 'Waldstein' Sonata and the *Pastoral* Symphony without considering their relation to Beethoven's revolutionary and long-term treatment of dynamics and tonality. One need only imagine how the rock-like strength of the triumphant C major opening of the finale of the Fifth Symphony would be shattered, in its context, by any change in its elementary but elemental harmonisation. It has been said light-heartedly that Beethoven could do more with the common chord or a couple of notes than any other composer; but the placing of that chord, the choice of those notes, and the long process of trial and error that they so often represent – these are the obvious but vital factors that make the sketchbooks such a revealing and rewarding study. Sibelius summed up this aspect of Beethoven's genius when he wrote home from Vienna during his own formative years and spoke of his own needs as a composer: 'The only thing I must have is criticism, self-criticism. The greatest composer of all, Beethoven, did not have the greatest *natural* talent but he subjected everything he did to the most searching self-criticism and by doing so achieved greatness.'[1]

Beethoven's fame was widespread enough during his lifetime to account for the crowds that flocked to his funeral. Yet he had often scorned the Viennese for their fickle and frivolous taste; and conversely there can have been few of his most serious devotees capable at that time of grasping the full spiritual significance of his very last works. For most of the people of Vienna, from the urchins who dogged his footsteps to Metternich's eavesdropping secret police, Beethoven must have remained a curiosity, an eccentric genius, to be respected for the respect he continued to inspire in the highest artistic and aristocratic circles. His rough outward demeanour, the notorious disorder of his various lodgings, and the fact that he could be

---

[1] Erik Tawaststjerna, trans. R. Layton: *Sibelius*, vol. 1, pp. 86–7.

mistakenly arrested as a tramp, must have been hard to reconcile with his noble and incomparable musical achievements. But the notion that he was ill-bred in all except music reveals a further dichotomy. Cherubini called him 'an unlicked bear' and Goethe spoke of him as 'utterly untamed'; yet the Countess Giulietta Guicciardi, with whom Beethoven had been in love during the first crisis over his deafness, remembered him for his nobility of character, his general culture and refinement. Magdalena Willmann, on the other hand, had rejected him in the 1790s because he was 'ugly and half-crazy'.

Such contrary reports have the ring of half-truths but indicate the strong conflicts in this character, symbolic of the age of turmoil in which he lived, and reflected too in his superhuman struggles with the material of music itself. The notion that he had no general education is also only partly true. Although he had no formal schooling after the age of ten, he had a working knowledge of French and Italian, and was widely read in subjects that interested him, such as philosophy and religion. If not conventionally religious, the composer of the *Missa Solemnis* and the late quartets was hardly the atheist Haydn made him out to be. His library included Bibles in Latin and French along with the great Roman and Greek classics, Homer, Virgil and Plutarch among them. His interest in poetry and drama, with their close relation to music, was to be expected; and his admiration for Goethe and Schiller was matched, if not surpassed, by his love of Shakespeare, whom he knew largely in German translation but cited more than once for his influence on his purely instrumental works. Probably many of these absorptions date back to his post-schooldays in Bonn and the benevolent influence of the Breuning family circle. For his lively interest in contemporary matters, whether war, politics, moral issues, or the music of other composers, we can turn to his letters, his *Tagebuch* and the conversation books. His views on politics and morals in particular may strike one as naive and contradictory, further examples of the conflict between ideas and ideals that seemed so deeply rooted in his nature.

Even the accounts of Beethoven's piano playing are confused enough, allowing for the tragic deterioration that followed in the wake of his growing deafness. His ability to hold an audience spellbound with his improvisations was generally agreed, even when his deafness was too far advanced for him to play in public any more. When it came to details Cramer had found his playing 'inconsistent, expressive but muddled', while Cherubini, who heard him in Vienna in 1805, summed it up as 'rough'. Clementi, a pioneer in piano technique, also spoke of roughness but praised its character and spirit. Rellstab and Schindler left widely contrasted impressions, reflecting Beethoven's changing moods and perhaps his changing manner at different stages of his career, the former describing his 'irresistible fire and mighty force', the latter his 'restraint and economy of movement'. It was Schindler who handed down detailed accounts of Beethoven's playing of specific sonatas, though since he was prone to exaggeration and knew the composer intimately only from 1814 onwards they can hardly be taken at face value. For a flamboyant account of Beethoven's earlier style of extempore playing one cannot resist quoting Ignaz von Seyfried, who was present at his meeting in 1799 with the Salzburg pianist and composer Joseph Wölffl. Wölffl's playing, we are told, was Mozartian and equable, whereas Beethoven improvised in 'the mystical Sanscrit language whose hieroglyphs can be read only by the initiated':

> Now his playing tore along like a wildly foaming cataract, and the conjurer constrained his instrument to an utterance so forceful that the stoutest structure was scarcely able to withstand it; and anon he sank down, exhausted, exhaling gentle plaints, dissolving in melancholy. Again the spirit would soar aloft, triumphing over transitory terrestrial sufferings, turn its glance upward in reverent sounds and find rest and comfort on the innocent bosom of holy Nature.[2]

In simple words Beethoven's improvisations, as expected, revelled in unprecedented extremes of moods and dynamics, taxing the instruments of the time to the utmost.

Yet instrumental (and vocal) limitations were also a source of strength in containing and disciplining a composer's thoughts. With Mozart the five-octave keyboard was hardly a hindrance and more often the mother of invention, so that when parallel passages returned in a higher key and had to be rethought they were usually enhanced in the process. In Beethoven's case some of the makeshift solutions show his frustration, but when keyboards were enlarged he changed his mind about a plan to bring his earlier sonatas 'up to date'. The rewritings could only have proliferated, threatening the

[2] Seyfried, quoted in *Beethoven: Impressions by his Contemporaries*, ed. O.G. Sonneck.

internal unity and the original character and sonority of the works. One exception was the solo part of the Third Piano Concerto, but this was expanded before publication. His attitude to this aspect of performance practice was, however, typically inconsistent: he objected to the liberties Czerny took with the piano part of the op. 16 Quintet, but had no qualms about producing drastic anachronisms in the cadenzas he later wrote for his first two piano concertos. Cadenzas, however, could claim a certain immunity in their nature as written-down improvisations, and this raises the question of improvised embellishments elsewhere, which had been an important feature in Mozart's playing of his own concertos. If this problem arises far less in Beethoven, even in his earlier works, this is because – unlike so many of Mozart's – they were mostly prepared for fairly prompt publication and hence filled in for general use. This did not prevent Beethoven from playing his B flat and C minor concertos from sketched-in solo parts and forgetting to complete them when he sent the scores to the publishers, cases where the first edition obviously takes precedence over the manuscript. This hardly affects the sonatas and chamber music, in which it would seem sacrilege to add or subtract a note; though with the composer's prerogative, and despite his later remarks to Czerny, Beethoven is said to have disconcerted his colleagues by adding unwritten flourishes in the rondo of the piano-and-wind Quintet at its first performance in 1797. He also approved, apparently, when Bridgetower threw in a short cadenza of his own on the violin in response to the piano's C major flourish in the first presto of the 'Kreutzer' Sonata.

Yet an overriding impression of Beethoven's finished works is their meticulous attention to detail, not merely in notes but in articulation and dynamics, despite the outward untidiness and often chaotic look of many of his autographs. His lifelong concern with accuracy is shown in his vehement letters to publishers and copyists, and a close study of any of his large-scale works, like the *Eroica*, will reveal the crucial relation between dynamics, harmony and tonality, on which the overall architectural strength depends. In his later years he set some store by the metronome and even attributed the Berlin success of the Ninth Symphony to this more precise method of indicating speeds; though his metronome marks, deserving of study but applied by a deaf composer with no chance of checking their practical application adequately, have long been a bone of contention and are seldom taken literally. Although the years following his death brought new waves of enthusiasm for his music, re-establishing neglected works like the Violin Concerto and introducing 'private music' such as the sonatas and quartets to the concert-going public, the Romantic age in general took its own unwarranted liberties. It was an age that thought little of replacing the scherzando movement in the Eighth Symphony with the popular Allegretto of the Seventh, or of publishing editions of the piano sonatas that played havoc with the original text at the whim of the virtuoso of the moment. Even Liszt, who gave memorable performances of the 'Hammerklavier', and Hans von Bülow, whose prodigious memory encompassed most of the Classical repertory, were no purists when it came to editing; though in fairness it must be added that Liszt's piano transcriptions of the Beethoven symphonies, so important in their time, were remarkable in reconciling effectiveness with fidelity, and in quite a different category from his virtuoso operatic paraphrases. Conductors with the noblest intentions, like Wagner and after him Weingartner, felt impelled to adjust Beethoven's scoring, notably in the Ninth Symphony, for the sake of balance and in view of the increased scope of horns and trumpets. By the turn of the twentieth century new attitudes reacted against Romantic excesses and liberties. Schnabel showed his devotion to Beethoven, as he was to do to Schubert, by reviving the less-played sonatas and the Diabelli Variations, and later produced a copiously annotated edition of the piano sonatas that nevertheless differentiated clearly between his own marks and the composer's original. Toscanini, with his principle of 'playing as written' and his genius for clarity and unity, also inaugurated a new era of respect for the score. He demolished many spurious traditions by playing the opening of the Fifth Symphony in the main tempo, and taking the Allegretto and the Trio in the Seventh at the speeds implied by Beethoven's markings; though even he made occasional retouches in scoring that would be frowned upon in the still more recent quest for authenticity. The recording age enables the Beethoven student to follow these changing twentieth-century attitudes to interpretation in detail and it is hoped that historic recordings, like Toscanini's, will continue to be available. Furtwängler's far more subjective approach is still influential and his 1951 performance of the Ninth Symphony at the Bayreuth Festival, eloquent but extremely personal, seemed to relive history in emphasising its link with Wagner. When Wagner had conducted it there himself in 1872 one of the violinists had been the 16-year-old Arthur Nikisch, and in due course it was Nikisch who made the first complete commercial recording of a Beethoven symphony, the Fifth, in 1913. Even the briefest historical discography of Beethoven must take note of the continuous reissues of Schnabel's records of the sonatas, concertos and other piano works; and of those made in the 1930s by the Busch Quartet, at once objective and profound and with a miraculous physical and spiritual unity, and especially of the late works.

Meanwhile Beethoven scholarship has grown apace and now demands the precision of an exact science, but the wisdom, humanity and readability of Tovey endure, and there may still be readers for the more romantic French accounts by Romain Rolland. More recent research has gained much from modern methods of detection and the greater ease of communication and cooperation, yet such scholars as Alan Tyson, Joseph Kerman and their colleagues have paid their own tributes to the earlier pioneers: to the analytical revelations of Heinrich Schenker and, going further back, the biographical zeal of Thayer or the researches into the sketchbooks by Gustav Nottebohm. The nineteenth century cannot be written off as an age of irresponsibility to Beethoven. In contrast to the many spurious editions of his works the Breitkopf and Härtel *Gesamtausgabe*, completed in 1888, aimed – like the *Bach-Gesellschaft* – to produce a true statement of the facts and paved the way for the later and still more precise 'Urtext' editions. Nottebohm, however, deserves a new paragraph for the impetus he gave to the study of the sketches.

Born at Lüdenscheid in Westphalia in 1817, Nottebohm moved to Vienna in 1846, where his Beethoven interests yielded an important catalogue of his works and some far-reaching essays and commentaries on the sketches, as noted in the bibliography below. The history of the sketchbooks, which give a unique insight into the workings of a great composer's mind, is fairly well known. Having been preserved carefully by Beethoven himself, they were casually auctioned off after his death with little thought of their importance for posterity. Only a handful of the fifty or more books survived intact, most were widely scattered with unknown destinations, and others mutilated or lost over the years. Nottebohm's difficult task was to locate the existing material and then to decipher Beethoven's rough notes, relating them where possible to known compositions or maybe relegating them to unfulfilled projects. He eventually analysed a fair cross-section of sketches from all periods, drawing attention to differing but complementary methods in the creative process:

the refinement of detail, as in the shaping of a theme or melodic fragment; and the sketching-out of a harmonic plan for a whole movement or section of a movement from which the details will emerge. The *Eroica* was a classic example of this architectural approach, and Nottebohm's commentary on its gradual evolution in the 'Landsberg 6' sketchbook was one of his greatest contributions. As a single-handed enthusiast working over a century ago, he was inevitably selective in his examples and to some extent subjective. Yet Kerman, in the preface to his masterly presentation and analysis of the 'Kafka' miscellany of sketches in the British Museum and after a century's refinement in musicological methods, wrote of Nottebohm: 'He made some mistakes, but it is to be doubted whether many musical scholars have maintained so high a standard of accuracy and objectivity, and so sharp a sense of the relevant, in treating a similar mass of difficult material.'

The existing sketches, spread around the world, still await a systematic publication, entailing expert analysis and the elucidation of Beethoven's hieroglyphics, often unclear or ambiguous and only intended for his own eyes; and for this reason there has been some reluctance on the part of serious musicologists to admit a more popular approach to the subject. It is too facile perhaps to arouse incredulity at the vast gulf between an early sketch, never intended to be played in that form, and the masterpiece that developed from it. Yet a close-up view of Beethoven at work may deepen the music-lover's appreciation of the finished product and provide valuable insights for the performer. No conductor of the *Eroica* or the Ninth should fail to study the sketches which help to clinch or clarify so many interpretative details; nor can pianists or string players afford to miss the new lights thrown by the sketchbooks on the sonatas and quartets, including the cross-influences between different media.

Beethoven's remarks about his approach to composition in general were recalled by Louis Schlösser, composer and court-conductor at Darmstadt, who visited him in 1822 and 1823:

I carry my thoughts about with me for a long time, sometimes a very long time, before I set them down. At the same time my memory is so faithful to me that I am sure not to forget a theme which I have once conceived, even after years have passed. I make many changes, reject and reattempt until I am satisfied. Then the working-out in breadth, length, height and depth begins in my head, and since I am conscious of what I want, the basic idea never leaves me. It rises, grows upward, and I hear and see the picture as a whole take shape and stand forth before me as though cast in a single piece, so that all that is left is the work of writing it down.[3]

Yet the sketchbooks seem to prove that the act of setting pen to paper, even as an aide-memoire, was a vital part of the process. As for the changes, rejections and reattempts, one recalls Carlyle's dictum on 'genius' as being the 'transcendent capacity of taking trouble, first of all'. From that standpoint, and on the evidence of the sketches alone, one might claim that Beethoven was the greatest genius, to our knowledge, that the art of music has ever produced.

[3] Ibid.

Appendix A

Calendar

Year	Age	Life	Contemporary Musicians and Events
1770		Ludwig van Beethoven baptised at Bonn, 17 Dec (born 16 Dec?), son of Johann, Court musician, and Maria Magdalena Leym, née Keverich.	Tartini (78) dies, 26 Feb. Albrechtsberger aged 34, Arne 60, C.P.E. Bach 56, J.C. Bach 35, W.F. Bach 60, Boccherini 27, Cherubini 10, Cimarosa 21, Clementi 18, Dittersdorf 31, Dussek 9, Galuppi 64, Gluck 56, Grétry 29, Haydn 38, Jommelli 56, Kozeluch 16, Martini 64, Méhul 7, Mozart 14, Paisiello 29, Piccinni 42, Salieri 20, Schenk 9, Steibelt 5, Wagenseil 55, Zelter 12.
771	1		Paër born, 1 June.
772	2		Daquin (78) dies, 15 June.
773	3	Death of paternal grandfather, Kapellmeister Ludwig (61), 24 Dec.	Quantz (76) dies, 12 July.
774	4	Caspar Anton Carl (brother) baptised, 8 Apr.	Jommelli (60) dies, 25 Aug. Spontini born, 14 Nov.
775	5	First music lessons from his father.	Boieldieu born, 16 Dec. Crotch born, 5 July.
776	6	Nikolaus Johann (brother) baptised, 2 Oct.	
777	7		Mozart sets out on tour to Munich, Augsburg, Mannheim and Paris, Sept. Wagenseil (62) dies, 1 Mar.
778	8	First public appearance as a keyboard prodigy at Cologne, 26 Mar. Lessons from Court organist, van den Eeden?	Arne (68) dies, 5 Mar. Hummel born, 14 Nov.

Year	Age	Life	Contemporary Musicians and Events
1779	9	Pfeiffer, actor-musician, assists with B.'s tuition.	Boyce (69) dies, 7 Feb.
1780	10		
1781	11	Becomes pupil of Neefe (33) and leaves school to devote himself to music. Other lessons with Koch (organ) and Rovantini (violin). Visits Holland with his mother?	
1782	12	Rapid musical progress with Neefe. B. deputises for him as organist.	Auber born, 29 Jan. J.C. Bach (47) dies, 1 Jan. Field born, 26 July.
1783	13	Assistant harpsichordist in Electoral Kapelle. Publication of Dressler Variations. Neefe reports on B.'s progress in Cramer's *Magazin der Musik*. Three keyboard sonatas, WoO 47, composed.	
1784	14	Death of Elector Maximilian Friedrich, 15 Apr. New Elector, Max Franz, reorganises music at Bonn. B. appointed second organist. Slanderous campaign against Neefe.	W.F. Bach (74) dies, 1 July. Martini (78) dies, 3 Oct. Onslow born, 27 July. Ferdinand Ries born, Nov. Spohr born, 5 Apr.
1785	15	Violin lessons with Franz Anton Ries (30). Neefe's salary restored. Three piano quartets, WoO 36, composed.	Galuppi (79) dies, 3 Jan.
1786	16		Bishop born, 16 Nov. Weber born, 18 Dec.
1787	17	Visits Vienna and plays to Mozart (31) but is hastily recalled to Bonn. Death of mother (40), 17 July.	Gluck (73) dies, 15 Nov.
1788	18	Friendship with von Breuning family and Franz Gerhard Wegeler. Meets Count Waldstein (26).	C.P.E. Bach (74) dies, 15 Dec.
1789	19	Granted half his father's salary to act as head of family. Plays	Outbreak of French Revolution with storming of Bastille,

Year	Age	Life	Contemporary Musicians and Events
		viola in opera orchestra.	14 July.
1790	20	Haydn (58) visits Bonn on his way to London, Dec. B. composes 'Joseph' and 'Leopold' cantatas.	Death of Emperor Joseph II and accession of Leopold II.
1791	21	Visits of Electoral court to Mergentheim and Aschaffenburg. B. plays to Sterkel (41). Righini Variations published. Helps Waldstein by composing music for *Ritterballet*.	Czerny born, 20 Feb. Herold born, 28 Jan. Meyerbeer born, 5 Sep. Mozart (35) dies, 5 Dec.
1792	22	Haydn's return visit to Bonn: after seeing one of B.'s cantatas he agrees to teach him in Vienna. B. leaves for Vienna, Nov. Compositions include Octet and Rondino for wind and String Trio op. 3. Death of father (*c*.52), 18 Dec.	Rossini born, 29 Feb. War between France and Austria, Apr. French army invades the Rhineland, Oct.
1793	23	Befriended by Prince Karl Lichnowsky (35) and other Viennese musicians. Lives with Lichnowskys. Lessons with Haydn supplemented by secret visits to Schenk (32).	
1794	24	Takes counterpoint lessons with Albrechtsberger (58) during Haydn's second visit to London.	Bonn occupied by the French.
1795	25	First public appearance in Vienna with Piano Concerto in B flat op. 19, 29 Mar. Publication of op. 1 trios and completion of op. 2 piano sonatas.	Marschner born, 16 Aug.
1796	26	Departs for Prague, Dresden and Berlin, Feb. Composes scena 'Ah! perfido' in Prague and op. 5 cello sonatas for performance with Duport in	Loewe born, 30 Nov.

Year	Age	Life	Contemporary Musicians and Events
		Berlin. Growing success as pianist and extemporiser. Quintet for piano and wind op. 16 composed.	
1797	27	Letter to Wegeler about 'improving health', 29 May, suggests previous illness. Publication of the song *Adelaide* and the Piano Sonata op. 7.	Donizetti born, 25 Nov. Schubert born, 31 Jan.
1798	28	Meets minister of French Directory in Vienna, General Bernadotte (35), who may have suggested the idea of a Bonaparte Symphony to B. Published works include the string trios, op. 9 and piano sonatas op. 10.	Gaveaux's *Leonore* produced in Paris.
1799	29	Publication of op. 12 violin sonatas, dedicated to Salieri, with whom B. has studied vocal composition. Other works of the year include the piano sonatas op. 13 (*Pathétique*) and op. 14. Work proceeds on the op. 18 string quartets and B. gives his friend Amenda the first version of the F major op. 18 no. 1. Recent visitors to Vienna include Cramer and Hummel.	Dittersdorf (60) dies, 24 Oct. Halévy born, 27 May.
1800	30	The Septet and the First Symphony are introduced in a benefit concert on 2 Apr, the programme probably including the C major Piano Concerto. B. composes his Horn Sonata op. 17 for Punto (45) which they perform in Vienna and Budapest. Visit to the Brunsvik family in Hungary. Defeats Steibelt (35) at an improvising 'contest'. Czerny (9) plays to B.	Piccinni (72) dies, 7 May.

Year	Age	Life	Contemporary Musicians and Events
		and becomes a favourite pupil. Third Piano Concerto in C minor written but withheld. Music for ballet *Prometheus* composed.	
1801	31	*Prometheus* produced with success, 28 Mar. Publication of op. 18 quartets. Prolific output of new works: violin sonatas op. 23 and op. 24; piano sonatas opp. 26 to 28; String Quintet op. 29. Falls in love with Giulietta Guicciardi but writes despairing letters to Wegeler and Amenda about his increasing deafness. Ries (17) becomes pupil of B.	Bellini born, 1 Nov. Cimarosa (52) dies, 11 Jan. Lanner born, 11 Apr.
1802	32	Spends the summer at Heiligenstadt, where he suffers deep depression on account of his deafness, culminating in the 'Heiligenstadt Testament', 6 and 10 Oct. He nevertheless completes the Second Symphony, the three piano sonatas op. 31 and the variations opp. 34 and 35.	
1803	33	Takes up lodgings in the Theater an der Wien in order to compose an opera, *Vestas Feuer*, for Schikaneder, which he later abandons. The oratorio, *Christus am Oelberge*, is performed there, 5 Apr. Writes the A major Violin Sonata op. 47 to play with George Bridgetower (24) on 17 May and dedicates it to Kreutzer (37). Spends summer in Oberdöbling and works on Third Symphony intended for Bonaparte.	Adam born, 24 July. Berlioz born, 9 Dec. Glinka born, 1 June. Lortzing born, 23 Oct. Süssmayr (37) dies, 16 Sept.

Year	Age	Life	Contemporary Musicians and Events
1804	34	Third Symphony completed, though when B. hears that Bonaparte (35) has proclaimed himself Emperor he removes the dedication and calls the work the *Eroica*, May. Composes piano sonatas op. 53 ('Waldstein') and op. 54.	Benedict born, 27 Nov. Paer's *Leonore* produced at Dresden.
1805	35	Having eventually decided on Bouilly's *Leonore* as suitable topic, B. composes opera to libretto by Sonnleithner. First performance as *Fidelio*, 20 Nov, partly frustrated by French occupation of Vienna: it is withdrawn after three nights and B. is persuaded to make cuts and revisions. Piano Sonata op. 57 ('Appassionata') composed.	Boccherini (62) dies, 28 May.
1806	36	*Fidelio* revised with help from Stephan von Breuning and overture 'Leonore no. 2' replaced by 'no. 3'. Revival, 29 Mar, but B. withdraws score after two performances. His brother Caspar Carl marries Johanna Reiss, 25 May. Visits Hungary and Silesia and refuses to play for French officers at Lichnowsky's. First performance of Violin Concerto by Clement (26), 23. Dec.	
1807	37	Fourth Symphony and G major Piano Concerto performed at Lobkowitz's palace, Mar. Clementi visits B. and contracts for London publication of recent works including 'Rasumovsky' quartets, Apr. Mass in C performed at Eisenstadt, Sept. The Deym 'affair' draws to a close.	

Year	Age	Life	Contemporary Musicians and Events
1808	38	Completion of Fifth and Sixth symphonies and op. 70 piano trios. Offered post of Kapellmeister at court of Jerome Bonaparte in Kassel, Oct. Marathon benefit concert at Theater an der Wien, mostly of new works and ending with 'Choral' Fantasy op. 80, 22 Dec.	Balfe born, 15 May.
1809	39	The Archduke Rudolph, Prince Kinsky and Prince Lobkowitz agree to pay B. an annuity to keep him in Vienna, 1 Mar. 'Lebewohl' Sonata op. 81a composed for Rudolph who is forced to depart during French occupation, May. B. seeks refuge at Caspar Carl's during bombardment, 12 May. Fifth Piano Concerto ('Emperor') and 'Harp' Quartet op. 74 composed.	Albrechtsberger (73) dies, 7 Mar. Haydn (77) dies, 31 May. Mendelssohn born, 3 Feb.
1810	40	Proposal of marriage to Therese Malfatti (18) rejected, May. Meets Bettina Brentano (25), friend of Goethe (61), and composes music for *Egmont*. Writes to Wegeler at Koblenz asking him to procure baptismal certificate and telling him of depression over increasing deafness, 2 May. Visits Baden, Aug–Oct; composes F minor Quartet op. 95 and works at 'Archduke' Trio op. 97.	Chopin born, 22 Feb. Nicolai born, 9 June. Schumann born, 8 June.
1811	41	Finishes 'Archduke' Trio, Mar. Writes music for *King Stephen* and *The Ruins of Athens* by Kotzebue (50). Visits Teplitz for health reasons, Aug.	Hiller born, 24 Oct. Liszt born, 22 Oct.

Year	Age	Life	Contemporary Musicians and Events
1812	42	Seventh Symphony finished, May. Returns to Teplitz in search of a cure and writes but does not send letter to 'Immortal Beloved', 6 and 7 July having recently met Franz and Antonie Brentano, probably in Prague. Meeting with Goethe (63). Visits his brother Johann in Linz, Oct. Completes Eighth Symphony and composes Violin Sonata op. 96 for performance by Rode (38) and the Archduke Rudolph, Dec. Prince Kinsky killed in riding accident, Nov.	Dussek (51) dies, 20 Mar.
1813	43	Letters to the Archduke refer to his depressed state and 'moral factors'; also writes to Princess Kinsky about his annuity. Seeks solace of the countryside in Baden, May–July, where he is found by the Streichers 'in deplorable condition'. No important works written but meets Maelzel (41), Nov, and composes so-called 'Battle Symphony', to celebrate Wellington's victory at Vittoria, which is performed with spectacular success, 8 Dec, in programme including Seventh Symphony.	Grétry (72) dies, 24 Sept. Verdi born, 10 Oct. Wagner born, 22 May. Alkan born, 30 Nov. Napoleon defeated at Leipzig, Oct.
1814	44	*Fidelio* again rewritten with libretto revised by Treitschke and at last produced with success, 23 May. Piano Sonata op. 90 composed. Makes last public appearance as pianist in 'Archduke' Trio with disastrous results, Apr. Composes occasional music for	Congress of Vienna, Sept. Rasumovsky's palace destroyed by fire, 31 Dec.

Year	Age	Life	**Contemporary Musicians and Events**
		Congress of Vienna including cantata, *Der glorreiche Augenblick*.	
1815	45	Two cello sonatas op. 102 composed, summer; also cantata, *Meeresstille und glückliche Fahrt*, dedicated to Goethe (66). B.'s brother Caspar Carl dies, 15 Nov, and B. claims legal custody of his son Karl (9).	Franz born, 20 June. Heller born, 15 May. Napoleon defeated at Waterloo, 18 June.
1816	46	B. granted custody of Karl, 19 Jan, and sends him to a school run by Giannatasio del Rio. Beginning of lengthy legal battle between B. and Karl's mother, each claiming the other unfit to bring up the child. Piano Sonata op. 101 completed, Feb; song-cycle *An die ferne Geliebte*, Apr, dedicated to Prince Lobkowitz (44) who dies, 15 Dec. Karl takes piano lessons from Czerny.	Paisiello (75) dies, 5 June.
1817	47	Intrigues and litigation over guardianship of Karl continue. Ries invites B. to compose two symphonies for London and to visit there the following year. B. accepts but later cancels plans for health reasons. Lengthy correspondence with Nanette Streicher (48) who helps B. to sort out his domestic disorders. Early sketches for the Ninth Symphony.	Gade born, 22 Feb. Méhul (54) dies, 18 Oct.
1818	48	Removes Karl from school, 24 Jan, and spends summer with him at Mödling, where he receives gift of Broadwood piano from London. Visited by	Gounod born, 17 June. Kozeluch (46) dies, 7 May.

Year	Age	Life	Contemporary Musicians and Events
		Cipriani Potter. Works on 'Hammerklavier' Sonata op. 106 and begins *Missa Solemnis*. Karl enters Gymnasium, Nov, but runs away to his mother, 3 Dec.	
1819	49	Johanna petitions for possession of Karl and gains temporary custody after case has been transferred from Landrecht to commoners' Magistrat, B. being unable to claim noble birth. He seeks advice from lawyer Johann Baptist Bach, Feb, but his counter-petition fails, Oct. 'Hammerklavier' Sonata finished, Mar. Work continues on *Missa Solemnis* and Ninth Symphony.	Offenbach born, 21 June.
1820	50	Court of Appeal appoints B. and Karl Peters co-guardians, Apr; and further appeal from Johanna rejected, 24 Jul. Piano Sonata op. 109 completed. Archduke Rudolph enthroned as Archbishop of Olmütz, Apr, but *Missa Solemnis* nowhere near ready for the occasion.	Vieuxtemps born, 20 Feb.
1821	51	Work on *Missa Solemnis* delayed by illness. Summer spent in Döbling and Baden. Piano Sonata op. 110 finished, 25 Dec.	
1822	52	Begins composition of Piano Sonata op. 111, 13 Jan. Unsuccessful attempt at reconciliation with his brother Nikolaus Johann and wife Therese, summer. Visited by Rochlitz and Rossini (30), whose operas have taken	Franck born, 10 Dec. Raff born, 27 May.

Year	Age	Life	Contemporary Musicians and Events
		Vienna by storm. Composes the overture *Die Weihe des Hauses* for opening of Josephstadt Theatre, Sept. *Fidelio* revived, 3 Nov. B. abandons attempt to conduct dress rehearsal owing to his deafness. Receives commission from Prince Galitzin to compose some new quartets, 9 Nov.	
1823	53	*Missa Solemnis* completed, Feb. Diabelli Variations published, June, and Ninth Symphony finished, autumn. Considers an operatic project, *Melusine*, with libretto by Grillparzer (32).	Lalo born, 27 Jan. Steibelt (58) dies, 20 Sept.
1824	54	Galitzin gives first performance of *Missa Solemnis* at St Petersburg, Apr. Premiere of Ninth Symphony in Vienna, 7 May, enthusiastically received, but repeat performance on 23 May poorly attended. First of the Galitzin quartets, op. 127, completed.	Bruckner born, 4 Sept. Cornelius born, 24 Dec. Reinecke born, 23 June. Smetana born, 2 Mar. Viotti (71) dies, 3 Mar.
1825	55	Karl enters Polytechnic and moves to independent lodgings, spring. Plans for B. to visit London for English premiere of Ninth Symphony fall through. He goes to Baden for his health, May–Oct, and composes the A minor Quartet op. 132. Visited by George Smart from London to discuss interpretation of the Ninth, Sept.	Gaveaux (64) dies, 5 Feb. Salieri (75) dies, 7 May. Strauss (J. ii) born, 25 Oct.
1826	56	First performance of Quartet op. 130, 21 Mar, with 'Grosse Fuge' as finale. B.'s attitude to Karl is increasingly possessive and suspicious. Karl (20)	Weber (40) dies, 4–5 June.

Year	Age	Life	Contemporary Musicians and Events
		attempts suicide, 30 Jul. B.'s health suffers but he completes the C sharp minor Quartet op. 131, autumn. Takes Karl to his brother Johann's at Gneixendorf to recuperate and composes his last Quartet op. 135 and a new finale for op. 130. Leaves hurriedly for Vienna with Karl, 1 Dec, and takes to bed with severe chill.	
1827	–	Karl joins army as cadet in Stutterheim's regiment, 2 Jan. B. confined to bed with pneumonia and dropsy: his condition deteriorates despite treatment from various doctors including Malfatti. Greatly touched at gift of £100 from London Philharmonic Society and promises them his tenth symphony. Visitors include Schubert (30) and Hummel (49). Receives last rites, 24 Mar, and dies two days later.	Auber aged 45; Balfe 19; Bellini 26; Benedict 23; Berlioz 24; Bishop 41; Boieldieu 52; Bruckner 3; Cherubini 67; Chopin 17; Clementi 75; Cornelius 3; Czerny 36; Donizetti 30; Field 45; Franck 5; Glinka 24; Gossec 93; Gounod 9; Halévy 28; Hérold 36; Hummel 49; Kuhlau 41; Liszt 16; Loewe 31; Lortzing 24; Marschner 32; Mendelssohn 18; Meyerbeer 36; Paër 56; Potter 35; Ries 43; Rossini 35; Schenk 66; Schubert 30; Schumann 17; Smetana 3; Spohr 43; Spontini 53; Verdi 14; Wagner 14; Weigl 61; Zelter 69.

Appendix B

List of works

Only completed and surviving works are included. For details of fragments and lost compositions the reader should consult the Kinsky-Halm catalogue (see Bibliography) or the list of works in *The New Grove*. A further source is the *Verzeichnis* by W. Hess (Wiesbaden, 1957) which lists works and fragments not included in the original collected edition. The accepted identification of Beethoven's works is by opus number (where applicable) or WoO number (Werk ohne Opuszahl, i.e. without opus number, from Kinsky-Halm) or Hess number. Since sketches for some works extended over a long and indefinable period the dates given below are those of completion (when known).

I PIANO MUSIC

(i) Sonatas

WoO47	3 Sonatas (E♭, F mi, D)	1783	'Kurfürsten' ('Electoral')
WoO50	Sonata in F	1790?	2 mvts only; pub. 1950
WoO51	Sonata in C	1792?	2 mvts only, the 2nd completed by Ries
op. 2	3 Sonatas (F mi, A, C)	1795	
op. 49	2 Sonatas (G mi, G)	1797?	no. 2 probably written first
op. 7	Sonata in E♭	1797	
op. 10	3 Sonatas (C mi, F, D)	1798	
op. 13	Sonata *Pathétique* in C mi	1799	
op. 14	2 Sonatas (E, G)	1799	
op. 22	Sonata in B♭	1800	
op. 26	Sonata in A♭	1801	
op. 27	2 Sonatas (E♭, C♯mi)	1801	each subtitled 'quasi una fantasia'; no. 2 nicknamed 'Moonlight'
op. 28	Sonata in D	1801	'Pastoral'
op. 31	3 Sonatas (G, D mi, E♭)	1802	
op. 53	Sonata in C	1804	'Waldstein'
op. 54	Sonata in F	1804	
op. 57	Sonata in F mi	1805	'Appassionata'
op. 78	Sonata in F♯	1809	
op. 79	Sonata in G	1809	

op. 81a	Sonata in E♭	1810	'Das Lebewohl' ('Les Adieux')
op. 90	Sonata in E mi	1814	
op. 101	Sonata in A	1816	
op. 106	Sonata in B♭	1818	'Hammerklavier'
op. 109	Sonata in E	1820	
op. 110	Sonata in A♭	1821	
op. 111	Sonata in C mi	1822	

(ii) Variations

WoO63	9 on a March by Dressler, C mi	1782	
WoO64	6 on a Swiss Air, F	1790?	for harp or pf
WoO65	24 on Righini's 'Venni amore', D	1790	1st ed lost, rev. (?) 1802
WoO66	13 on 'Es war einmal ein alter Mann' from Dittersdorf's *Das rote Käppchen*, A	1792	
WoO68	12 on 'Menuet à la Viganò' from Haibel's *Le nozze disturbate*, C	1795	
WoO69	9 on 'Quant'è piu bello' from Paisiello's *La Molinara*, A	1795	
WoO70	6 on 'Nel cor più non mi sento' from Paisiello's *La Molinara*, G	1795	
WoO71	12 on a Russian Dance from Wranitzky's *Das Waldmädchen*, A	1796	
WoO72	8 on 'Une fièvre brûlante' from Grétry's *Richard Coeur de Lion*, C	1796?	
WoO73	10 on 'La stessa, le stessissima' from Salieri's *Falstaff*, B♭	1799	
WoO75	7 on 'Kind, willst du ruhig schlafen' from Winter's *Das unterbrochene Opferfest*, F	1799	
WoO76	6 on 'Tändeln und scherzen' from Süssmayr's *Soliman II*, F	1799	
WoO77	6 on an Original Theme, G	1800	
op. 34	6 on an Original Theme, F	1802	
op. 35	15 and fugue on Theme from *Prometheus*, E♭	1802	'Eroica' Variations
WoO78	7 on 'God save the King', C	1803	
WoO79	5 on 'Rule Britannia', D	1803	
WoO80	32 on an Original Theme, C mi	1806	
op. 76	6 on an Original Theme, D	1809	later used as Turkish March in *The Ruins of Athens*

op. 120	33 on a Waltz by Diabelli, C	1823	

(iii) Miscellaneous

WoO48	Rondo in C	1783	
WoO49	Rondo in A	1783	
WoO82	Minuet in E♭	1785?	
WoO55	Prelude in F mi	1787?	
op. 39	2 Preludes through all the major keys	1789?	for pf or org
WoO81	Allemande in A	1793	
op. 129	Rondo a capriccio in G	1795	'The Rage over the Lost Penny'
Hess 64	Fugue in C	1795	
WoO52	Presto in C mi	1795?	
WoO10	6 Minuets	1795?	
WoO53	Allegretto in C mi	1797	
Hess 69	Allegretto in C mi	1797	
op. 51	2 Rondos (C, G)	1798?	
WoO11	7 Ländler	1798?	
op. 33	7 Bagatelles (E♭, C, F, A, C, D, A♭)	1802	
WoO54	'Lustig-traurig', C and C mi	1802?	
WoO57	Andante in F	1803	'Andante favori', orig. 2nd mvt of Sonata op. 53
WoO56	Allegretto in C	1803	
WoO83	6 Ecossaises in E♭	1806?	
op. 77	Fantasia in G mi	1809	
WoO58	2 Cadenzas for Mozart's Piano Concerto in D mi, K.466	1809?	
	Cadenzas for Beethoven's own concertos (see 'Orchestral Music')		
WoO59	Bagatelle in A mi	1810	'Für Elise'
op. 89	Polonaise in C	1814	
WoO200	Theme 'O Hoffnung'	1818	subj. of 40 vars by Archduke Rudolph
WoO60	Bagatelle in B♭	1818	
Hess 65	'Concert Finale' in C	1821	arr. of coda to finale of Pf. Con. no. 3 for Starke's *Wiener Pianoforte-Schule*
WoO61	Allegretto in B mi	1821	
op. 119	11 Bagatelles (G mi, C, D, A, C mi, G, C, C, A mi, A, B♭)	1822	nos. 1 to 5 written or sketched 20 or more years earlier

op. 126	6 Bagatelles (G, G mi, Eb, B mi, G, Eb)	1824	
WoO84	Waltz in Eb	1824	
WoO61a	Allegretto in G mi	1825	
WoO85	Waltz in D	1825	
WoO86	Ecossaise in Eb	1825	

(iv) Piano duets (one piano, four hands)

WoO67	8 Variations on a Theme by Count Waldstein	1792	
op. 6	Sonata in D	1797	
WoO74	Song 'Ich denke dein' (Goethe) with 6 Variations	1803	
op. 45	3 Marches (C, Eb, D)	1803	
op. 134	Grosse Fuge in Bb	1826	trans of op. 133 for str. quar.

Other Instruments

WoO31	Fugue in D for organ	1783	
WoO33	Movement for a mechanical clock	1799?	
Hess 107	Grenadiers' March in F for a mechanical clock	1798?	

II CHAMBER MUSIC

(i) with piano

WoO36	3 Piano Quartets (Eb, D, C)	1785
WoO37	Trio in G, pf, fl, bn	1786
WoO38	Piano Trio in Eb	1791
op. 44	Variations of Eb, pf trio	1792?
WoO40	Variations in F on 'Se vuol ballare' from Mozart's *Figaro*, pf and vn	1793
WoO41	Rondo in G, pf and vn	1794
op. 1	3 Piano Trios (Eb, G, C mi)	1794
WoO43a	Sonatina in C mi, pf and mand	1796
WoO43b	Adagio in Eb, pf and mand	1796
WoO44a	Sonatina in C, pf and mand	1796
WoO44b	Variations in D, pf and mand	1796
WoO42	6 German Dances, pf and vn	1796
op. 5	2 Cello Sonatas (F, G mi)	1796
WoO45	Variations in G on 'See the conqu'ring hero comes' from Handel's *Judas Maccabaeus*, pf and vc	1796

op. 66	Variations in F on 'Ein Mädchen oder Weibchen' from Mozart's *Die Zauberflöte*, pf and vc	1796	
op. 16	Quintet in E♭, pf, ob, cl, hn, bn	1796	
	Piano Quartet in E♭	1796	trans. of op. 16
op. 11	Trio in B♭, pf, cl, vc	1797	
op. 12	3 Violin Sonatas (D, A, E♭)	1798	
op. 17	Horn Sonata in F	1800	
op. 23	Violin Sonata in A mi	1801	
op. 24	Violin Sonata in F	1801	'Spring'
WoO46	Variations in E♭ on 'Bei Männern' from *Die Zauberflöte*, pf and vc	1801	
op. 30	3 Violin Sonatas (A, C mi, G)	1802	
op. 47	Violin Sonata in A	1803	'Kreutzer'
op. 42	Notturno in D, pf and va	1803	trans. of Serenade op. 8
op. 41	Serenade in D, pf and fl	1803	trans. of Serenade op. 25
op. 69	Cello Sonata in A	1808	
op. 70	2 Piano Trios (D, E♭)	1808	
op. 97	Piano Trio in B♭	1811	'Archduke'
op. 96	Violin Sonata in G	1812	
WoO39	Allegretto in B♭, pf trio	1812	
op. 102	2 Cello Sonatas (C, D)	1815	
op. 121a	Variations in G on Müller's 'Ich bin der Schneider Kakadu', pf trio	1816	first ver. 1803?
op. 105	6 National Airs and variations, pf and fl or vn	1818	
op. 107	10 National Airs and variations, pf and fl or vn	1818	

(ii) for strings

Hess 33	Minuet in A♭, string quar	1790?	
op. 3	String Trio in E♭	1792?	
op. 87	String Trio in C	1795	trans. of Trio for 2 ob and cor ang
op. 4	String Quintet in E♭	1795	trans. of Wind Octet op. 103
WoO32	Duet in E♭, va and vc, 'mit zwei obligaten Augengläsern'	1797?	for Zmeskall?
op. 8	Serenade in D, string trio	1797	
op. 9	3 String Trios (G, D, C mi)	1798	
Hess 28	New trio for minuet of op. 9 no. 1	1798	
op. 18	6 String Quartets (F, G, D, C mi, A, B♭)	1801	
op. 29	String Quintet in C	1801	

Hess 34	String Quartet in F	1802	trans. of pf Sonata in E op. 14 no. 1
op. 59	3 String Quartets (F, E mi, C)	1806	'Rasumovsky'
op. 74	String Quartet in E♭	1809	'Harp'
op. 95	String Quartet in F mi	1810	
op. 104	String Quintet in C mi	1817	trans. of pf Trio op. 1 no. 3
Hess 40	Prelude in D mi, string quintet	1817?	
op. 137	Fugue in D, string quintet	1817	
WoO34	Duet in A, 2 vln	1822	
op. 127	String Quartet in E♭	1825	
op. 132	String Quartet in A mi	1825	
op. 130	String Quartet in B♭	1825	new finale 1826
op. 133	Grosse Fuge in B♭, string quartet	1825	orig finale of op. 130
op. 131	String Quartet in C#mi	1826	
op. 135	String Quartet in F	1826	

(iii) for wind or wind and strings

WoO27	3 Duets, cl and bn	1792?	doubtful authenticity
WoO26	Allegro and Minuet in G, 2 fl	1792	
op. 103	Octet in E♭, 2 ob, 2 cl, 2 hn, 2 bn	1792	
WoO25	Rondino in E♭, 2 ob, 2 cl, 2 hn, 2 bn	1792	
op. 87	Trio in C, 2 ob and cor ang	1795	
WoO28	Variations in C on 'La ci darem la mano' from Mozart's *Don Giovanni*, 2 ob and cor ang	1795?	
op. 81b	Sextet in E♭, 2 hn and string quartet	1795?	
op. 71	Sextet in E♭, 2 cl, 2hn, 2bn	1796	
WoO29	March in B♭, 2 cl, 2 hn, 2 bn	1798	
op. 20	Septet in E♭, cl, hn, bn, vn, va, vc, db	1800	
op. 25	Serenade in D, fl, vn, va	1801	
WoO30	3 Equali, 4 trbn (D mi, D, B♭)	1812	
WoO17	11 'Mödlinger' Dances, 2 cl, 2 hn, 2 vn, db	1819	

III ORCHESTRAL MUSIC

(i) Symphonies

op. 21	Symphony no. 1 in C	1800
op. 36	Symphony no. 2 in D	1802
op. 55	Symphony no. 3 in E♭ (*Eroica*)	1803
op. 60	Symphony no. 4 in B♭	1806
op. 67	Symphony no. 5 in C mi	1808

op. 68	Symphony no. 6 in F (*Pastoral*)	1808	
op. 92	Symphony no. 7 in A	1812	
op. 93	Symphony no. 8 in F	1812	
op. 125	Symphony no. 9 in D mi (*Choral*)	1824	

(ii) Solo Instrument(s) and Orchestra

WoO4	Piano Concerto in E♭	1784	survives in pf score with orch cues
WoO6	Rondo in B♭ for pf and orch	1794?	orig. finale of op. 19
op. 19	Piano Concerto no. 2 in B♭	1795	rev. 1798
op. 15	Piano Concerto no. 1 in C	1795	rev. 1800
op. 50	Romance in F for vln and orch	1798?	
op. 37	Piano Concerto no. 3 in C mi	1800?	rev. 1803
op. 40	Romance in G for vln and orch	1802?	
op. 56	'Triple' Concerto in C for pf, vln, vc and orch	1804	
op. 58	Piano Concerto no. 4 in G	1806	
op. 61	Violin Concerto in D	1806	arr. for pf and orch 1807
op. 80	Fantasy in C for pf, chorus and orch	1808	
op. 73	Piano Concerto no. 5 in E♭	1809	'Emperor'
–	Cadenzas for op. 19, op. 15, op. 37, op. 58, and the pf version of op. 61	1809?	incl. 3 for 1st movt of op. 15 (1 unfin.) and 2 for 1st mvt of op. 58. Hess lists others

(iii) Overtures

Although most of these fall into other categories – opera, ballet, incidental music – their acceptance into the concert repertory calls for their inclusion here also.

op. 43	*Prometheus*	1801
op. 72a	*Leonore* no. 2	1805
op. 72a	*Leonore* no. 3	1806
op.138	*Leonore* no. 1	1807?
op. 62	*Coriolan*	1807
op. 84	*Egmont*	1810
op. 113	*The Ruins of Athens*	1811
op. 117	*King Stephen*	1811
op. 72b	*Fidelio*	1814
op. 115	*Namensfeier*	1815
op. 124	*Die Weihe des Hauses*	1822

(iv) Miscellaneous

| WoO7 | Twelve Minuets | 1795 |
| WoO8 | Twelve German Dances | 1795 |

243

WoO12	Twelve Minuets	1799	doubtful authenticity
WoO13	Twelve German Dances	1800?	survives in pf arr.
WoO14	Twelve Contredanses	1802	some written earlier
WoO16	Twelve Ecossaises	1806?	dubious arrangements
op. 91	*Wellington's Victory* or *The Battle of Vittoria*	1813	'Battle Symphony'
WoO3	Gratulations-Minuet in E♭	1822	

(v) Works for Wind Band (see also Chamber Music)

WoO18	March in F	1809	trio added 1823
WoO19	March in F	1810	trio added 1823
WoO21	Polonaise in D	1810	
WoO22	Ecossaise in D	1810	
WoO23	Ecossaise in G	1810?	
WoO24	March in D	1816	
WoO20	March in C	?	

IV MUSIC FOR THE STAGE

(i) Opera

WoO91	Two arias for *Die schöne Schusterin* by Umlauf	1796?
op. 72	*Fidelio* or *Leonore*, 1st version	1805
	2nd version	1806
	3rd version	1814
WoO94	'Germania', finale of Treitschke's Singspiel *Die gute Nachricht*	1814
WoO97	'Es ist vollbracht', finale of Treitschke's Singspiel *Die Ehrenpforten*	1815

(ii) Ballet

WoO1	Ritterballet	1791
op. 43	*Die Geschöpfe des Prometheus*	1801

(iii) Incidental Music

op. 62	Overture to *Coriolan* (Collin)	1807
op. 84	Music to *Egmont* (Goethe)	1810
op. 113	*The Ruins of Athens* (Kotzebue)	1811
op. 117	*King Stephen* (Kotzebue)	1811
WoO2	Triumphal March and Introduction to Act 2 of *Tarpeja* (Kuffner)	1813

WoO96	*Leonore Prohaska* (Duncker)	1815	
op. 114	March with chorus arr. from op. 113 for *Die Weihe des Hauses*	1822?	
op. 124	Overture, *Die Weihe des Hauses*	1822	
WoO98	'Wo sich die Pulse' (Meisl), chorus for the foregoing	1822	

V CHORAL MUSIC

(i) Chorus and Orchestra

(see also op. 80 and op. 125 under Orchestral Music)

WoO87	Cantata on the Death of the Emperor Joseph II (Averdonk)	1790	
WoO88	Cantata on the Accession of the Emperor Leopold II (Averdonk)	1790	
op. 85	*Christus am Oelberge* ('The Mount of Olives'), oratorio (Huber)	1803	rev. 1804
op. 86	Mass in C	1807	
WoO95	*Chor auf die verbündeten Fürsten* (Bernard)	1814	
op. 136	*Der glorreiche Augenblick*, cantata (Weissenbach)	1814	
op. 112	*Meeresstille und glückliche Fahrt*, cantata (Goethe)	1815	
–	*Opferlied* (Matthisson)	1822	1st chor. ver.
op. 123	Mass in D (*Missa Solemnis*)	1823	
op. 121b	*Opferlied* (Matthisson)	1824	2nd chor. ver.
op. 122	*Bundeslied* (Goethe)	1824	

(iii) Other Choral Works

WoO111	*Punschlied*, unison song	1790?	
WoO119	*O care selve* (Metastasio), unison song	1794	
WoO117	*Der freie Mann* (Pfeffel), unison song	1794	
WoO122	*Kriegslied* (Friedelberg), unison song	1797	
WoO102	*Abschiedsgesang* (Seyfried), unaccomp.	1814	
WoO103	*Un lieto brindisi* (Bondi), with pf	1814	
WoO104	*Gesang der Mönche* (Schiller), unaccomp.	1817	
WoO105	*Hochzeitlied* (Stein), with pf	1819	2 versions

WoO106	Cantata for Prince Lobkowitz's Birthday, with pf	1823	

VI MUSIC FOR SOLO VOICE(S)

(i) Voice(s) and Orchestra

WoO89	*Prüfung des Küssens*, aria	*c.*1790	
WoO90	*Mit Mädeln sich vertragen* (Goethe), aria	*c.*1790	
WoO92	*Primo amore*, scena and aria	*c.*1790	
op. 65	*Ah, perfido!* (Metastasio), scena and aria	1796	
WoO92a	*No, non turbati* (Metastasio), scena and aria	1802	
WoO93	*Nei giorni tuoi felici* (Metastasio), duet	1803	
op. 116	*Tremate, empi, tremate* (Bettoni), trio	1814	
op. 118	*Sanft wie du lebtest*, quartet	1814	with pf and str. qua

(ii) Songs with Piano

WoO107	*Schilderung eines Mädchens*	1783?	
WoO108	*An einen Säugling* (Döhring)	1784?	
WoO110	*Elegie auf den Tod eines Pudels*	1787?	
WoO113	*Klage* (Hölty)	1790?	
WoO119	*Trinklied*	1790?	
Hess 151	*Traute Henriette*	1792?	
WoO112	*An Laura* (Matthisson)	1792?	
WoO114	*Selbstgespräch* (Gleim)	1792?	
WoO115	*An Minna*	1792?	
op. 52	8 Songs	1793	
	Urians Reise um die Welt (Claudius)		
	Feuerfarb (Mereau)		
	Das Liedchen von der Ruhe (Ueltzen)		
	Maigesang (Goethe)		
	Mollys Abschied (Bürger)		
	Die Liebe (Lessing)		
	Marmotte (Goethe)		
	Das Blümchen Wunderhold (Bürger)		
WoO116	*Que le temps me dure* (Rosseau)	1793	2 versions (Hess 129, 130)
WoO126	*Opferlied* (Matthisson)	1794	rev. 1802; see also choral versions

WoO118	*Seufzer eines Ungeliebten* and		
	Gegenliebe (Bürger)	1795	
op. 46	*Adelaide*	1795	
WoO123	*Zärtliche Liebe* (Herrosee)	1795?	
WoO124	*La partenza* (Metastasio)	1796?	
WoO121	*Abschiedensgesang*		
	(Friedelberg)	1796	
WoO127	*Neue Liebe, neues Leben*		
	(Goethe)	1799	
WoO125	*La tiranna*	1799	
WoO128	*Plaisir d'aimer*	1799	
WoO120	*Man strebt die Flamme*	1800?	
op. 48	6 Songs (Gellert)	1802	
	Bitten		
	Die Liebe des Nächsten		
	Vom Tode		
	Die Ehre Gottes aus der		
	Natur		
	Gottes Macht und Vorsehung		
	Busslied		
WoO129	*Der Wachtelschlag* (Sauter)	1803	
op. 88	*Das Glück der Freundschaft*	1803	
WoO130	*Gedenke mein*	1805	
op. 32	*An die Hoffnung* (Tiedge)	1805	1st setting
WoO132	*Als die Geliebte sich trennen*		
	wollte (S von Breuning)	1806	
WoO133	*In questa tomba oscura*		
	(Carpani)	1807	
WoO134	*Sehnsucht* (Goethe)	1808	4 settings
WoO136	*Andenken* (Matthisson)	1809	
WoO137	*Lied aus der Ferne* (Reissig)	1809	
WoO138	*Der Jüngling in der Fremde*		
	(Reissig)	1809	
WoO139	*Der Liebende* (Reissig)	1809	
op. 75	6 Songs	1809	
	Mignon (Goethe)		
	Neue Liebe, Neues Leben		
	(Goethe)		
	Es war einmal ein König		
	(Goethe)		
	Gretels Warnung (Halem)		
	An den fernen Geliebten		
	(Reissig)		
	Der Zufriedene (Reissig)		
op. 82	4 Ariettas and a Duet	1809	
	Hoffnung		

	Liebes-Klage (Metastasio)		
	L'amante impatiente		
	(Metastasio)		'arietta buffa'
	L'amante impatiente		
	(Metastasio)		'arietta assai seriosa'
	Lebens-Genuss (Metastasio),		
	duet		
op. 83	3 Songs (Goethe)	1810	
	Wonne der Wehmut		
	Sehnsucht		
	Mit einem gemalten Band		
WoO140	*An die Geliebte* (Stoll)	1811	2 settings
WoO141	*Der Gesang der Nachtigall*		
	(Herder)	1813	
WoO142	*Der Bardengeist* (Hermann)	1813	
op. 94	*An die Hoffnung* (Tiedge)	1813?	2nd setting
WoO143	*Des Kriegers Abschied* (Reissig)	1814	
WoO144	*Merkenstein* (Rupprecht)	1814	
op. 100	*Merkenstein* (Rupprecht) duet	1815	
WoO135	*Die laute Klage* (Herder)	1815?	
WoO145	*Das Geheimnis* (Wessenberg)	1815	
WoO146	*Sehnsucht* (Reissig)	1816	
op. 98	*An die ferne Geliebte* (Jeitteles),		
	cycle of 6 songs	1816	
op. 99	*Der Mann von Wort*		
	(Kleinschmid)	1816	
WoO147	*Ruf von Berge* (Treitschke)	1816	
WoO148	*So oder so* (Lappe)	1817	
WoO149	*Resignation* (Haugwitz)	1817	
WoO150	*Abendlied unterm gestirnten*		
	Himmel (Goeble)	1820	
op. 128	*Der Kuss* (Weisse)	1822?	
WoO151	*Der edle Mensch* (Goethe)	1823	

(iii) Folksong Arrangements

The arrangements WoO152–7 and op. 108 were made for George Thomson o
Edinburgh between *c*.1809 and 1816 with accompaniments for piano, violin and cell
Though mostly for solo voice, they include duets and trios and some have choruse

WoO152	25 Irish Songs
WoO153	20 Irish Songs
WoO154	12 Irish Songs
WoO155	26 Welsh Songs
op. 108	25 Scottish Songs
WoO156	12 Scottish Songs
WoO157	12 Songs of various nationality
WoO158a	23 Songs of various nationality

WoO158b 7 British Songs
WoO158c 6 Songs of various nationality
Hess 168 Air français
Hess 133 *Das liebe Kätzchen*
Hess 134 *Der Knabe auf dem Berge*

(iv) Unaccompanied Vocal Music

WoO99 26 Italian duets, trios and
          quartets (Metastasio)   *c.*1792–1802

Apart from his serious contrapuntal and other vocal studies, including those for
Albrechtsberger and Salieri, Beethoven composed a large number of canons and
musical jokes between *c.*1795 and 1826, most of which have been catalogued under
WoO or Hess numbers, such as:

WoO100	*Schuppanzigh ist ein Lump*	1801	for Ignaz Schuppanzigh
WoO101	*Graf, Graf, Graf, Graf*	1802	for Nikolaus Zmeskall
WoO162	*Ta ta ta . . . lieber Maelzel*	1812?	possibly spurious?
WoO204	*Holz, Holz*	1825	for Karl Holz

Appendix C

Personalia

Albrechtsberger, Johann Georg (1736–1809), Viennese organist, composer and teacher who gave Beethoven counterpoint lessons in 1794–5 during Haydn's absence in London.

Amenda, Karl Friedrich (1771–1836), violinist and student of theology from Courland on the Baltic, who became a pastor. He visited Vienna in 1798–9 and acted as tutor to the Lobkowitz family. He soon became a close friend of Beethoven, who gave him a manuscript score of the String Quartet in F op. 18 no. 1. In 1801, however, Beethoven wrote telling him to disregard this early version of the work, and confiding in him about his encroaching deafness.

Artaria, a family of art dealers and music publishers in Vienna. Domenico Artaria (1775–1842) became head of the firm from 1802 and was responsible for the publication of many of Beethoven's works.

Averdonk, Severin Anton, whose father worked on the electoral Account Bureau at Bonn, wrote the texts for Beethoven's two cantatas in 1790. His sister Johanna, a singing pupil of Beethoven's father, took part in the concert at Cologne in 1778 at which Beethoven made his debut as a prodigy.

Bach, Carl Philipp Emanuel (1714–88), second surviving son of J.S. Bach, studied law at Leipzig, became harpsichordist to Frederick the Great of Prussia from 1738 to 1768 and then music director at Hamburg. His compositions were highly influential in bridging the gap between the High Baroque and the Classical styles. His 'Essay on the True Art of Playing Keyboard Instruments' (1753) was recommended by Beethoven to the young Czerny.

Bigot, Marie (1786–1820), pianist and wife of Count Rasumovsky's librarian, who is said to have sight-read the 'Appassionata' Sonata from the manuscript to Beethoven's astonishment and with whom he may have been in love. The Bigot family moved to Paris in 1809.

Bouilly, Jean-Nicolas (1763–1842), was in charge of a department near Tours during the French Revolution. His libretto for Gaveaux's *Leonore*, which was adapted for Beethoven's *Fidelio*, is supposed to derive from an actual incident of the time.

Braun, Baron Peter von (1758–1819), a wealthy banker, was in charge of the two Court Theatres in Vienna between 1794 and 1806. His wife Josephine was a pianist to whom Beethoven dedicated the two piano sonatas op. 14 and the Horn Sonata op. 17.

Breitkopf and Härtel, a famous music-publishing house at Leipzig, with which Beethoven had frequent dealings and correspondence. It was founded in 1719 by Bernhardt Christoph Breitkopf (1695–1777).

Brentano, Antonie, née von Birkenstock (1780–1869), wife of Franz Brentano from Frankfurt. The family visited Vienna from 1809 to 1812, and Antonie is favoured by Maynard Solomon as the 'Immortal Beloved' of Beethoven's much-debated letter from Teplitz. He later dedicated the monumental Diabelli Variations to her.

Brentano, Bettina (1785–1859), half-sister of Franz, married the poet Achim von Arnim in 1811. She was a poetess herself and a close friend of Goethe, and was helpful in introducing Beethoven to him after the composition of the music for *Egmont.*

Brentano, Maximiliane (1802–61), daughter of Franz and Antonie, for whom Beethoven composed the one-movement Trio in B flat WoO 39 in 1812 'for the encouragement of her piano-playing.' He also dedicated the Piano Sonata op. 109 to her.

Breuning, Stephan von (1774–1827) studied law in Bonn and Vienna and was appointed to the Imperial War Council. The von Breuning family, and especially Stephan's mother Helene, befriended Beethoven in his earlier days at Bonn; and his sister Eleonore von Breuning married Beethoven's friend Wegeler in 1802. Despite occasional frictions they remained life-long friends: Stephan helped to revise the libretto for the second version of *Fidelio* in 1806, and twenty years later was influential in obtaining a cadetship for Beethoven's nephew Karl.

Bridgetower, George Polgreen (1779–1860), mulatto violinist, son of an African father and Polish mother, who settled in England as a prodigy and led the Pavilion Orchestra at Brighton. He visited Vienna in 1803 and gave the first performance of the 'Kreutzer' Sonata op. 47 with Beethoven.

Browne-Camus, Count von (1767–1827), a wealthy officer in the Russian Imperial Service in Vienna, and one of Beethoven's most generous patrons. He received the dedications of the String Trios op. 9, the Piano Sonata op. 22, and the Gellert songs op. 48. Beethoven dedicated the Piano Sonatas op. 10 to the Countess Browne.

Clementi, Muzio (1752–1832), Italian pianist and composer who settled in England in his youth and later took to piano-making and publishing. He travelled widely, took part in a famous piano-playing 'contest' with Mozart in 1782, and visited Beethoven in 1807 to negotiate English publications of his works. He was a pioneer in piano technique and his possible influence on Beethoven's earlier sonatas has been noted.

Collin, Heinrich Joseph von (1771–1811), Austrian poet and author of the play *Coriolan,* for which Beethoven composed the Overture op. 62 in 1807. Their proposed cooperation over an operatic project came to nothing.

Cramer, Johann Baptist (1771–1858), pianist and composer, was born in Mannheim but brought to London in infancy. Like Clementi, with whom he studied, he founded a publishing firm. Although a voluminous composer, he is largely remembered for his piano studies. Ferdinand Ries maintained that he was the only pianist Beethoven really admired.

Czerny, Carl (1791–1857), Viennese pianist and composer, studied with Beethoven from 1800 to c.1803 and wrote a vivid account of their first meeting. He was a prolific composer of piano studies and Liszt was his most famous pupil.

Deym, Countess Josephine (1779–1821), née Brunsvik, took lessons from Beethoven along with her sister Therese before marrying Count Deym in 1799. After the Count's death in 1804 she formed a close relationship with Beethoven, who was clearly in love with her and hoped to marry her. She left Vienna with her family in 1808 and married Baron von Stackelberg two years later.

Diabelli, Anton (1781–1858) was an Austrian composer who joined the Viennese publisher Peter Cappi in 1818 and took over the firm in 1824. His chief claim to fame was through the waltz he sent out to fifty or more composers inviting each to contribute a variation to a composite work, the *Vaterländische Künstlerverein*, and on which Beethoven wrote a complete set of thirty-three himself, the Diabelli Variations op. 120.

Dressler, Ernst Christoph (1734–79), singer and composer from Thuringia who joined the court chapels at Bayreuth and Gotha, became Kapellmeister at Wetzlar in 1767, and ended his career as an opera singer in Vienna and Kassel. Beethoven's first known composition was a set of keyboard variations on a march by Dressler.

Dussek, Jan Ladislav (1760–1812), Bohemian pianist and composer whose keyboard works contributed much to the development of piano writing, even foreshadowing Schumann and Brahms at times.

Eeden, Gilles van den (c.1710–82), Court organist at Bonn, who may have given Beethoven lessons in keyboard and composition in the late 1770s.

Erdödy, Countess Anna Marie (1779–1837), married a Hungarian Count in 1796. She was a good pianist, a great admirer of Beethoven, and promoted his works at her private concerts. He shared her apartment in 1808–9, at which time she helped to negotiate his annuity. She received the dedications of two important pairs of chamber works, the piano trios op. 70 and the cello sonatas op. 102.

Fischer, the name of a family in Bonn who knew Beethoven as a child and in whose house his grandfather Ludwig had apartments. In much later years Gottfried and Cäcilia Fischer recorded their memories of the composer's youth in the so-called 'Fischer manuscript'.

Förster, Emanuel Aloys (1748–1823), a Silesian composer who settled in Vienna in 1809 and taught piano and theory. His quartets, though little known, are said to have influenced Beethoven, who called him his 'old master'. Beethoven gave his son piano lessons in 1802.

Fries, Count Moritz von (1777–1826), an Austrian banker, art collector and patron. Beethoven dedicated some important works to him including the Seventh Symphony. It was at his house in 1800 that the celebrated improvising contest took place between Beethoven and Steibelt, to the latter's disadvantage.

Galitzin, Prince Nikolas (1794–1860), an amateur cellist and musical enthusiast from St Petersburg. In 1822 he commissioned Beethoven to write some more string quartets, and op. 127, op. 130 and op. 132 were dedicated to him. He also organised the first complete performance of the *Missa Solemnis*, which was given in St Petersburg in April 1824.

Gardiner, William, author and musical amateur from Leicester. He was a great admirer of Haydn, and his enthusiasm for Beethoven dated back to 1793, when he was shown a manuscript of the String Trio op. 3 which had been brought to England by the Abbé Dobbeler from Bonn.

Gelinek, Abbé Joseph (1758–1825), a Bohemian pianist, composer and priest, who became chaplain and piano teacher to Prince Kinsky in 1786 and to the Esterházy household from 1795. He met Beethoven in Vienna in 1793 and was overwhelmed by his extempore playing. Hearing of his dissatisfaction with Haydn's counterpoint lessons, he introduced Beethoven to Joseph Schenk.

Gellert, Christian Fürchtegott (1715–69), a German poet admired by generations of composers. Beethoven set six of his sacred odes to music in 1802.

Grétry, Andre Ernest Modeste (1741–1813) was born in Liège but settled in Paris where he became a prolific composer of comic operas. Two of his operas, *L'amant jaloux* and *La fausse Magie*, were performed in Bonn in 1789.

Grillparzer, Franz (1791–1872), the famous Austrian dramatic poet who wrote Beethoven's funeral oration. Their collaboration in 1823 over an operatic project, *Melusine*, was abandoned.

Holz, Karl (1798–1858), a keen amateur violinist who became a close friend of Beethoven in 1824–6 at the time of the late string quartets, to the disapproval of Schindler. Holz sometimes played second violin in Schuppanzigh's quartet.

Huber, Franz Xaver (1760–1810), a popular Viennese poet and librettist who wrote the text for Beethoven's oratorio *Christus am Oelberge*, in 1803.

Hummel, Johann Nepomuk (1778–1837) was born in Bratislava and became a well-known pianist and composer. As a child he studied with Mozart, for whose concertos he later wrote anachronistic cadenzas and embellishments over-exploiting the higher reaches of the extended keyboard. He travelled widely as a prodigy. In 1804 he became Kapellmeister to Prince Esterházy, and was to hold similar posts at Stuttgart and Weimar. His florid piano writing influenced the early Romantics, including Chopin.

Kant, Immanuel (1724–1804), German philosopher admired by Beethoven, who possessed some of his works. Extracts from his *Allgemeine Naturgeschichte* were copied out in Beethoven's *Tagebuch* of 1812–18.

Kinsky, Prince Ferdinand (1781–1812) was a patron of Beethoven's and the major contributor to the annuity agreed with the Archduke Rudolph and Prince Lobkowitz in 1809. He was killed in a riding accident in November 1812.

Kotzebue, August von (1761–1819) was born at Weimar and became a popular poet and dramatist. Beethoven wrote the overtures and incidental music for his plays, *The Ruins of Athens* and *King Stephen*, to celebrate the opening of a new theatre in Pest in 1812. Kotzebue lived in Estonia from 1811, but was eventually assassinated in Mannheim.

Kozeluch, Leopold (1752–1818), a Bohemian composer, settled in Vienna in 1778 and became a popular piano teacher of the aristocracy. He declined an invitation to succeed Mozart at Salzburg in 1781 but took over his post as Court composer in Vienna in 1792. He was a versatile and prolific composer, especially of symphonies and piano music, and like Haydn and Beethoven he arranged Scottish airs for Thomson of Edinburgh.

Kreutzer, Rodolphe (1766–1831), French violinist and composer, who met Beethoven in Vienna when in the entourage of General Bernadotte in 1798. Though naturally famous for his violin works, ranging from studies to concertos, he also composed a large number of operas. Beethoven dedicated his Violin Sonata in A op. 47 to Kreutzer.

Krumpholz, Wenzel (1750–1817) was a violinist at the Court opera in Vienna. He became a great admirer and close friend of Beethoven and introduced him to the young Czerny in 1800. He was also a virtuoso on the mandolin, and Beethoven's works for mandolin and piano were probably written for him.

Lichnowsky, Prince Karl (1756–1814) was a pupil and patron of Mozart and accompanied him on his travels in 1789. He became Beethoven's first benefactor in Vienna, invited him to live in his apartment, and granted him an annuity from 1800 onwards. He received several important dedications, beginning with the op. 1 piano trios which were first performed at his house.

Lichnowsky, Count Moritz (1771–1837), a younger brother of the above, also became a staunch admirer of Beethoven. In 1814 Beethoven composed the two-movement Piano Sonata op. 90 for him, humorously relating its changing moods to the Count's forthcoming marriage to a singer.

Linke, Joseph (1783–1837) was the cellist in Count Rasumovsky's quartet from 1808 until its disbandment in 1815, when he was engaged as house musician by the Countess Erdödy. Beethoven's two cello sonatas op. 102, dedicated to the Countess, were written with him in mind. He also participated in performances of the late quartets.

Lobkowitz, Prince Franz Joseph (1772–1816), of Bohemian origin, was one of Beethoven's greatest patrons. From 1796 he had a private orchestra which gave concerts in his palace in Vienna. The *Eroica* Symphony was first played there, repeated at Lobkowitz's request, and subsequently dedicated to him. He was one of the guarantors of Beethoven's annuity in

1809, though he ran into financial trouble during the post-war inflation.

Maelzel, Johann Nepomuk (1772–1838), the inventor of the metronome, came from Regensburg to Vienna in 1792. One of his earlier inventions was a mechanical orchestra or 'panharmonicon', for which he invited Beethoven to compose the 'Battle Symphony' in 1813.

Malfatti, Dr Giovanni (1775–1859), was an Italian-born physician who made a great reputation in Vienna. It was on his advice that Beethoven visited Teplitz in 1811 and he also attended the composer in his final illness. In 1810 Beethoven made an unsuccessful proposal of marriage to his young niece Therese.

Matthisson, Friedrich von (1761–1831), a German lyrical poet. Beethoven made settings of several of his poems, most notably 'Adelaide' and 'Opferlied'.

Méhul, Etienne (1763–1817), French organist, pianist and composer. He was influenced and helped by Gluck and produced a continuous flow of operas from 1790 onwards. As a representative of the new French school his dramatic works were greatly admired by Beethoven.

Moscheles, Ignaz (1794–1870), pianist, conductor and composer, came from Prague to Vienna in 1808. He studied with Salieri and Albrechtsberger and soon became a friend of Beethoven. In 1814 he was commissioned by Artaria to make the piano score of *Fidelio* under the composer's supervision. In 1826 he settled in London, and in 1841 he produced an English edition of Schindler's biography of Beethoven.

Neate, Charles (1784–1877), English pianist, cellist and composer, who studied with John Field, and was a founder member of the London Philharmonic Society. He met Beethoven in Vienna in 1815 and corresponded with him on his return. In 1824 he invited him to visit London for the Society's performance of the Ninth Symphony, but in vain. Neate gave the first performance in England of the 'Emperor' Concerto.

Neefe, Christian Gottlob (1748–98), studied law at Leipzig but soon abandoned it for music. As a composer of Singspiele he came to Bonn in 1779 to direct the music for Grossman's theatrical company, but his more serious musical qualities led to his appointment as Court organist in 1781. He took the young Beethoven under his wing and was his first important teacher.

Oliva, Franz (d.1848) was a clerk and traveller with the Viennese firm of Offenheimer and Herz, and a good linguist. Though not a musician he was a close friend of Beethoven from around 1810 to 1813 and again from 1818 to 1820 when he left for Russia. Beethoven dedicated the piano variations op. 76 to him.

Paër, Ferdinando (1771–1839), an Italian opera composer who was adopted by Napoleon as his *maître de chapelle* in 1807. During his previous tenure as Kapellmeister at Dresden he composed the opera *Leonore* (1804) to an Italian version of Bouilly's libretto, which Beethoven was to adopt a year later and eventually immortalise.

Pleyel, Ignaz Joseph (1757–1831), an Austrian composer and publisher who studied with Haydn. He later moved to Strassburg and London and settled in Paris where he founded a famous firm of piano-makers and publishers in 1807. He returned to Vienna and had several meetings with Beethoven in 1805.

Potter, Cipriani (1792–1871), a well-known English pianist, conductor and composer, who became Principal of the Royal Academy of Music in London from 1832 to 1859. He visited Beethoven in 1818 while studying composition with Förster. In 1824 he gave the first English performance of the Third Piano Concerto for the Philharmonic Society, following it with the Fourth Concerto in 1825.

Punto, Giovanni (1755–1803), alias Johann Wenzel Stich, was a horn virtuoso for whom Beethoven wrote his Sonata op. 17 to perform with him in Vienna and Budapest in 1800.

Rasumovsky, Count Andreas (1752–1836), was Russian ambassador in Vienna from 1792 and became Prince Rasumovsky in 1815. He was an amateur violinist and maintained a resident quartet, including Schuppanzigh and Linke, that was disbanded after a fire at his palace in 1814. He commissioned Beethoven's three string quartets op. 59.

Ries, Franz Anton (1755–1846) was a violinist and musical director at Bonn under the Elector Max Franz. He had studied with Salomon, and his pupils included the young Beethoven.

Ries, Ferdinand (1784–1838), son of Franz, visited Vienna from about 1801 to 1805, studying the piano with Beethoven and theory from Albrechtsberger. He was then obliged to return to Bonn for military service. From 1813 to 1824 he lived in London and had much correspondence with Beethoven over the English publication and performance of his works. He spent his later years in Godesberg and Frankfurt, and cooperated with Wegeler in compiling the *Biographische Notizen* about Beethoven's life which were published at Koblenz in 1838.

Rochlitz, Johann Friedrich (1769–1842), German critic and theologian, founded the important Leipzig *Allgemeine Zeitung* in 1798. He sent Beethoven an opera libretto in 1803 which was politely rejected because it dealt with magic. In 1822 he visited the composer and wrote a perceptive account of his character.

Rode, Pierre (1774–1830), a French violinist and pupil of Viotti for whom Beethoven wrote the Violin Sonata op. 96 in 1812 for performance with the Archduke Rudolph. His restrained style of playing influenced the intimate character of the work, and especially the finale, as Beethoven explained in a letter to the Archduke.

Romberg, Bernhard (1767–1841), cellist, and his cousin Andreas Romberg (1767–1821), violinist, were in the Bonn Court orchestra during Beethoven's last years there. Bernhard lived in Berlin from 1805 and became Kapellmeister ten years later. He met Beethoven again in Vienna in 1822.

Rudolph, the Archduke (1788–1831) was a son of the Emperor Leopold II. Although born in Florence he came to Vienna as a child of two and established his own court there at the age of fifteen. He studied piano and composition with Beethoven from about 1803 and became a lasting friend and patron. His musical gifts seem to be reflected in the large number of important works that were dedicated to him. Beethoven also sought his help in the final stages of the Karl crisis.

Salieri, Antonio (1750–1825), Italian composer, mostly of operas, who spent much time in Vienna and became notorious for his supposed jealousy of Mozart's genius. He was appointed Kapellmeister to the Imperial Court at Vienna in 1788. Beethoven thought highly enough of him to study vocal writing, and especially Italian word-setting, with him over a long period.

Salomon, Johann Peter (1745–1815), violinist and composer whose parents lived at Bonn during Beethoven's childhood. He held the post of concert-master and opera composer to Prince Henry of Prussia before moving to London in 1781. He was a great admirer of Haydn and was responsible for arranging his visits to London in 1790 and 1794.

Schikaneder, Emanuel (1751–1812), actor, singer, librettist and theatre manager, who arrived in Vienna from Germany in 1784 and is best remembered for his cooperation in Mozart's *Die Zauberflöte*, in which he took the part of Papageno as well as writing the libretto. In 1801 he became manager of the new Theater an der Wien and in 1803 commissioned Beethoven to write an opera, *Vestas Feuer*, which was abandoned.

Schindler, Anton (1796–1864), was a law student from Moravia who took to music and became leader of the orchestra at the Josephstadt theatre. He met Beethoven in 1814 and eventually became his factotum, but he is known to have suppressed or destroyed important material and his biography of the composer is notoriously inaccurate.

Schuppanzigh, Ignaz (1777–1830), Viennese violinist and conductor who was associated with Beethoven's works from the days of Lichnowsky's musical parties in the 1790s up to the time of the late quartets. From 1808 he led the Rasumovsky Quartet until its disbandment in 1815, when he departed on a long tour and settled in St Petersburg, returning to Vienna in 1823.

Sebald, Amalie (1787–1846), singer, was born in Berlin and joined the Singakademie there under Zelter's direction. Beethoven met her at Teplitz in 1811 and 1812. He wrote several letters to her in the autumn of 1812 reporting on his ill-health, and she was considered by some as a candidate in the 'Immortal Beloved' mystery.

Simrock, Nikolaus (1750–1832) was a horn-player at Bonn from whom Beethoven took some lessons in his youth. He later founded a famous publishing firm and was responsible for the first editions of important works by Beethoven, including the 'Kreutzer' Sonata and the op. 102 cello sonatas.

Smart, Sir George (1776–1867) had a long and eventful musical career. During Haydn's second visit to London he received an unexpected lesson in timpani-playing from the composer. Eighteen years later, in 1813, he became a founder member of the London Philharmonic Society, which brought him into direct dealings with Beethoven. His visit to Vienna in 1825 to discuss the Ninth Symphony was amusingly recorded in his journals.

Sonnleithner, Joseph (1766–1835), lawyer, publisher and librettist, was secretary of the Court theatres in Vienna from 1804 to 1814. He wrote the libretto, based on Bouilly's French original, for the first version of *Fidelio*.

Steibelt, Daniel (1765–1823) was a German pianist and composer renowned for his fantasias, pot-pourris and programme music. He enjoyed a great but ephemeral popularity, travelled widely, and was demolished by Beethoven at an improvising 'duel' at the home of Count Fries in 1800.

Sterkel, Johann Franz Xaver (1750–1817), known as the Abbé Sterkel, was a German priest and gifted amateur musician. He was renowned as a pianist and a prolific composer. In 1791 he heard and admired the twenty-year-old Beethoven when the Bonn musicians visited Aschaffenburg.

Streicher, Nanette (1769–1838) was the daughter of the Augsburg pianomaker Johann Andreas Stein. As a child prodigy she played to Mozart on his visit there in 1777. In 1794 she married Johann Andreas Streicher and together they established a similar firm in Vienna. They became close friends of Beethoven, and Nanette helped him with his domestic problems during the crisis over his nephew Karl.

Stumpff, Johann Andreas (1769–1846) was born in Thuringia but moved to London in 1790. He was a harp-maker by profession, visited Beethoven at Baden in 1824, and sent him a gift of Handel's works during his last illness.

Swieten, Baron Gottfried van (1734–1803), Court Librarian in Vienna, was a well-known musical enthusiast and patron of the arts. As an admirer of the older 'learned' style he introduced Mozart to Bach's '48', then still in manuscript, and prepared the libretti for Haydn's *Creation* and *The Seasons*. Beethoven dedicated his First Symphony to him.

Thomson, George (1757–1851), a Scottish folksong collector and publisher. He planned a long series of arrangements of Irish, Scottish and Welsh airs, with piano accompaniments and 'ad lib' parts for other instruments, and engaged famous composers for the task – not only Kozeluch and Pleyel, but Haydn and Beethoven.

Treitschke, Georg Friedrich (1776–1842), poet, actor and producer, came from Leipzig to Vienna around 1800. He held posts at the Theater an der Wien and the Kärntnertor Theatre and was engaged by Beethoven to revise Sonnleithner's libretto for the final version of *Fidelio* in 1814.

Unger, Caroline (1803–77) was the contralto who sang the solo parts in the first performance of the Ninth Symphony and the extracts from the *Missa Solemnis* on 7 May 1824. Although she complained at rehearsal about Beethoven's harsh treatment of the voice, it was she who turned him round at the end of the symphony to witness the applause he could no longer hear.

Wegeler, Franz Gerhard (1765–1848) was born at Bonn and became a well-known medical consultant, setting up a practice in Koblenz. In the *Notizen* which he later compiled with Ferdinand Ries he claimed to have known Beethoven in Bonn from 1782, and Wegeler also saw much of him in his early years in Vienna from 1794 to 1796. They never met again and only corresponded on rare occasions. In Bonn they had mutual friends in the von Breuning family, and Wegeler was to marry Eleonore in 1802.

Weiss, Franz (1778–1830), a viola player from Silesia, was a regular member of Schuppanzigh's quartet both before and during the Rasumovsky period, and he rejoined it after the leader's return to Vienna in 1823.

Wölffl, Joseph (1773–1812), pianist and composer, was born in Salzburg where he studied with Leopold Mozart and Michael Haydn. His music covered a wide range of forms though he only had a modest success as an opera composer. As a piano virtuoso however he was highly regarded. He met Beethoven in Vienna in 1798 and dedicated some sonatas to him.

Zelter, Carl Friedrich (1758–1832), a German composer and versatile performer, mainly remembered for his vocal music and friendship with Goethe. He became Director of the Berlin Singakademie in 1800. On a visit to Vienna in 1819 he exchanged letters with Beethoven, expressing admiration for his works and sympathy for his ailments. Mendelssohn studied with him for a time, during which he introduced his pupil to a manuscript score of Bach's *St Matthew Passion*, resulting in its famous revival in 1829.

Zmeskall von Domanovecz, Nikolaus (1759–1833), was awarded the title of Hofrat for his services to the Hungarian Chancellery. He spent most of his life in Vienna, took to Beethoven soon after his arrival in 1792 and formed a long and steady friendship with him. Zmeskall was an amateur cellist and he also cut Beethoven's quill-pens for him.

Appendix D
Select bibliography

The following list is naturally extremely selective. For a comprehensive bibliography the Beethoven entry in *The New Grove* is highly recommended, though it includes many historic and specialised works not readily available. Most of the books listed below are in English, or English translation, but one or two foreign texts are mentioned for their important contribution to Beethoven scholarship.

GENERAL REFERENCE

Abraham, Gerald (ed.), *The New Oxford History of Music*, Vol. VIII: 'The Age of Beethoven' (London, 1982).

Anderson, Emily (ed. and trans.), *The Letters of Beethoven* (London, 1961).

Kinsky and Halm, *Das Werk Beethovens: thematisch-bibliographisches Verzeichnis* (Munich and Duisburg, 1955). [The standard catalogue of Beethoven's works, supplanting the classic Nottebohm volume of 1868.]

Pestelli, Giorgio, trans. Cross, Eric, *The Age of Mozart and Beethoven* (Cambridge, 1984).

Sadie, Stanley (ed.), *The New Grove Dictionary of Music and Musicians*, Vol. 2. (London, 1981).

COLLECTIONS OF ESSAYS

Arnold, Denis and Fortune, Nigel (eds.), *The Beethoven Companion* (London, 1971).

Nottebohm, Gustav, '*Beethoveniana*' (Leipzig, 1872) and '*Zweite Beethoveniana*' (Leipzig 1887). [The latter, published posthumously and edited by Mandyczewski, amounts to a wide-ranging survey of Beethoven's sketches from all periods. Both volumes were reprinted in the original German in 1970.]

Tovey, Donald Francis, *Essays in Musical Analysis* (London, 1935–44). [The title should not deter the average reader. Many of the essays derived from programme-notes for the Reid concerts in Edinburgh and Vol. 2 contains Tovey's famous discussion of the Ninth Symphony.]

Tyson, Alan (ed.), *Beethoven Studies* (New York, 1973, London, 1974);

Beethoven Studies 2 (London, 1977); *Beethoven Studies* 3 (London, 1982). [Extremely specialised studies by various writers on aspects of Beethoven's life and work, representing the highest standards of modern research and analytical methods.]

BIOGRAPHY AND RELATED STUDIES

Cooper, Martin, *Beethoven: The Last Decade, 1817–1827* (London, 1970). [A life-and-works study of the late period, covering rather more than the decade of the title and incorporating an appendix on Beethoven's medical history by Edward Larkin.]

Landon, H.C. Robbins, *Beethoven: a Documentary Study* (London and New York, 1970). [A lavishly produced anthology and iconography.]

Schindler, Anton, *Beethoven as I knew him* (London, 1966). [An English version of Schindler's original biography, dating back to 1860 in its final form. The 1966 translation was by Constance S. Jolly, with invaluable editorial notes by Donald W. MacArdle.]

Solomon, Maynard, *Beethoven* (New York, 1977). [A single-volume biography recommended for its up-to-date research, especially concerning the 'Immortal Beloved', and including some discussion of the music at each stage of the composer's career.]

Sterba, E. and R., *Beethoven and his Nephew* (New York, 1954).

Thayer, A.W., *Life of Beethoven* (Princeton, 1967). [The most extensive of all Beethoven biographies, revised by Elliot Forbes from Krehbiel's 1921 English edition.]

Wegeler, F.G. and Ries, Ferdinand, *Biographische Notizen über Ludwig van Beethoven* (Koblenz, 1838). [Important personal reminiscences of the composer's early life. A supplement was published at Bonn in 1845. Both were revised by A.C. Kalischer in 1906 and reprinted in 1972.]

CHARACTER STUDIES

Closson, Ernest, *The Fleming in Beethoven* (London, 1936).

James, Burnett, *Beethoven and Human Destiny* (London, 1960).

Mellers, Wilfrid, *Beethoven and the Voice of God* (London, 1983). [Though basically an analysis of selected works, especially the piano sonatas and the *Missa Solemnis*, Mellers proceeds 'to relate these musical events to their physiological and psychological consequences'.]

Sonneck, O.G., *Beethoven: Impressions by his Contemporaries* (New York, 1926).

Sullivan, J.W.N., *Beethoven: His Spiritual Development* (London, 1927).

THE MUSIC: GENERAL STUDIES

Newman, Ernest, *The Unconscious Beethoven* (London, 1927).
Rosen, Charles, *The Classical Style* (New York, 1971).
Tovey, D.F., *Beethoven* (London, 1944).

ORCHESTRAL WORKS

Fiske, Roger, *Beethoven Concertos and Overtures* (London, 1970). [BBC Music Guide.]
Grove, George, *Beethoven and his Nine Symphonies* (London, 1898).
Hopkins, Antony, *The Nine Symphonies of Beethoven* (London, 1981). [An eminently readable and not too technical approach by an author well known for his 'Talking about Music' broadcasts.]
Schenker, Heinrich, *Beethovens Neunte Sinfonie: eine Darstellung des musikalischen Inhaltes* (Vienna and Leipzig, 1912). [An exhaustive analysis of the Ninth Symphony including many references to the sketches, and a classic example of Schenkerian methods.]
Simpson, Robert, *Beethoven Symphonies* (London, 1970). [BBC Music Guide.]
Weingartner, Felix, *On the Performance of Beethoven's Symphonies* (London, 1907). [English translation by Jessie Crosland of a German text giving a bar-by-bar account of problems of tempo, phrasing and balance. The many suggested adjustments in scoring are now generally discredited but are interesting relics of performance practice by a conductor renowned for his Beethoven interpretations.]
Vaughan Williams, Ralph, *Some Thoughts on Beethoven's Choral Symphony, with other Musical Subjects* (London, 1953).

CHAMBER MUSIC

Kerman, Joseph, *The Beethoven Quartets* (New York, 1967). [The most important and extensive English study of the string quartets.]
Radcliffe, Philip, *Beethoven's String Quartets* (London, 1965).
Robertson, Alec (ed.), *Chamber Music* (London, 1957). [A Penguin paperback including a general survey of Beethoven's chamber works by Roger Fiske.]

PIANO MUSIC

Fischer, Edwin, *Beethoven's Piano Sonatas* (London, 1959).
Kaiser, Joachim, *Beethovens 32 Klaviersonaten and ihre Interpreten* (Frank-

furt am Main, 1975). [This German work is included for its observations of recorded performances and its useful discography.]

Newman, W.S., *Performance Practices in Beethoven's Piano Sonatas: an Introduction* (New York, 1971).

Reti, Rudolph, *Thematic Patterns in the Sonatas of Beethoven* (London, 1965).

Tovey, D.F., *A Companion to Beethoven's Pianoforte Sonatas* (London, 1931).

SPECIAL STUDIES

Kerman, Joseph, *Ludwig van Beethoven: Autograph Miscellany from circa 1786 to 1799* (London, 1970). [A facsimile and transcription of the so-called 'Kafka' miscellany of sketches and autographs from the early period.]

Nottebohm, Gustav, trans Katz, Jonathan, *Two Beethoven Sketchbooks* (London, 1979). [Nottebohm's commentaries on these two sketchbooks from the years 1801 to 1803 were originally published separately in German in 1865 and 1880 but reprinted in one volume at Leipzig in 1924. The second of the books, dating from 1803 and known to scholars as 'Landsberg 6', is the celebrated 'Eroica' sketchbook.]

Prod'homme, J.-G. (ed. and trans.), *Les cahiers de conversation*, 1819–1827 (Paris, 1946).

Schmidt, H. *Verzeichnis der Skizzen Beethovens* (*Beethoven-Jahrbuch* 1965–8). [A catalogue of the known surviving sketches and sketchbooks. For a brief introduction to the subject, its background and problems, readers are directed to Alan Tyson's article on sketches and autographs in *The Beethoven Companion*.]

Tyson, Alan, *The Authentic English Editions of Beethoven* (London, 1963).

Willetts, Pamela J., *Beethoven and England: an Account of Sources in the British Museum* (London, 1970).

Winter, Robert and Carr, Bruce, *Beethoven, Performers and Critics* (Detroit, 1980). [Papers given during the International Beethoven Congress in 1977.]

Young, Percy, Beethoven: *A Victorian Tribute*, based on the papers of Sir George Smart (London, 1976).

Appendix E

The Heiligenstadt Testament

To Caspar Anton Carl and [Nikolaus Johann]
van Beethoven

Heiligenstadt, *October* 6, 1802

For my Brothers Carl and [Johann] Beethoven

O my fellow men, who consider me or describe me as unfriendly, peevish or even misanthropic, how greatly do you wrong me. For you do not know the secret reason why I appear to you to be so. Ever since my childhood my heart and soul have been imbued with the tender feeling of goodwill; and I have always been ready to perform even great actions. But just think, for the last six years I have been afflicted with an incurable complaint which has been made worse by incompetent doctors. From year to year my hopes of being cured have gradually been shattered and finally I have been forced to accept the prospect of a *permanent infirmity* (the curing of which may perhaps take years or may even prove to be impossible). Though endowed with a passionate and lively temperament and even fond of the distractions offered by society I was soon obliged to seclude myself and live in solitude. If at times I decided just to ignore my infirmity, alas! how cruelly was I then driven back by the intensified sad experience of my poor hearing. Yet I could not bring myself to say to people: 'Speak up, shout, for I am deaf'. Alas! how could I possibly refer to the impairing *of a sense* which in me should be more perfectly developed than in other people, a sense which at one time I possessed in the greatest perfection, even to a degree of perfection such as assuredly few in my profession possess or have ever possessed – Oh, I cannot do it; so forgive me, if you ever see me withdrawing from your company which I used to enjoy. Moreover my misfortune pains me doubly, in as much as it leads to my being misjudged. For me there can be no relaxation in human society, no refined conversations, no mutual confidences. I must live quite alone and may creep into society only as often as sheer necessity demands; I must live like an outcast. If I appear in company, I am overcome by a burning anxiety, a fear that I am running the risk of letting people notice my condition – And that has been my experience during the last six months which I have spent in the country. My sensible doctor by suggesting that I should spare my hearing as much as possible has more or less encouraged my present natural inclination, though indeed when carried away now and then by my instinctive desire for human society, I have let myself be tempted to seek it. But how humiliated I have felt if somebody standing beside me heard the sound of a flute in the distance and *I heard nothing*, or if somebody heard *a shepherd sing* and again I heard nothing – Such experiences almost made me despair, and I was on the point of putting an end to my life – The only thing that held me back was *my art*. For indeed it seemed to me impossible to leave this world before I had produced all the works that I felt the urge to compose; and thus I have dragged on this miserable existence – a truly miserable existence, seeing that I have such a sensitive body that any fairly sudden change can plunge me from the best spirits into the worst of humours – *Patience* – that is the virtue, I am told, which I must now choose for my guide; and I now possess it – I hope that I shall persist in my resolve to endure to the end, until it pleases the inexorable Parcae to cut the thread; perhaps my condition will improve, perhaps not; at any rate I am now resigned – At the early age of 28 I was obliged to become a philosopher, though this was not easy; for indeed this is more difficult for an artist than for anyone else – Almighty God, who look down into my innermost soul, you see into my heart and you know that it is filled with love of humanity and a desire to do good. Oh my fellow men, when some day you read this statement, remember that you have done me wrong; and let some unfortunate man derive comfort from the thought that he has found another equally unfortunate who, notwithstanding all the obstacles imposed by nature, yet did everything in his power to be raised to the rank of noble artists and human beings. – And you, my brothers Carl and [Johann], when I am dead, request on my behalf Professor Schmidt, if he is still living, to describe my disease, and attach this written document to his record, so that after my death at any rate the world and I may be reconciled as far as possible – At the same time I herewith nominate you both heirs to my small property (if I may so describe it) – Divide it honestly, live in harmony and help one another. You know that you have long ago been forgiven for the harm you did me. I again thank you, my brother Carl, in particular, for the affection you have shown me of late years. My wish is that you should have a better and more carefree existence than I have had. Urge your children to be *virtuous*, for virtue alone can make a man happy. Money cannot do this. I speak from experience. It was virtue that sustained me in my misery. It was thanks to virtue and also to my art that I did not put an end to my life by suicide – Farewell and love one another – I thank all my friends, and especially *Prince Lichnowsky* and *Professor Schmidt*. I would like Prince L[ichnowsky]'s instruments to be preserved by one of you, provided this does not lead to a quarrel between you. But as soon as they can serve a more useful purpose, just sell them; and how glad I shall be if in my grave I can still be of some use to you both – Well, that is all – Joyfully I go to meet Death – should it come before I have had an opportunity of developing all my artistic gifts, then in spite of my hard fate it would still come too soon, and no doubt I would like it to postpone its coming – Yet even so I should be content, for would it not free me from a condition of continual suffering? Come then, Death, *whenever* you like, and with courage I will go to meet you – Farewell; and when I am dead, do not wholly forget me. I deserve to be remembered by you, since during my lifetime I have often thought of you and tried to make you happy – Be happy –

Ludwig van Beethoven

For my brothers Carl and [Johann]
To be read and executed after my death –
Heiligenstadt, October 10, 1802 – Thus I take leave of you – and, what is more, rather sadly – yes, the hope I cherished – the hope I brought with me here of being cured to a certain extent at any rate – that hope I must now abandon completely. As the autumn leaves fall and wither, likewise – that hope has faded for me. I am leaving here – almost in the same condition as I arrived – Even that high courage – which has often inspired me on fine summer days – has vanished – Oh Providence – do but grant me one day *of pure joy* – For so long now the inner echo of real joy has been unknown to me – Oh when – oh when, Almighty God – shall I be able to hear and feel this echo again in the temple of Nature and in contact with humanity – Never? – No! – Oh, that would be too hard.

(*The Letters of Beethoven*, trans. and ed. Emily Anderson, Macmillan, 1961)

Appendix F

The letter to the 'Immortal Beloved'

[Teplitz], *July 6 and 7*, [1812]
July 6th, in the morning

My angel, my all, my very self. – Only a few words today, and, what is more, written in pencil (and with your pencil) – I shan't be certain of my rooms here until tomorrow; what an unnecessary waste of time is all this – Why this profound sorrow, when necessity speaks – can our love endure without sacrifices, without our demanding everything from one another; can you alter the fact that you are not wholly mine, that I am not wholly yours? – Dear God, look at Nature in all her beauty and set your heart at rest about what must be – Love demands all, and rightly so, and thus it is *for me with you, for you with me* – But you forget so easily that I must live *for me and for you*; if we were completely united, you would feel this painful necessity just as little as I do – My journey was dreadful and I did not arrive here until yesterday at four o'clock in the morning. As there were few horses the mail coach chose another route, but what a dreadful road it was; at the last stage but one I was warned not to travel by night; attempts were made to frighten me about a forest, but all this only spurred me on to proceed – and it was wrong of me to do so. The coach broke down, of course, owing to the dreadful road which had not been made up and was nothing but a country track. If I hadn't had those two postilions I should have been left stranded on the way – On the other ordinary road Esterházy with eight horses met with the same fate as I did with four – Yet I felt to a certain extent the pleasure I always feel when I have overcome some difficulty successfully – Well, let me turn quickly from outer to inner experiences. No doubt we shall meet soon; and today also time fails me to tell you of the thoughts which during these last few days I have been revolving about my life – If our hearts were always closely united, I would certainly entertain no such thoughts. My heart overflows with a longing to tell you so many things – Oh – there are moments when I find that speech is quite inadequate – Be cheerful – and be for ever my faithful, my only sweetheart, my all, as I am yours. The gods must send us everything else, whatever must and shall be our fate –

Your faithful
Ludwig

Monday evening, July 6th
You are suffering, you, my most precious one – I have noticed this very

267

moment that letters have to be handed in very early, on Monday – or on Thursday – the only days when the mail coach goes from here to K. – You are suffering – Oh, where I am, you are with me – I will see to it that you and I, that I can live with you. What a life!!!! as it is now!!!! without you – pursued by the kindness of people here and there, a kindness that I think – that I wish to deserve just as little as I deserve it – man's homage to man – that pains me – and when I consider myself in the setting of the universe, what am I and what is that man – whom one calls the greatest of men – and yet – on the other hand therein lies the divine element in man – I weep when I think that probably you will not receive the first news of me until Saturday – However much you love me – my love for you is even greater – but never conceal yourself from me – good night – Since I am taking the baths I must get off to sleep – Dear God – so near! so far! Is not our love truly founded in heaven – and, what is more, as strongly cemented as the firmament of Heaven? –

Good morning, on *July 7th*

Even when I am in bed my thoughts rush to you, my eternally beloved,[1] now and then joyfully, then again sadly, waiting to know whether Fate will hear our prayer – To face life I must live altogether with you or never see you. Yes, I am resolved to be a wanderer abroad until I can fly to your arms and say that I have found my true home with you and enfolded in your arms can let my soul be wafted to the realm of blessed spirits – alas, unfortunately it must be so – You will become composed, the more so as you know that I am faithful to you; no other woman can ever possess my heart – never – never – Oh God, why must one be separated from her who is so dear. Yet my life in V[ienna] at present is a miserable life – Your love has made me both the happiest and the unhappiest of mortals – At my age I now need stability and regularity in my life – can this coexist with our relationship? – Angel, I have just heard that the post goes every day – and therefore I must close, so that you may receive the letter immediately – Be calm; for only by calmly considering our lives can we achieve our purpose to live together – Be calm – love me – Today – yesterday – what tearful longing for you – for you – you – my life – my all – all good wishes to you – Oh, do continue to love me – never misjudge your lover's most faithful heart.

ever yours
ever mine   L.
ever ours

(*The Letters of Beethoven*, trans. and ed. Emily Anderson, Macmillan, 1961.)

---

[1] 'Unsterbliche Geliebte' is appropriately translated as 'eternally beloved', though 'Immortal Beloved' is universally accepted for the intended recipient.

Index